HOMELAND SIEGE

15.95

MORE INTELLIGENCE/TACTICS SUPPLEMENTS FROM POSTERITY PRESS:

THE LAST HUNDRED YARDS: THE NCO'S CONTRIBUTION TO WARFARE
ONE MORE BRIDGE TO CROSS: LOWERING THE COST OF WAR
PHANTOM SOLDIER: THE ENEMY'S ANSWER TO U.S. FIREPOWER
THE TIGER'S WAY: A U.S. PRIVATE'S BEST CHANCE FOR SURVIVAL
TACTICS OF THE CRESCENT MOON: MILITANT MUSLIM COMBAT METHODS
MILITANT TRICKS: BATTLEFIELD RUSES OF THE ISLAMIC MILITANT
TERRORIST TRAIL: BACKTRACKING THE FOREIGN FIGHTER
DRAGON DAYS: TIME FOR "UNCONVENTIONAL" TACTICS
TEQUILA JUNCTION: 4TH-GENERATION COUNTERINSURGENCY

HOMELAND

SIEGE

TACTICS FOR POLICE AND MILITARY

ILLUSTRATED

H. JOHN POOLE
FOREWORD BY
MAJ.GEN. RAY L. SMITH USMC (RET.)

POSTERITY
PRESS

Published by Posterity Press
P.O. Box 5360, Emerald Isle, NC 28594
(www.posteritypress.org)

Cataloging-in-Publication Data
Poole, H. John, 1943-
Homeland Siege.
    Includes bibliography and index.
    1. Infantry drill and tactics.
    2. Military art and science.
    3. Military history.
I. Title.   ISBN: 978-0-9818659-1-1   2009   355'.42
Library of Congress Control Number: 2009925336

Cover art © 2009 by Michael Leahy
Edited by Dr. Mary Beth Poole
Proofread by William E. Harris

Second printing, United States of America, December 2009

To all who protect U.S. citizens at home.

Disclaimer:

Much of what is true never makes it into the political or media limelight. "Ultimate truth" is so tremendously complicated that only God may be able to fully appreciate it. The best that mortal men (and government agencies) can generally manage is a single perspective. And often, there are several—equally valid—ways of looking at the same issue.

This book contains a number of little-known, U.S.-security-related facts. Most of these facts have been carefully checked and come from highly reputable sources. Then—within the context of world history, current events, U.S. tactics, and enemy patterns—they are woven together to show which new threats may now face the American homeland. While parts of the book are somewhat "forward looking," they are far from fictional. Unlike most extensions of the U.S. defense establishment, Posterity Press is in no way obligated to assess all problems from a "politically correct" standpoint. It can therefore be more objective in its analyses. Through a working knowledge of Eastern thought processes and battlefield methods, it has amassed a fairly respectable threat assessment record. It identified the trouble in Iraq as an insurgency long before the U.S. government acknowledged that fact. It pointed to Iran as the primary instigator four years before that paradox became officially recognized.[1] And it identified northern Somalia as a safe haven for al-Qaeda three years before the U.S. media made that momentous discovery.[2]

As a highly centralized "top-down" organization, the U.S. military is still predicated on all members being absolutely certain that "headquarters always knows what it's doing." To acknowledge any exception would run the risk of orders not being followed. Thus, those who object to such a free-wheeling style of research may too closely affiliate with organizational policy. America's foes are also well versed in U.S. military procedure. That's why they so easily work outside the "box." Thinking like them has never been required of GIs (possibly because it would highlight the need for tactical reform). But the U.S. heartland now faces a new kind of invasion. International organized crime factions are well connected and highly secretive. To combat them, law enforcement agencies have little choice but to extrapolate "known modus operandi" into "probable intentions." Deployed U.S. forces should try this sometime; it works.

Contents

————————————————————————————

Illustrations

Figures

Chapter 10: *Collateral-Damage-Free Defense*

Chapter 11: *Using Basic-Service Volunteers*

Afterword:

Foreword

In *Homeland Siege,* Poole again uses recent enemy intelligence as a lead-in to advanced tactical technique. But this intelligence does not come from some distant shore. It is from the borders, highways, and cities of America—with the enemy being international organized crime. For open-source intelligence gathering, a private researcher has little choice but to test some hypothesis against available facts. Poole's hypothesis is that Communist China may have had something to do with the increased flow of drugs and aliens into the U.S. from Mexico. After closely analyzing all of America's Asian and Hispanic gangs, he arrives at an objective assessment to that hypothesis. As a veteran of the U.S. invasion of Grenada, I can assure all readers that Communist influence in Latin America did not end with the Soviet Union. Should any of that influence now spring from Asia, every ruse I encountered in Vietnam may be in play.

The Chinese are the acknowledged masters of deception, because they first determine how an adversary thinks. Throughout America's security establishment, decision making is decidedly top down. Leaders arrive at conclusions from the most readily available information, and then expect subordinates to apply those conclusions. While most American leaders have a good view of the "big picture," they too seldom get to see "where the rubber meets the road." Self-serving subordinates will sometimes misreport it. Then, a senior officer's only hint of how things are really going at the bottom are his own enlisted experience and conversations with his driver. Once a Private First Class myself, I can remember how less well-oiled the "train" sometimes looked from its undercarriage.

To confuse what is normally a Western adversary, Asian armies like to operate from the bottom up. Instead of constantly going for the knockout punch, they will bleed a well-endowed foe to death with a thousand razor cuts. As many of those razor cuts are directed against seemly inconsequential targets by phantom-like saboteurs, Western leaders easily underestimate their collective damage. Often, foul play is only suspected by first responders to various "accidents." Thus, American E-6's and below can more easily see what an Asian adversary is up to.

As an E-7 at retirement, Poole shares this perspective of E-6's and below. That's why his books are so popular among that category of reader. As a two-tour veteran of Vietnam and longtime student of squad tactics, he can also see how a "bottom-up" adversary thinks. U.S. forces are now facing a very difficult challenge in Afghanistan. To succeed where 120,000 Soviets could not will take more insight than was achieved in Vietnam. Expeditionary force commanders might have better luck this time if they were to pay more attention to the "bottom-up" perspective—for it is shared by their junior enlisted and enemies alike. I urge all company grade, field grade, and flag rank officers to become better acquainted with this alternative way of operating. They can most easily do so through Poole's entertaining analyses. Now that the nation itself is threatened, U.S. law enforcement personnel may also want to exploit this valuable resource. In *Homeland Siege,* Poole's chapters on collateral-damage-free offense and defense should be required reading at all infantry, special-operations, and police academies.

M.Gen. Ray L. Smith USMC (Ret.)

Preface

Within the United States [U.S.] government, "terrorism" has become nearly synonymous with "Muslim extremism." Yet, there are many kinds of fanatics, and those Islamist were not the first to push their agenda through terror. After the Bolshevik Revolution of 1917, Lenin and his Communist henchmen only managed to coalesce their fellow Russians into a Red State by executing all who wouldn't cooperate. After Lenin was nearly assassinated in 1918, his secret police applied the "Red Terror." This was nothing more than an extrajudicial campaign of mass arrest in which suspected foes of the State could be "legitimately" tortured or killed. Over a quarter of a million Russians were to die in this internal house cleaning.[1] From 1918 to 1922, eight million more perished in the fighting between Red and White forces and its concurrent "class conflict."[2] Throughout Lenin's time in office, he remained a staunch believer in mass terror.[3] Then, his record of brutality was eclipsed by his successor—"Uncle Joe" Stalin. From 1922 to 1953, somewhere between 20 and 43 million people succumbed to Uncle Joe's psychopathic rule.[4] And, sadly, Stalin's legacy still lives on today. Russia's new "State-approved" textbook will assert that Stalin acted "entirely rationally" during his many purges.[5] Of course, the Soviet Union is not the only Communist nation to have taken such a horrific approach to governance. China has also depended—for the abject loyalty of its massive population—on the implicit threat of death. That's why 25 to 58 million of its citizens ceased to exist from 1946 to 1976. Since the end of Mao's "Cultural Revolution," an additional 20 million have quietly expired in Chinese Labor Camps.[6] Though no longer openly antagonistic toward the West, the People's Republic of China (PRC) is still run by the same one-party system it had in 1950. Thus, for any terrorist threat to America, there is always the possibility of Communist instigation.

Most Asians are "holistic" thinkers. That means they consider the whole of something to be greater than the sum of its parts. Over the years, this alternative way of looking at the world has created quite a challenge for the U.S. military. While each Chinese private gets continually briefed on the battlefield intentions of all senior commanders, the U.S. private is lucky to know what his platoon commander wants to do next. And while each North Korean private has been shown how single-handedly to make a strategic difference, his American counterpart is routinely punished for displays of initiative.

In combat, Asians also prefer to operate from the bottom up. Before any combined-unit offensive is even envisioned, some lone scout has to spot a weakness in the adversary's defenses. This is quite different from what happens in the West. Most U.S. offensives are based on the overall commander's preferred plan of attack. Because of this distinctly different way of problem solving, Asian armies, insurgent movements, and criminal enterprises are generally better at short-range combat than U.S. forces. Their infantry squads have more surprise-oriented tactical techniques (like football plays), and their squad members are more self-sufficient.

However, this "perspective-inspired" edge is not limited to the Asian's small-unit tactics. It also applies to his operational arts. Within every U.S. military headquarters is a commander, an executive officer, and several task-oriented sections. When the commander gets a mission, he tells his training (S-3), logistics (S-4), intelligence (S-2), and administration (S-1) section heads to work out a solution. Those section heads further assign the most obvious parts of their piece of the puzzle to subordinate specialists. And those specialists may, in turn, delegate various segments. In essence, the commander's mission has been arbitrarily dissected and farmed out to people who best understand one thing. But what if that mission involves subtle nuances that don't conveniently fit into any established category? And how can the specialist in one field know when he is infringing on the requirements of another? More often than not, the sections end up working at cross-purposes, and only the most magnificent of "Ex Os" can sufficiently reconnect the pieces to achieve a feasible solution. The classic example is the S-3's chronic inability to muster enough people for squad training because of the S-4's constant need for working parties and S-1's equally urgent obligation to administratively record any change in individual status.

Unfortunately, that's not the extent of the bad news. This "top-down" way of doing things that the U.S. security establishment has inherited from the French and British also makes it extremely difficult to spot impending danger in time. In an age where foreign attack is routinely accompanied by feints and disinformation, American intelligence analysts are overly focused on their own narrow areas of responsibility. That's why *Hezbollah* contractors working for Chinese proxies end up looking like Muslim conspirators. And *al-Qaeda* operations on Sulawesi don't translate into PRC interest in one of Southeast Asia's two largest petroleum reserves. Though theoretically attuned to the "big-picture," U.S. security agencies thus have trouble learning enough about a pending attack's specifics to stop it. Their sacred responsibility to America could better be served by learning to think holistically and "bottom-up" like a crime- or insurgency-oriented foe. Only then will they allow enough bottom-echelon initiative to defeat America's current conglomeration of loosely structured opponents.

H. John Poole

Introduction

While America Was Chasing Osama bin Laden

With U.S. intelligence, military, and police officials dutifully focused on Sunni extremism, the Shiite radicals have been having a field day. Iran has moved inexorably closer to its own nuclear weapon. *Hezbollah* has forcefully arranged veto power over the Lebanese government.[1] One of *Hezbollah's* proxies has emerged victorious in the Gaza elections.[2] And al-Sadr has made a nonaggression pact with Iraq's pro-Iranian regime.[3] Still, these are just the setbacks in Muslim regions. Throughout the rest of the world, America's leaders have fared less well. There, they have stood idly by while Communist regimes and their allies freely intruded on any number of sovereign nations. Russia's invasion of Georgia not withstanding, China has clearly emerged as the Free World's most serious threat. Russia, North Korea, Sudan, Iran, Venezuela, Cuba, and several other nations now regularly function as PRC surrogates. This should come as no surprise. Two of those nations have Communist governments, while three of the remaining four have the "revolutionary" variety. When any one of those PRC proxies comes under too much international scrutiny, another always seems to divert everyone's attention with another act of aggression. And thus, much of the Free World has been steadily falling under the Chinese sphere of economic and political influence.

Most Americans are still unaware of losing a proxy war to the Communists in southern Africa in the 1980's. Because of the concurrent (and very important) issue of apartheid, they don't realize that the Rhodesian and South African armed forces were also confronting blatant Communist aggression. There was, after all, no shortage of Cuban troops, Soviet Navy personnel, and Chinese advisors in the region. Then, the United Nations [U.N.] and Britain stepped in to stop the fighting with hastily held elections. When those elections were over, the largely uneducated and news-media-deprived peoples of southern Africa had mostly done the bidding of their "terror-wielding" Communist commissars. To this day, all but two on the nations in this region have one-party "democracies."

The parallels between those and subsequent events elsewhere should serve as a warning to U.S. policy makers. Communist governments already see themselves as "democratic." In theory, they too support the will of the people. When China finally makes her bid to remove all Western influence from the Asian mainland, her chief instrument of expansion will be the Democratic People's Republic of Korea (DPRK). While the African resistance movements of the late 20th Century had the word "People's" or "Liberation" in their titles, those of today have the word "Democratic." In essence, the Communists are now playing off the West's commitment to the democratic process. And like the Islamists, they have learned how to win the elections of targeted countries. The Communist Party of China's (CPC's) true opinion of Western democracy should be apparent from its slaughter of thousands of unarmed students in Tiananmen Square. It is not America's friend, nor is it her arch rival. It is simply the autocratic ruler of a country with a mushrooming need for natural resources, little regard for human rights, a knack for deception, and expansionist tendencies. Though initially economic and then political, those tendencies must be countered wherever possible.

The Chances of Chinese Retribution

When the Soviet Union was bankrupted by the West in 1990, could the paranoid rulers of the only other Communist power have decided to defend themselves? How tough could an appropriate response have been for Sun-Tzu-like thinkers with an unlimited supply of cheap labor? Their principal threat was a nation whose armed forces had yet to embrace the nuances of 4th-Generation War (that fought in political, economic, psychological, and martial arenas simultaneously). In democracy- and trade-oriented America, who would notice a 4th-Generation Warfare (4GW) attack—if all violence were applied by proxy?

The operative concept here is 4GW. Though somewhat difficult for Western traditionalists to appreciate, its power has been more than adequately demonstrated by the Iraqi opposition. In 4GW, firefights may be intentionally lost to make progress in one of the non-martial arenas. The most powerful is obviously politics. This fact has not been lost on the Chinese. Though decidedly totalitarian themselves, they have been sending "election observers" to other countries.[4] One of their more obscure African allies has even been combining peacekeeper security with election "training" in the outlying villages of Democratic Republic of the Congo (DRC). According to Human Rights Watch, there are problems with such an approach. "The institutions that are organizing the elections are politicized [themselves]."[5] How many more "Chinese-style" elections will the West permit, and the world have to endure? The PRC's ultimate objective is, by all available indicators, eventually to dominate global affairs.

> China's "comprehensive warfare" strategy wears down [an] enemy using non-military means. . . .
> . . . [Chinese] National Defense University Senior Col. Meng Xiansheng . . . defined the term as "the means of defeating enemies without waging a war through deploying a wide range of political, economic, cultural, diplomatic and military tactics."
> [Col.] Meng said "comprehensive warfare" advocates the use of non-violent means in handling state-to-state disputes, . . . but [it] also fits with China's grand strategy of "peaceful development."[6]
> —*Geostrategy-Direct,* 2 August 2006

The PRC Has Just Stolen Asia's Crown Jewel

On 19 August 2008, a tiny news item appeared at the very bottom of an interior page of the *Christian Science Monitor*. It read, "A former Maoist guerrilla was sworn in today as Nepal's first prime minister . . . [after being] picked . . . by a special assembly meant to write a new Constitution and double as an interim parliament."[7] Only those who had tracked Nepal's slow strangulation seemed to sense the significance of those few words. In two short sentences, the last step in the PRC's latest expansionary formula had been disclosed. Nepal lies between China and India. Eastern India also suffers from a long-running Maoist rebellion.[8] In fact, Calcutta already has its own Communist government.[9] With full access to the Indian Ocean, China would no longer have to risk wartime oil shipments to the Straits of Malacca.

For the West to learn from its most recent 4GW defeat, all other steps in Pranchanda's takeover must now be remembered. Something similar will almost certainly occur elsewhere. Involving 19 years of alternating threats and pseudo-democratic reforms, the blow-by-blow account has been reserved for the Appendix.

While U.S. leaders basked in China's professed friendship at Beijing's Olympic Games, the crown jewel of South Asia had quietly slipped away. The person who had led a PRC-inspired insurgency costing 13,000 lives was now poised with no fewer than 20,000 experienced guerrillas to support the Naxalite rebellion in India and its Bangladeshi equivalent. For those who still doubt the significance of this event to world peace, the following epilogue is offered:

> The Maoists, originally inspired by Peru's Shining Path, are guided by the principle of Pranchanda Path, a Nepalese derivative of Marxism, Leninism, and Maoism. Pranchanda Path is an ideology of "tactical flexibility and strategic rigidity," according to [Nepalese] Maoist military commander Bipav.[10]
>
> —*Christian Science Monitor,* 21 August 2008

The most disturbing part of Pranchanda's method was his mezmerization of Nepal's young voters. In the past, Communists have attempted to generate popular support at universities, but Pranchanda went far beyond that—possibly into 4GW's psychological arena. Hopefully, this kind of "popular delusion" could not happen any closer to home.

> The Maoists' success came not just from Maoist sympathizers, but also from Nepali *[sic]* youths who wanted a new political force in power after seeing former political parties not deliver for decades, says . . . a political scientist at Nepal's biggest university.
>
> "The voters generally did not vote for their ideology, but for change," he says. "It became a fashion, a reaction to the nonperformance of other political parties."[11]
>
> — *Christian Science Monitor,* 21 August 2008

The PRC Has Also Just Snagged the Biggest Prize in Africa

After the "Red-Guard" insurgencies of the 1970's, China took full advantage of Africa's vulnerability. Communist-backed "freedom fighters" won U.N.-arranged elections in Mozambique, Zimbabwe, Angola, and South Africa. Only the first and last of those countries have managed to avoid one-party rule. In April 2009, a former Communist was poised to become South Africa's next president. Now there are untold numbers of Chinese contract laborers in Sudan, Eritrea, Djibouti, Nigeria, Angola, and Zimbabwe.[12]

After Angola's war, the nation most highly contested in Africa has been the DRC. Since 1998, some 5.4 million DRC citizens have died in interfactional fighting.[13] Most of this fighting has occurred in that nation's mineral-rich northeastern provinces. While this region is generally known for its copper and cobalt, it also has huge uranium deposits. To acquire those and other minerals, China has been refurbishing the Benguela Railroad that runs from the Angolan seaport of Lobito to the Zambia-DRC border.[14] In June 2008, it managed to trade a 1,000-mile truck-and-train conduit to the DRC's mining district from this Benguela railhead for all the minerals it could extract in the foreseeable future. It and the DRC would form a joint mining company in which only 32% was DRC owned. The DRC would then foot its part of the construction bill by allowing China to take minerals for free.[15] As this incredible "arrangement" was trade oriented, the U.S. never admitted that Kabila may have been manipulated. Nor did it suspect China of keeping that part of the Congo destabilized to discourage Western business interests.

> Congo and China are forming a massive mining company . . . with Congo owning 32 percent and China . . . 68 percent.
> The Chinese are putting up all the money. . . .
> But the money isn't free—it will [be] . . . loans. . . . Congo will pay back China with copper, cobalt and road tolls.[16]
> —National Public Radio (NPR), 30 July 2008

To recognize the deception, one must look a few hundred miles to the north—at the Darfur region of Sudan. There, China is interested in oil and also wants no competition from Western companies. As such, it cooperates with, and provides U.N. protection to, the Islamist regime behind Darfur's genocide. Not surprisingly, the Congo's mining-region problems also involve ethnic rivalries. Here, the Congolese Army has secretly allied itself with the Forces Democratiques de Liberation du Rwanda (FDLR) to suppress what it calls a Tutsi rebellion. In fact, the two forces have already run joint raids on Tutsi villages.[17] This is the same FDLR that committed Rwanda's horrendous genocide. To fund the "allied militia," the Congolese Army further allows the FDLR to control much of the trade in tin, tungsten, and coltan.[18] Thus, one starts to see an unhappy resemblance between the Arab *Janjaweed* of Sudan and the Hutu FDLR of the Congo. And he or she can't help but notice the same aspiring superpower waiting nonchalantly in the wings to monopolize both sets of natural resources.

As of November 2008, troops from China's most militarily proficient African proxy (Angola) were helping DRC forces to defend Goma.[19] Also coming were troops from China's most blatant surrogate, Zimbabwe.[20] While the Tutsi rebel leader—Gen. Laurent Nkunda—was far from perfect, he claimed to be just defending the Congo's huge Tutsi population from further atrocities. Who can really blame him? Most deserving of the world's condemnation is any foreign power that would take unfair advantage of the area's misery. As often happens in Africa, the whole situation became a little murky in January 2009. In exchange for arresting Nkunda, Kabila invited Rwandan troops onto Congolese soil to purportedly confront the FDLR. What resulted was a loose alliance with Nkunda's former National Congress for the Defense of the People (CNDP), with the CNDP now being led by indicted war criminal, Gen. Bosco Ntaganda.[21]

Within Africa as a whole, the PRC's expansionist *modus operandi* has several variants. In Zimbabwe, it involves openly bolstering a failed state with no natural resources. In Nigeria, it has to do with Chinese oil companies patiently waiting while non-Muslim rebels discourage Western companies.[22] In Sudan and Angola, it involves so many Chinese immigrants that local politics cannot help but be affected.[23] While the obvious thread is oil and mineral removal, there have been serious political consequences. The PRC has a "revolutionary" government that still considers insurgency to be helpful to the progress of developing nations. To many of Africa's inhabitants, China's ongoing good will feels more like sabotage or invasion.

[A]long with the infrastructure come Chinese laborers and companies. . . . In addition, cheap Chinese goods . . . have flooded African markets, wiping out competition, crippling local enterprises, closing factories and adding to widespread unemployment.[24]
— National Public Radio, 28 July 2008

Michael Sata, nicknamed King Cobra, is Zambia's feisty opposition leader. . . . Sata speaks of exploitation.
"Today, the Chinese are not here as investors, they are here as invaders," Sata says.[25]
— National Public Radio, 1 August 2008

Adama Gaye, a Senegalese author and commentator, says Chinese merchants were the vanguard of Beijing's [strategy]. . . .
The Chinese merchants, he says, were "the advance force that has allowed opening . . . territories, . . . they were followed . . . by the big companies and . . . political leaders."[26]
— National Public Radio, 1 August 2008

China More Subtly Encroaches on the Western Hemisphere

In recent years, China has been much more careful about subverting the sovereign nations in America's backyard. There has been a big influx of Chinese immigrants into Paraguay's Tri-Border Area (TBA), Panama, and Venezuela,[27] but nowhere near the numbers that have poured into Sudan and Angola. Around the Caribbean, most of the PRC's expansionist agenda has been discreetly accomplished through regional proxies—like Cuba,[28] Venezuela,[29] Fuerzas Armadas Revolucionarias de Colombia (FARC),[30] and local triad chapters.[31]

Through imaginative ways of funding strategic initiatives, China has maintained its deniability. Three of its favorites have been foreign aid, "goods-for-services barter," and drug trafficking. After all, the CIA's (Central Intelligence Agency's) *World Factbook* still describes China as a "major trans-shipment point for heroin produced in the Golden Triangle."[32] And the Venezuelan government is now so well endowed that its "socialist production projects" easily extend into other sovereign countries. Clearly, the same Eastern government has implicitly authorized both challenges to Western society.

> Chavez will first travel to close ally Cuba, and then to China, which Chavez calls a strategic ally, for the capitalization of a six-billion-dollar bilateral investment fund. He says Caracas will use it for "socialist productive projects."
>
> China is contributing four billion dollars and Venezuela two billion dollars, said Chavez, who is to meet with Chinese President Hu Jin Tao.[33]
>
> — Agence-France Presse, 20 September 2008

Leftist candidates have now been elected in fourteen of Latin America's twenty nations. Of the remaining six, three—Mexico, Peru, and Colombia—have the hemisphere's only active insurgencies. Peru's Maoist Shining Path has recently experienced a resurgence.[34] While most leftist political advice has come from Cuba, that country's new sponsor can't be directly linked to the takeover. That's because both candidates and guerrillas have been largely funded through local drug trafficking. In March 2009, tiny El Salvador was added to the growing list of openly Marxist regimes (Cuba, Venezuela, Ecuador, Bolivia, and Nicaragua). Farabundo Marti National Liberation Front (FMLN) candidate Mauricio Funes had effectively evicted the incumbent conservative party.[35]

Most of the PRC's more flagrant incursions into Latin America have had military ramifications. Hutchison Whampoa—a known business extension of the People's Liberation Army (PLA) [36]—already controls the port facilities at both ends of the Panama Canal. Before long, China will be docking ships of its navy at the now-leased Rodman Naval Station.[37] Additionally, U.S. Air Force personnel and equipment will be replaced by their Chinese counterparts at the Ecuadorian airbase of Manta. In the meantime, PRC engineers are building a railroad from Manta to South America's mineral-rich interior.[38] Coupled with China's support for Venezuela's "Bolivarization" of Latin America, one senses the presence of a very hungry Sino-tiger. That tiger and its assorted proxies also prowl all the way up to the U.S. border.[39] Mexico's 5,376 organized-crime slayings during the first 11 months of 2008 were more than double the number for the previous year.[40] One wonders how many were to preclude witnesses, undermine the government, or terrorize the population. As the draft of FMFM 1-3A had warned in August, non-governmental entities are fully capable of waging war against the Americas.[41] Part One will investigate the extent to which that war has already spilled over into U.S. territory.

Limitations to the Research Method

This book goes far beyond the "philosophical overview of events and procedures" that constitute most nonfiction writing. Such works are often lacking in detail. That's because their nitty-gritty particulars would be too hard to fully substantiate or sell to the average reader. This book is not for the average reader. It is for professional soldiers and policemen.

The world is a very complicated place. *Homeland Siege* attempts to zero in on some of the more obscure threads in a convoluted carpet of evidence. In the process, it may have overlooked a few competing threads. And, any in-depth look into the highly secretive world of international crime must always be an educated guess. To justify such an approach to research, the author has relied on historical trends worldwide and the law enforcement concept of *"modus operandi."* *Modus operandi* is a way in which policemen solve current crimes through past observations. They do so by comparing the characteristic patterns and operating style of known felons to ongoing circumstances. Though strictly circumstantial, such evidence can still augment, and at times supplant, hard evidence (like fingerprints) in all U.S. courts of law.

The Book's Utility

The international trade in narcotics has been concurrently harming Americans at home and helping their enemies abroad. It undermines Western society, while funding Maoist or Islamist expansion (to include FARC and the Taliban).

Like all the other books in the Posterity Press series, *Homeland Siege* is an intelligence and tactics manual supplement. Its three parts are equally applicable to police departments, security agencies, and military units. Part One points out the parallels between criminal-gang activity and armed insurrection. Part Two shows how most law enforcement procedures can be applied to counterinsur-

gency or 4GW. And Part Three sheds some much needed light on
how to rescue hostages in peacetime and kill fewer noncombatants in
war. It also shows how to operate a tiny smuggler-spotting outpost
in Mexico or infiltration-monitoring station in Afghanistan without
much risk to its occupants. As such, it should be as useful to the
War on Crime as it is to the War on Terror (now wisely renamed
"Overseas Contingency Operations").[42]

Acknowledgments

This work has been based on the research of many dedicated Americans. Most value the Judao-Christian ideals upon which this nation was founded. They worry about the increase in youth gangs and how it may correlate with more availability of their greatest money-maker—drugs. They know that the Mexican cartels will try to flood the United States with Colombian cocaine and Asian heroin. They also realize that their criminal justice system is already overloaded. When too many Americans can no longer walk their streets in safety, the world's last "bastion of freedom" will no longer be as able to protect others from the Communist tiger or Islamist lion. As history has repeatedly proven, such a scenario too easily leads to world war. Thanks be to God for whatever wisdom may be contained herein.

Part One

The Most Serious Threat to America

"Our constitution was made only for a moral and religious people.
It is wholly inadequate to the government of any other."
— President John Adams, 11 October 1798

(Source: Attributed to President John Adams)

1 Far Too Much Foreign Activity on U.S. Soil

- From which country have most U.S. cyber attacks come?
- Do PLA-affiliated triads prey on American cities?

Which nation still actively expands its global influence?

(Source: Public domain image "1950-sl_ec06.jpg" as retrieved from http://timpanogos.wordpress.com/2007/09/13)

Time to Reassess the Homeland Challenges

Once again, Americans are dealing with a whole series of what appear to be natural or self-inflicted hardships. At the top of the list are a troubled economy, two long-running overseas wars, and a virtual assault on their heartland by foreign drug smugglers. Having endured the McCarthy and Cold War eras, they are in no hurry to admit the possibility of non-Muslim sabotage. But, those who have fought in East Asian wars remember how readily their foes attacked from the rear. When the Soviet Union was bankrupted by the West in 1990, is it not possible that the world's only other

3

Communist power decided to defend itself. With limitless funding and a new "4GW" format, that power might now be able to so undermine America at home that she could no longer democratize the world. Thus, America's most pressing internal problems must now be reassessed from the standpoint of foreign instigation.

Who Besides *al-Qaeda* Has Eroded America's Functioning?

Chinese citizens have been hacking into U.S. agency computers since before 9/11. Two events seem to have precipitated this intrusion—the mistaken bombing of their Belgrade embassy in May 1999 and the U.S. spy plane bumping by one of their fighter jets in April 2001.[1] The extent of this hacking has been massive. In addition to the Pentagon, the following departments have been penetrated: (1) State; (2) Commerce; (3) Energy; (4) Health and Human Services; (5) Labor;[2] and (6) Homeland Security.[3] Unfortunately, those Chinese hackers have been guilty of more than just reconnaissance. Two massive U.S. power outages have also been attributed to them—one that covered much of the Northeast in 2003 and another in Florida in 2007.[4] The most recent computer break-ins from the People's Republic of China (PRC) involve espionage. Two separate U.S. Congressmen claim Chinese hackers have stolen sensitive information on the world's political dissidents from their files. One further asserts that U.S. government officials urged him not to go public with the allegation.[5]

The Chinese People's Liberation Army (PLA) has openly endorsed cyber-warfare for ten years. It trains "many individuals" in cyber operations in its military academies, and its parent regime "devotes a tremendous amount of human resources to cyber activity for government purposes."[6] Thus, one could easily conclude that the U.S. is now under "cyber-reconnaissance" or "cyber-attack" from the PRC. This does not come as particularly good news for U.S. leaders who prefer to see Muslim extremism as their only challenge. That's because *al-Qaeda's* first website was developed in southern China.[7]

> Computer hackers in China, including those working on behalf of the Chinese government and military, have penetrated deeply into the information systems of U.S. companies and government agencies, stolen proprietary

information from American executives in advance of their business meetings in China, and, in a few cases, gained access to electric power plants in the United States, possibly triggering two recent and widespread blackouts in Florida and the Northeast, according to U.S. government officials and computer-security experts.

One prominent expert told National Journal he believes that China's People's Liberation Army played a role in the power outages. Tim Bennett, the former president of the Cyber Security Industry Alliance, a leading trade group, said that U.S. intelligence officials have told him that the PLA in 2003 gained access to a network that controlled electric power systems serving the northeastern United States. The intelligence officials said that forensic analysis had confirmed the source, Bennett said. "They said that, with confidence, it had been traced back to the PLA." These officials believe that the intrusion may have precipitated the largest blackout in North American history, which occurred in August of that year. A 9,300-square-mile area, touching Michigan, Ohio, New York, and parts of Canada, lost power; an estimated 50 million people were affected.[8]

— *National Journal Magazine,* 31 May 2008

While cyber-security experts and some U.S. intelligence heads suspect that the PRC is behind the hacking, Washington has yet to lodge an official complaint.

Brenner [head of U.S. counterintelligence] . . . looks for vulnerabilities in the government's information networks. He pointed to China as a source of attacks against U.S. interests. "Some [attacks], we have high confidence, are coming from government-sponsored sites," Brenner said. "The Chinese operate both through government agencies, as we do, but they also operate through sponsoring other organizations that are engaging in this kind of international hacking, whether or not under specific direction. It's a kind of cyber-militia."[9]

In November [2007], the . . . [U.S-China Economic and Security Review Commission (USCC)] reported that "Chinese military strategists have embraced . . . cyberattacks" as a weapon in their military arsenal. Gen. James Cartwright, the former head of U.S. Strategic Command and now the vice chairman of the Joint Chiefs, told the commission that China was engaged in cyber-reconnaissance, probing computer networks of U.S. agencies and corporations. . . .

A former CIA official cast the cyber-threat in . . . similarly dire terms. "We are currently in a cyberwar, and war is going on today," Andrew Palowitch, who's now a consultant to U.S. Strategic Command, told an audience at Georgetown University in November. . . . Palowitch cited statistics . . . that 37,000 reported breaches of government and private systems occured [sic] in fiscal 2007. The Defense Department experienced almost 80,000 computer attacks, he said. Some of these assaults "reduced" the military's "operational capabilities," Palowitch noted.[10]

— *National Journal Magazine,* 31 May 2008

Despite the apparent indifference of U.S. leaders, this problem is ongoing and serious. A Chinese ally has already softened up its expansionist targets with cyber attacks.

There have been a series of high-profile attacks against the U.S. since last summer. . . . *Newsweek* reported that computers used by both the Obama and McCain campaigns were hacked. . . [A] variety of news sources have reported . . . successful breaches on . . . the White House, the World Bank, and the Department of Defense (DoD).

There were 43,880 incidents of malicious activity from all sources against DoD and defense company computers in 2007, a 31 percent increase from the year before, according to a recent annual report from the . . . (USCC). . . .

The USCC report also points to links between hackers and the Chinese government. . . . [I]t states, there are 250 hacker groups in China that are "tolerated and may even be encouraged" by the Chinese government. . . .

. . . Heli Tiirmaa-Klaar, a senior advisor in the Estonian Ministry of Defense, said attacks in Estonia in 2007 and Georgia in 2008 were both "culturally traceable" and involved "similar paradigms."

She indicated that official ties were particularly likely in

the Georgia attacks, which struck news, police, government, and other websites mainly during the beginning of Russia's Georgian incursion last August.[11]
— *Security Management,* 19 December 2008

No Big Deal?

Those who have yet to appreciate the importance of computer networks to the everyday functioning of America may now be saying, "So what!" They see China as a rising star that yearly donates billions of dollars to developing-nation infrastructure, and believe Western-style democracy will inevitably spring from her new market economy. And, as far as they are concerned, China is guilty of nothing more than copying America's "superior" technologies and methodologies.

The PRC is now seldom criticized by Washington or the U.S. news media, but hints of its impropriety still slip through. On 25 April 2009, ABC's Nightly News reported that foreign computer hackers had not only caused a shutdown of America's electrical grids, but also interfered with her financial systems. Then, the former U.S. anti-terrorism czar announced, "A country like China could do either thing to the United States and make it look as if someone else had."[12]

The U.S. may be great in many ways, but it is not the world's only source of technology. And Asia's "bottom-up" agencies have already proven themselves more responsive to localized predicaments than are America's "top-down" bureaucracies. That's why Chinese authorities were able to react more quickly to the Sichuan earthquake than did their U.S. counterparts to Hurricane Katrina. Pride in one's country must always be tempered with an objective view of opposition strengths.

It is true that China has now massively embraced a warped version of free enterprise. In the process, it has so flooded the Third World with cheap goods that local manufacturers have been forced out of business. This has, in turn, resulted in less self-sufficiency for developing nations, and more Chinese influence over their political affairs. In many places, vast arrays of cottage industries have been replaced with the few enterprises that support China's strategic agenda. Those enterprises have mostly to do with the growing/mining, refining, and transportation of natural resources. And the local populations will either have to work there or starve. Among the commodities thus reshaping many Third World economies are oil, minerals, and drugs. In essence, China has—through infrastructure assistance and massive emigration—infiltrated the political fabric of its targeted countries. With every new Chinese road comes an incumbent-regime concession. That concession may be anything from breaking diplomatic ties with Taiwan to forfeiting mineral rights. Once the PRC has established a strong enough power base in each of those countries, it will craftily introduce its version of democracy. While such talk may be a little too negative for *rapprochement* enthusiasts, it is nothing more than an objective look at recent history. Zimbabwe provides a perfect example of what happens to developing nations that accept too much help from the PRC.

As for China's apparent switch to capitalism, things in the Orient are not always what they seem. China is still a Communist state, according to the CIA's *World Factbook*. Every Chinese business must have its own Communist Party cell. In 2007, the Public Broadcasting System's (PBS's) *China from the Inside* reported all village elections rigged and an "election process that made the Communist Party more secure."[13] So, it is illogical to conclude that China's new economic system will eventually lead to Western-style democracy. The ruling party's opinion on that subject has been adequately demonstrated in Tiananmen Square and Tibet. It already considers its style of government to be democratic. The only difference between it and its 1950's forerunner is its ability to win a Western-style election. As demonstrated in the Introduction, nowhere is that more evident than Nepal.

If one can acknowledge the threat to world peace that a "revolutionary" government poses, then one must also admit that Chinese leaders may not always act in America's best interests. Any aggressive act against the U.S. would, of course, be carefully masked. That brings up a very unpleasant, yet totally plausible, possibility. What if the Chinese government were to delve deeply into the most profitable of all business enterprises—organized crime. Avowedly atheistic, it might not consider all such deals to be morally inappropriate. Through drug trafficking alone, it could locally fund elections, rebellions, or anything in between—without ever implicating itself.

America's New Vulnerability

When the U.S. government legalized "direct-to-consumer" advertising of prescription drugs several years ago, it unwittingly exposed America's underbelly. In a country when lobotomies were all the rage in the late 1940's,[14] it should have expected a rush on anti-depressants and pain killers. Now growing numbers of young Americans consider any downswing in mood to be a medical problem and regularly medicate their overactive children. This and the on-going abuse of prescription drugs have not been lost on the world's organized-crime syndicates.

> Officials in treatment facilities throughout the country report that many abusers of prescription opiates such as OxyContin, Percocet, and Vicodin eventually begin abusing heroin because it is typically cheaper and easier to obtain.[15]
> — NDIC Drug Threat Assessment for 2009,
> National Drug Intelligence Center

The Chinese Government's Link to the Hong Kong Triads

When the Communist Chinese received Hong Kong from the British in 1997, they were worried its Taiwan-affiliated triads would make trouble. (See Map 1.1.) Soon, they realized that—as criminal enterprises—those triads could be "financially influenced." And that's precisely what happened with at least one of the biggest.

> So he [Deng Xiaoping] bought them: the Sun Yee On, the largest Hong Kong triad society, no longer requires initiates to pledge allegiance to Taiwan; now it is to the People's Republic of China that they swear.[16]

By that point in time, the Chinese Premiere had been thinking for almost fifteen years about how to harness the Hong Kong triads. After adding Hong Kong to the PRC, he was at first only interested in how its triads could help to fund his regime. Then, he must have realized the role they could play in unconventional warfare. One has to wonder why the U.S. government has never acknowledged the threat they now pose to national security.

Map 1.1: Red China Has Owned Hong Kong since 1997
(Source: Courtesy of General Libraries, University of Texas at Austin, from their website for map designator "hong_kong_pol_1998.pdf")

Of all of the treacherous aspects of Hong Kong's reunification with China, the most treacherous—and the least noticed—is . . . a cooperation pact between the triad societies and the Communist Party. This dreadful alliance, of the world's largest criminal underground and the world's last great totalitarian power, has received surprisingly little attention in this country, even though the U.S. Justice Department has identified triad racketeering as a significant global threat. Even more ominously, this alliance is not accidental. It was part of Deng Xiaoping's reunification plan for Hong Kong from the very beginning, and dates from the early 1980's.[17]

The West's apparent blindness to the ramifications of a working alliance between a great power and a great criminal network is striking for its persistence [and a bit suspicious]. Deng had been openly hinting at an underworld accord for years. In September 1983 and June 1984, while China was still negotiating with Britain to regain Hong Kong, and again in early October 1984, only days after a handover agreement had been reached, he made remarks about triads at the Great Hall of the People that were surprisingly and pointedly positive. . . . Many of them were good. Many of them, he said, were patriotic.[18]

Soon, the PLA was making money off the triad with the biggest overseas operation (Sun Yee On), and very possibly thinking about how to use it against China's only legitimate competitor.[19]

One authority on triads says the "great fear" of the Hong Kong police is arms smuggling by triads in alliance with the People's Liberation Army. . . .
For the United States and other parts of the world, China's accord with organized crime is cause for considerable alarm—triads are great exporters of misery.[20]

[The triads'] powerful influence is felt worldwide in counterfeiting, arms dealing, alien smuggling and money laundering. Hong Kong is a key transit point for the Southeast Asian heroin and methamphetamine that pour into the United States, and triads play a key role in the drugs' transshipment.[21]

Hong Kong Has Another Big Triad in Latin America

South America's smuggling activity has been coordinated from the Tri-Border Area (TBA) of Paraguay, and that in Central America from Panama. Hong Kong's other large "foreign-oriented" triad is 14-K. Both it and Sun Yee On have been seen in the TBA.[22] "Triad

11

gangs" of uncertain parentage have also been reported in Panama City. Their allegiance may be different from the 18 Chinese gangs known to operate throughout Central America. Those 18 affiliate with an obscure Hong Kong triad by the name of Fa Yen.[23]

Triads in Canada

The two most active triads in Canada are 14-K and Luen Kung Lok (a member of the Hong-Kong-based Luen Group). In some Canadian cities, there are also Sun Yee On, Wo Hop To, and Wo On Lok. The last two are branches of the Hong-Kong-based Wo Group.[24]

The Triads That Prey Directly on Americans

Three of Hong Kong's four biggest triads operate within the continental U.S.—Sun Yee On, 14-K, and Wo Hop To.[25] Though the Triad Police in now-Communist Hong Kong vehemently deny it,[26] all three have been peddling illicit narcotics in America. The fourth—Wo Shing Wo [27]—apparently targets only Europe.[28]

> In 1997, the . . . FBI [Federal Bureau of Investigation] office initiated . . . [a] heroin trafficking investigation . . . targeting Weng Keek Hoo. . . . Hoo had successfully re-established ties to heroin distributors in several United States cities and was now residing in New York City.
> . . . New York FBI agents identified associates of Hoo in Philadelphia, Detroit, Atlanta, Los Angeles, and Gary, Indiana. . . .
> Agents determined that large quantities of heroin were regularly being shipped from Southeast Asia to Vancouver, Canada, then on to Toronto, Canada before being smuggled into the United States. New York FBI agents identified four distinct trafficking organizations directing the operations from Southeast Asia. . . . [E]vidence was uncovered showing that several of the leaders of these organizations were members of the 14K Triad criminal enterprise based in Hong Kong.[29]
> — Federal Bureau of Investigation Case Study

[G]roups with a major foothold in the United States are the 14K triad (in New York, California, Chicago, Boston, and Houston) and the Sun Yee On triad (in New York, Miami, San Francisco, and Los Angeles) (Bolz, "Chinese Organized Crime . . . ," *Asian Affairs,* fall 1995, 22).[30]

— Library of Congress Research Paper, April 2003

Members of the Sun Yee On [or San Yee On] triad have settled in Toronto, Edmonton, and Vancouver . . . ("Asian Organized Crime," International Crime Threat Assessment 2000). They are involved in the trafficking of heroin and methamphetamines . . . to the United States. The triad appears to have ties to New York's Tung On gang (The Protection Project, "A Human Rights Report on Trafficking," 2002). . . .

The Wo Group has 10 sub-groups and approximately 20,000 members worldwide (Bolz, "Chinese Organized Crime . . . ," *Asian Affairs,* fall 1995, 22). . . . [T]he Wo Hop To sub-group is involved in both heroin trafficking and alien smuggling in the United States.[31]

—Report for the Library of Congress, July 2003

Probable Triad Middlemen

For any Hong Kong triad now working for the PLA, all dope trafficking within the U.S. would be handled by a proxy. That's how the PRC has traditionally maintained its veneer of propriety. Most appropriate for this role would be an America-based Chinese organization. On the West Coast, there is Wah Ching. With 300-year-old roots in Hong Kong, it has close ties to two of Hong Kong's biggest triads and considerable animosity toward a third. Its allies are Sun Yee On and 14-K, while its rival is Wo Hop To. Wah Ching was headquartered in San Francisco when Wo Hop To arrived there in the 1980's. At first, the two were partners in crime. Then, the bullets started flying, and Wah Ching was forced by Wo Hop To to leave San Francisco. While Wah Ching then moved its headquarters to Los Angeles, it continues to operate in other cities.[32]

The dominant groups in California (notably in Long Beach, Los Angeles, and San Francisco) are the Wah Ching and the Wo Hop To. The former was described in 1995 as the most powerful Asian crime group in San Francisco. Boston, Chicago, Dallas, Honolulu, Houston, Las Vegas, Miami, Phoenix, and Seattle are other U.S. cities where Chinese gangs have been active (Ko-lin Chin, *Chinatown Gangs*, Oxford Univ. Press, 1996, 8).[33]

— Library of Congress Research Paper, April 2003

For the two friendly triads, Wah Ching could now be coordinating all drug trafficking operations in the southwestern U.S. But, that would take the cooperation of certain Hispanic factions. Without them, it would have trouble taking delivery on any product that had been off-loaded at Hutchison Whampoa ports in Panama and Mexico.

Also present in America is a Chinese syndicate known as the Big Circle Boys. With its roots also in China, it has Vancouver and Toronto as its North American headquarters. Though not itself a triad, it has an interesting history and membership. For at least one of the big Hong Kong triads, it could be coordinating the drug flow into the northeastern U.S. from Canada.

[It] originated in the late 1960's from a group of purged or imprisoned Red Guard soldiers who initially engaged in armed robberies. . . . After expanding operations successfully into Hong Kong from its mainland bases, [it] diversified its criminal activities and became prosperous. Key members emigrated to Canada, South America, and the United States, establishing operations in those countries and ultimately diversifying into credit card fraud, counterfeiting, and trafficking humans and narcotics. Now [it's] one of the largest and most successful Chinese crime groups in the world. Organized in cells, some with their own names. Although not a traditional triad group, [it] includes substantial numbers of triad members and has secret membership rites (Huston, *Tongs, Gangs, and Triads,* Authors Choice Press, 2001, 109-110). Estimated membership [is] 5,000.[34]

— Library of Congress Research Paper, April 2003

Heroin moves from the source in Southeast Asia through China's Guangdong Province to Vancouver, which is a central distribution point for North American sales. Big Circle and Hong Kong-based triads regularly have used commercial transport to move large shipments of heroin into Canada (Criminal Intelligence Service of Canada, "Annual Report 1998").[36]

— Library of Congress Research Paper, April 2003

Like Wah Ching, the Big Circle Boys cooperate easily with other ethnic groups. That could prove very useful in making final distribution of the drugs.

The loosely structured group [Big Circle] uses its connections in many countries and with other types of crime, such as trafficking in heroin and luxury automobiles, to maintain a large amount of working capital. Big Circle also is known to cooperate with other ethnic criminal groups.[35]

— Library of Congress Research Paper, April 2003

Only missing is a hybrid Chinese criminal organization to act as middleman/recipient for the drugs coming via Mexico into the Midwest and Middle Atlantic states from Texas. The only other known candidate is Fuk Ching (or Fu Ching). But Fuk Ching is more probably another New York distribution hub for triad drugs from Canada. Of note, its roots are also in Hong Kong, just like those of Wah Ching and Big Circle Boys.

Following the Tiananmin Square incident of 1989, liberalization of U.S. policy toward Chinese immigrants brought . . . new gangs such as the Big Circle and the Fu Ching groups from China to challenge [or provide a covered link for] . . . the traditional triad groups.[37]

— Library of Congress Research paper, April 2003

What All of This May Mean to National Security

That Chinese hackers have been sabotaging the internal functioning of the U.S. should be of great concern to America's newly elected leaders. So should China's growing ownership of U.S. debt. That debt was estimated by NPR to be at $10 trillion in November 2008. Two months later, NPR reported that the U.S. had already sold China $2 trillion worth of treasury bonds and was planning to sell it $2 trillion more in 2009. If the PRC were suddenly to dump those bonds, not only would the value of the dollar plummet but possibly much more.[38] Simply the threat of such a thing might cause U.S. leaders to avert their gaze from the next blatant example of Chinese expansionism. Thus, one worries that the PRC may be in the midst of an extra-low-intensity 4GW attack against not only large parts of Asia, Africa, the Middle East, and Latin America,[39] but also the U.S. itself. Smuggling conduits easily double as infiltration routes. Wherever drugs and people can be smuggled in, so too can technology and spies be smuggled out.

The United States constitutes the world's largest illicit drug market. Chinese triads traffic in both people and drugs. Most of their heroin and methamphetamines have been reaching this country via U.S. ports, Canada, and Mexico. Hong Kong's two biggest triads now operate as PLA business extensions. If those same triads have been additionally facilitating the flood of Colombian cocaine into America, then their ultimate objective may be more than just money. Fully to assess their intentions and progress, one must closely examine every player—whether Chinese or otherwise—in the highly convoluted U.S. smuggling network.

2 — More Than Just a Crime Wave

- Where is America most vulnerable?
- How could too many drugs destroy her societal structure?

Some nations see drugs as legitimate "trade goods."

(Source: Corel Gallery Clipart, Totem Ship #37C019)

Lincoln's Warning

In particularly trying times, U.S. citizens will sometimes heed the advice of past leaders. Their most revered president clearly identified the only real threat to their homeland.

All the [foreign] armies of Europe, Asia, and Africa combined . . . could not, by force, take a drink from the Ohio [River]. . . .
At what point, then, is the approach of danger to be expected? I answer, if it [is] ever reach us, it must spring

up amongst us; it cannot come from abroad.[1]
— Abraham Lincoln
in "Perpetuation of Our Political Institutions"

But, what if that internal danger were to be instigated or accelerated from abroad? With "an open society" and "free trade" comes a certain amount of inherent risk. Enough drug peddling can so corrupt local officials as to politically undermine an entire government. This has already occurred in Afghanistan and several of the Latin American countries. Thus, any competing power that could pump enough dope into America's political heartland might seriously compromise her governance. In the process, it would damage the very fabric of U.S. society. More drug-related crime (to include that by cash-deprived addicts) might so overload the U.S. criminal justice system as to virtually preclude any rehabilitation of offenders. Then, instead of discouraging law breakers, this country's prisons would mass-produce sociopaths. And, while freedom-loving Americans stewed in their own juice, that competing power would continue to expand its worldwide influence. Only with relative security at home could the U.S. military mount any serious opposition.

Financial Crisis Seen Coming by U.S. Justice Department

In April 2008, the U.S. Justice Department divulged eight threats that were posed to homeland security by international organized crime. That was five months before the U.S. credit and stock market crashes of October. Below are the most shocking of those eight findings:

* International organized criminals exploit the U.S. and international financial system to move illegal profits and funds, including sending billions of dollars in illicit funds through the U.S. financial system annually. . . .
* International organized criminals are manipulating securities exchanges and engaging in sophisticated fraud schemes that rob U.S. investors, consumers, and government agencies of billions of dollars.
* International organized criminals have successfully corrupted public officials around the world . . . and con-

tinue to seek ways to influence—legally or illegally—U.S. officials.[2]
      — U.S. Justice Dept. Press Release, 23 April 2008

Now-Communist Hong Kong has powerful organized-crime factions with overseas operations. And, following the worldwide financial crash of October 2008, too few U.S. leaders noticed that Beijing had barely suffered. In fact, the PRC's banking-system assets actually rose by 14% in 2008. By March 2009, that country had so much extra cash that it went on a spending spree for Western oil and mining interests.[3]

> Chinese banks have been barely affected by the financial crisis that has brought some of America's and Europe's biggest financial institutions to the brink of disaster.
> The [Communist] Chinese financial system is . . . less international . . . than its Western counterparts. The largest Chinese banks are state owned. . . .
> Chinese companies do not rely on money markets or on the commercial paper market for their daily operational capital. They keep cash reserves instead.[4]
>   — *Christian Science Monitor*, 21 October 2008

Nor did most U.S. leaders realize that the economy of China's closest new ally—Russia—had also been protected by large reserves of foreign currency and gold.[5] It may have been just a coincidence that the economic crisis came at a time when it would so discredit America's incumbent rightists as to virtually assure a leftist victory at the polls. Still, America was in trouble, and it needed to make very certain that all of that trouble had been self-inflicted.

Could Crime Function As Part of a 4GW Attack?

In 1999, the Chinese PLA published *Unrestricted Warfare*—a document containing what is still the most comprehensive list of 4GW attack options in existence. Among other things, *Unrestricted Warfare* said the "source country for drugs" would be safe from military attack from the U.S. In the very next sentence, it admits "special funds can be set up to influence another country's government through lobbying." Then, within the footnote of a concluding

19

section, it touts the safety of a "nation state attack" that had been made to look like organized crime.[6] Its underlying point is that the U.S. security establishment considers martial assault as the only retaliatory act of war.

> The U.S. military does not treat transnational companies which seize monopolistic profits as security threats, and in addition to their deeply-rooted awareness of economic freedom, this is also related to the fact that they still limit threats to the military arena.[7]
> — Concluding section of *Unrestricted Warfare*

As is most evident in Africa, the PRC has become highly skilled at 4GW. By progressively destabilizing a targeted nation, it gives its own political and economic agendas a better chance. If it could somehow foster chaos in America, it would also enjoy more world-wide influence. What better way to destabilize a free society than to flood it with drugs. The PRC need not personally smuggle those drugs into the U.S., it has only to provide a neighboring country's organized-crime faction with sufficient product.

There's big money to be made from drug trafficking. After a little laundering, that money can pay for candidates, lobbies, or strikes. And the resulting discord creates more difficult decisions at the polls. This is as true for U.S. citizens, as it is for those of any other country. These same pressures have plagued Latin America's voters for the last 20 years. (See Map 2.1.) Of its 20 or so nations, only six still enjoy conservative governments: (1) Mexico; (2) Honduras; (3) Panama; (4) Colombia; (5) Guianas; and (6) Peru. And, of those six rightist regimes, two came very close to going Socialist in the last election. While the reasons for the ideology swing are many, it's clear that the whole Hemisphere is still under Communist at-tack. While most of those six regimes are suspected of extrajudicial excesses,[8] all must deal with leftist-opposition support from beyond their borders. The political advice comes from Cuba, and the money from Venezuela or local drug traffickers. Russia is no longer strong enough to have instigated so widespread a conspiracy.

U.S. Highly Susceptible to Any Hemispheric Problem

Through generous trade and immigration policies, the United

Map 2.1: Americas Linked by Land Bridge and Trade Accords
(Source: Courtesy of General Libraries, University of Texas at Austin, from their website for map designator "world_pol02.pdf")

States has fully participated in the community of Caribbean nations. As such, much of what happens to the peoples of Central America will eventually impact upon U.S. residents. There has been a recent example in the realm of adolescent crime. A gang with Salvadorian roots has so quickly established itself across America that a new National Gang Task Force and Intelligence Center have been specifically dedicated to its control. But this gang's rapid ascent was no *al-Qaeda* plot or fluke of criminal avarice. According to the FBI, U.S. intelligence community, and several Central American governments, MS-13 has no ties to radical Islam. As in Central America, MS-13 has a specific role with regard to the drug trade. There, it protects the smuggling conduits.[9] So, one wonders which of America's other foes may have helped the U.S. branch of MS-13 so rapidly to expand and why. To find out, one must delve deeply into the obscure world of international drug trafficking. Whether or not any direct links can be found between Chinese and Central American factions, the clever PRC may still have induced the crisis.

An Overview of the Current Drug Onslaught

Contributing to America's ongoing narcotics addiction are cocaine, heroin, MDMA (3,4-methylenedioxymethamphetamine or "ecstasy"), and methamphetamine. Most of the highly refined "white" heroin now comes from South America and is consumed between New York City and Washington, D.C. Its Asian counterpart is currently in limited supply. While some Southeast Asian heroin still enters the Northeast through Canada, most smuggled drugs now have the Southwest border region as their principal "arrival zone." As such, the Mexican border may be the portal through which international drug traffickers plan to flood this country with Southwest Asian (Afghan) heroin. The *NDIC Drug Threat Assessment for 2009* says that "traffickers are increasingly relying on smuggling routes through the Southwest Border to supply heroin to U.S. drug markets." It goes on to warn that "Southwest Asian heroin availability may increase in some U.S. cities" and that "Mexican DTOs [Drug Trafficking Organizations] will most likely continue to establish new markets for Mexican heroin in northeastern states."[10] What it fails to mention is that Chinese triads easily deliver Southwest Asian heroin to Mexican DTOs.

Most of the Colombian cocaine and heroin used to come up

Central America's Pacific Coast to Mexican ports. A submarine carrying five tons of cocaine was seized from Mexico's offshore waters in July 2008, and a Mexico-flagged fishing vessel with seven tons in February 2009. Because of such interdiction successes, more of the trade is now "land-based." However, this term applies not only to overland smuggling, but also to coastline maritime shipping and short-range aerial trafficking. As such, some legs of the drug route may still be by local-fishing or "go-fast" boat. Still, more drugs are clearly coming overland. In March 2009, the U.S. Ambassador to Guatemala estimated that 300-400 tons of cocaine were now passing through his nation per year (as much as half of everything that left South America for the U.S. in 2007).[11]

From Mexican ports like Acapulco and Zihuatenejo, the drugs pass into South Texas under the auspices of the Mexican cartels. There is an ongoing struggle between the Gulf Cartel and an alliance of other cartels to handle this product and to control the various points of entry, particularly Nuevo Laredo. As the Sinaloa Cartel is also known as the "Alianza de Sangre," it is obviously the nucleus of this new "Alliance" or "Federation." (See Map 2.2.) But the Jaurez and Milenio Cartels are also members. In turn, the Gulf Cartel is allied with the Tijuana and tiny Oaxaca Cartels. Both criminal partnerships maintain highly proficient paramilitary security detachments. Sinaloa has "Los Pelones" and "Los Negros," whereas the Gulf Cartel has "Los Zetas."[12]

> The Alliance, also known as The Federation, is a cooperating group of Mexican . . . (DTOs) that share resources such as transportation routes and money launderers. The Alliance was formed to counter the Gulf Cartel. The Alliance includes organizations headed by Joaquín Guzman-Loera [Sinaloa Cartel], Ismael Zambada-Garcia [Juarez Cartel], Juan Jose Esparragosa-Moreno [formerly of Guadalajara and now of Juarez Cartel], Arturo and Hector Beltran-Leyva [Los Negros part of Sinaloa Cartel], Edgar Valdez-Villareal [Los Negros part of Sinaloa Cartel], Armando Valencia-Cornelio [Milenio or Valencia Cartel], and Ignazio Coronel-Villareal [Guadalajara Cartel].[13]
> — *NDIC Drug Threat Assessment for 2008*

Both Mexican drug-trade partnerships have long vied for the Colombian cartels' product. And wherever there are Colombian

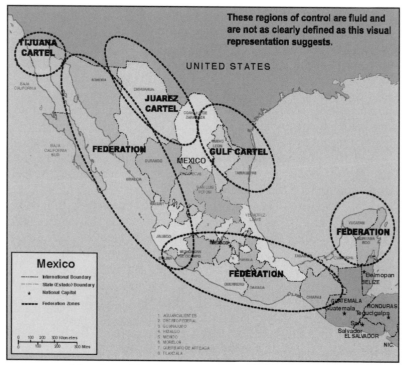

These regions of control are fluid and are not as clearly defined as this visual representation suggests.

Map 2.2: Mexican Cartel Areas of Influence
(Source: "Mexico's Drug Cartels," by Colleen W. Cook, CRS Report for Congress, Order Code RL34215, 25 February 2008)

drugs, there is Colombian "muscle." Most often, that muscle comes from FARC. There were financial problems between the Tijuana Cartel and Colombian cocaine producers, so the Juarez Cartel was chosen to move the majority of Colombian cocaine into the U.S. It established close ties with a cocaine-producing organization run by Miguel and Victor Mejia Munera [of the rightist paramilitary Autodefensas Unidas de Colombia (AUC)].[14]

According to the U.S. Drug Enforcement Administration (DEA), "Colombian DTOs increasingly rely on Mexican DTOs to smuggle South American heroin [across the Southwest Border] into the United States." That goes for South American cocaine as well. In late 2004, a Mexican cartel leader by the name of Ignacio Coronel-Villareal was indicted in the U.S. for helping Colombian drug organizations to smuggle tons of cocaine across Mexico "in tractor trailers and tanker trucks."[15] From this indictment, two things were apparent: (1) how the drugs were getting across the border; and (2) how the Colombians had started to cede distribution headaches to the Mexicans.

Colombian DTOs are dominant cocaine and heroin traffickers, particularly in the Northeast; however, they are increasingly relinquishing control of drug transportation and wholesale distribution to Mexican DTOs in order to shield themselves from law enforcement detection [and interdiction].[16]

—NDIC Drug Threat Assessment for 2008

As a result, the Mexican cartels now buy more South American product with the intention of distributing it themselves. Much of that product comes by go-fast or fishing boat to Mexico's Pacific ports and then by truck or train to Nuevo Laredo. While there is no Colombian cartel on the DEA's latest list of U.S. street gang distributors,[17] some Colombian cocaine is still being delivered to Colombian criminal groups in the Northeast. In those instances, the Mexican DTOs are only contracted to transport the drugs.

[I]ntelligence . . . indicates that Colombian DTOs are contracting with Mexican DTOs to transport heroin from the Southwest Border to Colombian criminal groups in eastern drug markets, such as New York City. As payment, Mexican DTOs receive transportation fees from the Colombian DTOs in cash or by wire after the heroin is delivered by the Mexican organization. Mexican DTOs typically transport the South American heroin in vehicles, on buses and trains, and on commercial aircraft through southern California, South Texas, and West Texas POEs [points of entry] using the overland routes that they had established to transport cocaine as well as Mexican marijuana, methamphetamine, and heroin; they often use low-level couriers in doing so.[18]

— NDIC Drug Threat Assessment for 2008

Meanwhile, the Asian DTOs and their gang affiliates in Canada have been significant producers, transporters, and distributors of high-potency marijuana and MDMA to the various drug markets throughout the U.S. Yet, the Mexican DTOs have still controlled the transportation and wholesale distribution of cocaine and heroin to every place except the Northeast. And those Mexican DTOs are now gaining a larger share of the Northeastern drug market as well.[19] That's why the Mexican DTOs have been purchasing more drugs outright from the Colombian DTOs to distribute themselves.

> Traditionally, Mexican DTOs transported illicit drugs to New England on consignment for Colombian . . . DTOs. However, Mexican traffickers are beginning to bypass Colombian . . . DTOs and are increasingly transporting and distributing cocaine, marijuana, heroin, and limited quantities of ice methamphetamine in New England on their own behalf.[20]
>
> — *NDIC Drug Threat Assessment for 2008*

In essence, the whole northeastern U.S. drug market is being taken over by the Mexicans. That would explain the huge influx of MS-13 cliques into that region. (See Map 2.3.) The Mexican cartels most probably pay MS-13 to guard the drug conduits and keep the street gangs that do the selling in line. As MS-13 also guards such conduits in Mexico, it may also help to sneak product across the border. With all providers consolidated, more society-damaging drugs could be pumped into America from a narco-state neighbor.

Back to the Chinese for a Moment

If the PRC had wanted to add a deluge of drugs to its ongoing 4GW attack on America, would it not work through organized crime contacts in both Canada and Mexico? That liaison could be most easily accomplished through the Hong Kong triads it "financially enlisted to its Communist agenda" in 1997.[21]

> There is a well-documented history of both Russian and Chinese organized crime organizations working as tools of their governments.
>   In Panama, . . . there is a dangerous convergence of well-financed Chinese . . . mobs with Cuban government operatives and Latin American drug lords. . . . This dark

partnership is a . . . direct long-term threat to Mexico and
the United States.[22]
— American Foreign Policy Council Report, 1999

Chinese criminal groups will cooperate with those of other eth-
nicities whenever it is advantageous to do so. And, according to a
Federal Research Study, "[Chinese] cooperation is known to occur
with Hispanic groups." So, the smuggler of Asian dope into Acapulco or any Hutchison Whampoa port along the Pacific Coast may
pay MS-13 to guard their shipping containers as they make their
way north. Or MS-13 may monitor the transport of Asian heroin
from the Port of New York.[23] Either way, the final recipient would
be some Chinese criminal faction—like the Wah Ching, Big Circle
Boys, Fuk Ching, or some other ostensibly homegrown outfit. They,
in turn, would farm out the drugs to local street gangs for resale. A
few triad-affiliated street gangs—like the Black Dragons [24]—might
even take direct delivery and then do their own selling. MS-13
would be nowhere in the chain of custody, but still of great use for
protection.

Or, there may be a more symbiotic relationship between the
Mexican and the Asia DTOs. One primarily deals in methamphetamines and cocaine, while the other handles MDMA and high-potency marijuana. MDMA is often mixed with methamphetamine
to make it more addictive. Why shouldn't the Mexican and Asian
DTOs also cooperate on heroin?

U.S.-based Asian DTOs are expanding their working relationships with other DTOs . . . to increase their whole-
sale- and retail-level high-potency marijuana and MDMA
distribution operations. . . . [S]ome Asian DTOs also trade
their marijuana and MDMA for cocaine supplied by Mexican
DTOs.[25]
— National Drug Threat Assessment for 2009

But, like the Colombian cocaine, most Asian heroin is now
probably sold outright to Mexican cartels that in turn distribute
it through their U.S. gang networks. That way, only the Mexican
cartels would use MS-13 for delivery and collections, and the original supplier would remain anonymous. To maintain deniability on
strategic matters, Asian nations often use proxies. They can do so

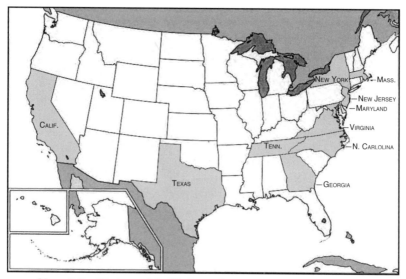

Map 2.3: States with Highest Concentrations of MS-13
(Sources: Nat. Drug Intell. Center, map MS-13map2.gif, n.d.; General Libraries, University of Texas at Austin, from their website for map designator "usa_blank.jpg")

as easily with drug trafficking as in open warfare. Chinese DTOs are known to work through Hispanic cartels and gangs. Such an unholy alliance would pose a significant risk to U.S. security.

> The connections between Mexican and Asian DTOs, the principal suppliers of illicit drugs in the United States, and gangs, the primary retail-level distributors of drugs in many suburban areas, according to reports from law enforcement officials, are an increasing concern to federal, state, and local law enforcement officials.[26]
> — National Drug Intelligence Center, April 2008

How Mexican DTOs Interact with MS-13

While the Mexican DTOs that are most often associated with MS-13 are the Carrillo-Fuentes (Juarez) Cartel and Gulf Cartel, the Sinaloa Alliance also uses MS-13 and the Mexican Mafia.[27] If those DTOs were delivering the drugs on consignment to MS-13, MS-13 would only have to reimburse them for a percentage of what was actually sold. MS-13 has become so sophisticated that it now resembles an organized-crime family itself. Its cliques bother local politicians, offer immediate legal assistance to arrested members, and seem to have their own networks of street vendors. Still, it's difficult to imagine a Mexican cartel being that trusting of a loose confederation of Salvadorian youth.

More probably, MS-13 provides transportation protection for Mexican-cartel shipments and then helps with collections. It may also provide "emergency transpo" whenever normal loads become threatened. "For drug trafficking enterprises, . . . responsibilities such as . . . transport . . . are [often] subcontracted out."[28] To accomplish all three missions at once, MS-13 would need political, economic, and managerial advice. The most probable source of that advice will be discussed later. First, MS-13's known history must be closely reviewed.

MS-13's Background

MS-13 (or *Mara Salvatrucha*) began in Los Angeles in the late 1980's when refugees from El Salvador's civil war banded together to protect themselves from existing neighborhood gangs. In time, many MS-13 members turned to illegal activities. By the 1990's, U.S. law enforcement had deported them back to El Salvador, where they set up local branches or returned to the United States. Soon, this L.A.-born street gang was operating in 34 states, the District of Colombia, and five other countries. By 2005, the states with the largest concentrations (more than six cliques each) were California, Texas, Tennessee, Georgia, North Carolina, Virginia, Maryland, New Jersey, New York, and Massachusetts. (Refer back to Map 2.3.) Within Central America, the sovereign countries with more than six MS-13 cliques were Mexico, Guatemala, El Salvador, and Honduras.[29]

29

MS-13's Organizational Structure

MS-13 currently has no command structure other than that loosely created by clique longevity. Groups all over the United States operate nearly autonomously. Most "strategic guidance" appears to emanate telephonically from the cliques in Los Angeles. It is then relayed by those in mid-country (as in a "calling tree"). L.A. members also do their fair share of traveling and relocating to other States.

Right now, MS-13 has no official national leadership structure. MS-13 originated in Los Angeles, but when members migrated eastward, they began forming cliques that for the most part operated independently. These cliques, though, often maintain regular contact with members in other regions to coordinate recruitment/criminal activities and to prevent conflicts. We do believe that Los Angeles gang members have an elevated status among their MS-13 counterparts across the country, a system of respect that could potentially evolve into a more organized national leadership structure.[30]
— FBI Headline Story, January 2008

"Bottom-up movements" are able be more opportunistic than "top-down bureaucracies." They have ways to compensate for any lack of organizational structure. Among those ways are regional centers to support (instead of direct) local initiatives. For a while, *al-Qaeda* had just such an arrangement. MS-13 may now have regional support centers. They would most likely be near its biggest concentrations. Some 3,000 MS-13 members operate in the Washington, D.C., area alone.[31]

MS-13 is over 10,000 in the United States with the largest concentration in Los Angeles, Northern Virginia, Maryland, and New York.[32]
— FBI Press Release, September 2005

According to an NDIC assessment in 2004, MS-13 "may be increasing its coordination with . . . chapters in Los Angeles, Washington, D.C./Northern Virginia, and New York City, . . . [in] an attempt to build a national command structure."[33] Those who believe that this gang poses little threat because of its lack of organizational structure must still equate efficiency with stratified bureaucracy. That may be true for certain things, but not for short-range combat or criminal behavior.

MS-13's Greatly Expanded U.S. Operating Area

Since starting in Los Angeles in the late 1980's, MS-13 has mysteriously matured into a full-blown criminal enterprise. Its overall membership has not increased that much, just the number of States in which it operates. By July 2005, it had an estimated 8,000-10,000 members nationwide and was in 33 states and the District of Columbia.[34] Nine months later, 10,000 U.S. members were confirmed and five times that number (50,000) in Central America.[35] As of October 2007, MS-13 was in 40 U.S. states and 10 nations (to include Canada) across two continents.[36] As of late 2008, the number of host states had risen to 42 while the nationwide membership remained at 8,000-10,000.[37] *Mara Salvatrucha* was being cautious about who it joined to its ranks.

MS-13 has tried moderately to expand its membership through recruitment and migration. Within the U.S., it mostly targets middle and high school students. It will form tenuous alliances or vicious rivalries, depending on its needs at the time. It recruits new members by glorifying its lifestyle (often over the Internet) and by absorbing smaller gangs. Some long-time MS-13 members have also been relocating—ostensibly to get jobs or be near family members, but more probably to start new cliques. Currently, the largest membership increases are occurring in the northeastern and southeastern U.S. *Mara Salvatrucha's* colors are blue and white, like in the flag of El Salvador. Only its original members still sport elaborate tattoos or body art.[38]

Greater D.C.'s MS-13 Concentration

As the study unfolds, a disturbing question looms. What are so many MS-13 members doing so close to the nation's capital? They may be just exploiting the country's second largest drug market, or they may somehow intend to disrupt its governance. Most Americans would not ordinarily consider the latter possibility. But, at this crucial juncture in their great nation's history, they must be absolutely certain that the current rash of street crime is nothing more than that. Therefore, all *Mara Salvatrucha* activity within 50 miles of D.C. should be closely monitored.

The Other Central American Gang

The 18th Street Gang evolved in the early 1960's from L.A.'s older Hispanic factions. The M-18 *mara* was then started in Central America in the 1990's by 18th Street members who had been deported.[39] Thus, America's 18th Street Gang now includes the U.S. chapters of M-18. In fact, the 18th Street Gang is really just a federation of smaller factions. As such, it is the fastest growing gang in Los Angeles with some 8,000 to 20,000 members in that location alone. The latest NDIC figures show 18th Street membership at 30,000 to 50,000 nationwide. Various 18th Street cliques have been identified in 37 states and the District of Columbia, as well as 10 foreign countries.[40] Within the U.S., M-18 may or may not yet provide the DTOs with "transpo protection" or "distribution to and collections from other gangs."

> The gang's main source of income is retail-level distribution of cocaine and marijuana and, to a lesser extent, heroin and methamphetamine.[41]
> — *Attorney General's Report,* April 2008

Still, many 18th Street factions have become more sophisticated and organized than other gangs. That's because of the close ties their predominantly Mexican members have nurtured with Mexican and Colombian cartels. Some even help to smuggle drugs from Mexico. It's clear from 18th Street rules that most members plan to deal in illegal narcotics. That's why all 18th Street gang members are forbidden from personally using crack cocaine or any other hard drug.[42]

MS-13 controls most of the rail routes in Mexico, but it has been aggressively vying with M-18 for Guatemala's northernmost rail yards. The two gangs have also had big prison brawls in El Salvador and Guatemala.[43] While 18th Street and MS-13 are still rivals inside the U.S., they don't actively fight each other as much here.

MS-13's Function in the Central American Smuggling

Within Central America, *Mara Salvatrucha* "protects" smuggler conduits. Like the guerrillas in Colombia, its members exact a toll or tariff on all contraband that passes through their zones of responsibility.[44] This is quite different from providing the actual means of shipment.

While the Security Minister of Honduras has warned that *al-Qaeda* might try to use MS-13 channels to smuggle terrorists into the U.S.,[45] one can safely say that MS-13 is not part of any *al-Qaeda* plot.

> The FBI . . . [and other intelligence agencies] determined that there is no [evidence of] . . . radical Islamic ties to MS-13 (Mara Salvatrucha)," says Robert Clifford, director of the new [MS-13] task force."[46]
> — *USA Today*, 23 February 2005

In April 2005, that same Security Minister intercepted an overland shipment of small arms from a Central American gang that wanted to trade weapons to Colombian guerrillas for narcotics.[47] That means one or more of the *maras* may be starting to do more than just safeguard other people's routes.

MS-13's Expanded Role within the Continental U.S.

As in Central America,[48] the drug syndicates (whether cartel or triad) have most likely incorporated *Mara Salvatrucha* into their U.S. distribution network. MS-13 does have about 10,000 members in this country with the largest concentrations around Los Angeles, the District of Colombia, and New York. Those 10,000 members could sell a lot of drugs. But main-street U.S.A. is not like the slums of Guatemala, Honduras, and El Salvador. Here, MS-13 would have far less access to schools and neighborhoods. And in the world's biggest drug market, organized crime syndicates might be more interested in a good collection agent. How else could they capitalize on all the gangs available to sell drugs? That collection agent would need the reputation of being utterly ruthless. From 2003 to 2005, there were no fewer than 18 MS-13 related killings in North Carolina, 11 in Northern Virginia, and eight more in L.A. Within the Charlotte area alone, MS-13 has murdered 11 human beings over the last eight years.[49]

Inside the U.S., *Mara Salvatrucha* cliques may have also added another dimension to their "conduit protection" role. After helping to smuggle product across the border, some may monitor its northward progress. Others may off-load any threatened truck and shuttle its contents the rest of the way by car. As is clearly evident from Map 1.1, MS-13 has already established "vehicular protection lanes" that stretch all the way from the Mexican border to America's largest metropolitan areas. In the dangerous world of big drug deals, reliable "transpo" needs not only its own "muscle," but also an alternate shipping means.

The Triads Could Have Easily Linked Up with MS-13

When the British Protectorate of Hong Kong was ceded to Communist China in 1997, large numbers of its citizens immigrated to Vancouver, British Columbia. Many a triad member was among them, because 14-K and Sun Yee On are both now well established in Canada and the United States.[50] The West Coast has long been regarded as America's "stronghold of Asian organized crime activity," particularly the communities of Santa Ana and Garden Grove in Orange County, California.[51] Of course, MS-13 originated in the Rampart area of nearby Los Angeles. Since that time, its cliques have spread to northern California, Oregon, Washington, Alaska, Idaho, Nevada, Arizona, and Colorado.[52] Those cliques now transport "multi-kilogram quantities of powdered cocaine . . . and kilogram quantities of heroin and methamphetamine throughout the Southwest, particularly [in] southern California, Nevada, and Texas."[53] It's doubtful that some MS-13 "headquarters" is sending the drugs it has bought to far-flung subordinate locations to be resold. More probably (and as in Central America), the various cliques shuttle cartel drug shipments from one to another as "transpo" subcontractors. With regard to the Asian product, they may do likewise for a triad.

Of all the police departments polled in every corner of the U.S., over 28% reported local gangs associating with Asian organized-crime groups. To increase criminal activity and profit, such groups readily work with street gangs.[54] According to FBI-approved research, "Asian organized crime groups and street gangs [frequently] work with non-Asian groups, usually for the purposes of drug trafficking."[55] Thus, they could easily be affiliated with MS-13 and Southern California's other Hispanic gangs.

Wah Ching has grown over 40 years from a San Francisco street gang to the "organized crime group" that controls most of the criminal activity in L.A.'s Chinatown. It has "strong associations" with Oriental crime factions in Seattle, Vancouver, Toronto, Boston, and New York. That means close ties to Sun Yee On and 14-K, but not Wo Hop To.[56] Wah Ching is known to traffic in narcotics.[57] Its probable relationship with 14-K and Sun Yee On is best illustrated by what its initial arrangement was with Wo Hop To.

> In the 1990's, . . . Wo Hop To set foot in San Francisco to take over all Asian organized crime in the United States. At that time Wah Ching and Wo Hop To became partners in crime activities. Later, they turned into rivals after one of the Wah Ching leaders was gunned down . . . by members of the Wo Hop To.[58]

Wah Ching is the most likely intermediary for all 14-K and/or Sun Yee On drug transactions on the U.S. West Coast. Only missing is a link between Wah Ching and MS-13. Roughly equivalent numbers of Asian and Hispanic gangs share Los Angeles, Long Beach, Carson, Pomona, and Torrance. Torrance is also known to be a Wah Ching stronghold. It would only allow allied gangs on its turf. "There are Asian gangs that 'down' with the Surenos."[59] Unfortunately, the term may have more than one meaning in the gang world.

Mexican DTOs Already Using Triad Tricks

Many of the illegal aliens and narcotics move north through Mexico in MS-13-watched passenger trains,[60] but bulk currency heads south on Mexican bus lines.[61] There are many more bus routes in America than train routes, so here buses may carry more of the drugs. Mexican DTOs are already known to ship drugs across the southwestern U.S. by private bus.[62] With little trouble, they could collocate watchful passengers with drug-laden packages on public buses. That may be what happens in other parts of the country.

Chinese triads also use buses to transport contraband. To further copy the triads, Mexican DTOs and MS-13 could simply ship their drugs through a food or merchandize supplier to markets or stores they already control.[63] Such suppliers often have their own fleets of trucks.

In his research, Chin (1996) found that Chinese gangs were quite active in legitimate businesses in New York City's Chinatown. For example, they owned or operated restaurants, retail stores, vegetable stands, car services, ice cream parlors, fish markets, and video stores.[64]

MS-13 Services All Comers at the Border

Mara Salvatrucha regularly targets U.S. Border Patrol personnel for impeding its "people smuggling."[65] There is other violence against law enforcement officials at the Southwest Border to deter them from seizing illicit drug shipments or as a diversion during drug smuggling operations.[66]

MS-13 is thought to have established a major smuggling center in Matamoros, Mexico, just south of Brownsville, Texas. From that center, it arranges to bring illegal aliens into the U.S. from countries other than Mexico.[67] It could not be doing so without the explicit permission of the Gulf Cartel. Mexican DTOs also collect fees from people-trafficking organizations for the use of specific smuggling routes.[68]

If MS-13 can bring illegal immigrants across the border, it can also bring in narcotics. It definitely does so for the cartels. According to the NDIC, *Mara Salvatrucha* is frequently employed by both Gulf and Tijuana Cartels for precisely that purpose.[69] It could just as easily work for the triads.

Members [of MS-13] smuggle illicit drugs, primarily powder cocaine and marijuana, into the United States and transport and distribute the drugs throughout the country. Some members also are involved in alien smuggling.[70]
— *Attorney General's Report,* April 2008

Human "mules" are a good way to carry narcotics across the border, but tunnels—something at which Asians have long been expert—would make that trip less obvious. Many such tunnels have already been found on both sides of the traditional Chinese smuggling hub of Mexicali. Why should anyone then doubt that the Mexican DTOs have obtained Chinese or North Korean excavation advice?

MS-13's West Coast Affiliations Point to a Different Mentor

During the 1980's, California's Hispanic street gangs were nominally separated into *Surenos* (Southerners) and *Nortenos* (Northerners). The two terms designated whether the gang was from the northern or southern part of the state. As *Mara Salvatrucha* grew in size, it aligned with the Mexican Mafia prison gang *(Le Eme* or "M")* under the *Los Surenos* umbrella. Once so aligned, it incorporated the number "13" into its name. Before long, the Mexican Mafia (which also operates outside of prison) had formed a coalition that encompassed most of L.A.'s Hispanic gangs.[71]

These Surenos . . . became convenient and expendable instruments to be utilized by the EME to further its criminal enterprise. Their loyalty to EME is often expressed by identifying their respective gangs and adding "13" (for M—the 13th letter of the alphabet) or "X13" after their gang name.

. . . In the 1970's the Black Hand of the Mexican Mafia expanded outside the prison walls and evolved into a criminal organization specializing in extortion, narcotics trafficking, and other crimes. . . .

Around 1992, Orange County law enforcement discovered that the Mexican Mafia was conducting mass meetings of numerous rival Hispanic gangs. Video surveillance of a meeting in El Salvador Park with hundreds of gang members was obtained. . . . Ojeda [the senior EME representative] instituted a "no drive-by" edict . . . [and] the taxation of all drug dealers operating in areas controlled by the EME or its surrogate Sureno army.[72]
— *Police Magazine,* July 2007

"Sureno, or Sur 13, is a banner under which most southern California Hispanic gangs gather." And, according to a reliable source, it is now virtually synonymous with the Mexican Mafia. "Southern California's branch of the Mexican Mafia calls itself the Surenos (or Sur-13)." Thousands of former convicts are still members of the Mexican Mafia and mostly live in California, Texas, and Arizona. While there is allegedly a *Le Eme* "headquarters" in San Antonio, that city more probably hosts a regional trade consulate. There are as many as "30,000 [Mexican Mafia members] throughout the Unites States."[73]

Within the Mexican Mafia's list of "criminal accomplishments" lies implicit proof of MS-13's new role. What was once just a street gang of youthful Salvadorian immigrants must minimally help to bring drugs up from Central America, across the U.S. border, and then over to America's biggest cities. The Mexican cartels supply all *Sureno* street gangs with drugs through the Mexican Mafia and then depend upon the Mexican Mafia to control all *Sureno* drug trafficking activity.[74]

> According to the NDIC, the "Mexican Mafia smuggles the drugs from Tijuana into southern California for distribution and is suspected of smuggling drugs from Mexico into Arizona, New Mexico, and Texas." It also distributes drugs throughout northern California, Washington, and Hawaii and, to a lesser degree, [in] Idaho, Nevada, and Oregon (NDIC, Drugs and Crime Gang Profile: Mexican Mafia, July 2003). . . . California's Mexican Mafia has recently increased the extent to which it controls the street-level drug trade through its dominance of Sureno gangs. Sureno street gangs sell drugs and must pay a 10 percent tax to the Mexican Mafia in return for protection in prison. Failure to pay the tax will result in . . . the gang's members . . . be[ing] shot on sight. As the Mexican Mafia's control increases, some evidence suggests that "Sureno gangs are rebelling against the process and fighting back" (McBride, President of Cal. Gang Investigators Assoc.).[75]
>
> — FBI's National Gang Threat Assessment, 2005

To collect this tax, who would be better qualified than MS-13? To handle an expanding market, the Mexican Mafia may now be also grooming another protege for "transpo," "collection," or both. It continues to influence the policies that guide both MS-13 and M-18 in Mexico and Central America. There is even talk of MS-13 and M-18 forming some kind of alliance. But, instead of letting by-gones be bygones, both will probably manage different segments of an expanding drug network. According to the DEA, MS-13 is most closely connected with the Carillo-Fuentez (Juarez) and Cardenas-Guillen (Gulf) Cartels, whereas M-18 works with the Arellano-Felix (Tijuana) and Guzman-Loera (Sinaloa) Cartels. MS-13 is most active in 38 states, whereas M-18 operates in 28.[76]

> There has also been some speculation that MS-13 leaders would like to bring 18th Street and MS-13 together to become the strongest Hispanic gang in Central America and the United States. Recent violence occurring between MS-13 and 18th Street, and within the gangs themselves in several jurisdictions, indicates that attempts to align the two gangs have not yet been successful.[77]
> — FBI's National Gang Threat Assessment, 2005

According to a *New York Times* article in August 2007, there have already been attempts to merge M-18 with MS-13. It first cites a 2004 report by the NDIC. That report indicated M-18 "may be increasing its coordination with MS-13 chapters in Los Angeles, Washington, D.C./Northern Virginia, and New York City, possibly signaling an attempt to build a national command structure." On Long Island in 2006, there was another hint of this merger. A *Mara Salvatrucha* leader came in from the West Coast "to try to organize the various cliques or sets into a more formal structure," says Robert Hart, supervisory special agent with the FBI. "That's a significant step in the development of MS-13." And in northern Virginia, U.S. Attorney Paul McNulty observed that "in some of the violent crimes, there seems to be a kind of approval process in some kind of hierar-chy beyond the clique." According to the National Council for Public Security, the lead Hispanic gang is "highly organized and disciplined . . . with semi-clandestine structures and vertical commands."[78]

The Mexican Mafia's *Modus Operandi*

While the Mexican Mafia's highly deceptive methods simulate Asian 4GW thinking, they may simply spring from the criminal mind. Thus, the Mexican Mafia appears to be MS-13's only men-tor.

This system of infiltration and takeover of "self help" and gang prevention organizations continues to be one of the Mexican Mafia's favorite tactics today. They utilize corrupt and gullible politicians, policemen, churches, and attorneys to gain control of these resources.[79]
— *Police Magazine,* July 2007

The Mexican Mafia also likes to extort (demand a protection fee from) drug distributors. In turn, the *Surenos* extort money from the street dealers. Still, everyone's main source of income is the retail-level distribution of cocaine, heroin, marijuana, and methamphetamines.[80] Thus, the Mexican Mafia may want MS-13 and now M-18 to recruit and tax more vendors. That would be the same as mobilizing gangs of varying ethnicity and, as such, a fairly terrifying prospect. While only Latino or Asian gangs might be included, there is no guarantee of that.

For the PRC's strategic agenda to be realized, there need not be any direct link between it and the *Surenos*. To divert and hamstring the American military, its PLA proxies have only to encourage enough chaos within the continental U.S. to preclude foreign deployment. Wherever there is greed and anti-social behavior, this should not be all that hard to accomplish.

The Texas Version of the Mexican Mafia

The Lone Star equivalent of the Mexican Mafia *(Le Emi or Mexikanemi)* was formed within the Texas Prison System in the 1980's.[81] While *Le Emi* works with the Carrillo-Fuentes (Juarez) and Cardenas-Guillen (Gulf) Cartels, its California cousin—*Le Eme*—works most closely with the Curillo-Fuentes (Juarez), Arellano-Felix (Tijuana), and Guzman-Loera (Sinaloa) Cartels.[82] As *Mexikanemi* and MS-13 both associate with the Gulf Cartel, MS-13 must also help *Mexikanemi* to smuggle narcotics across the border and transport them inland. There is little doubt that *Le Emi* has been deeply involved in both endeavors.

Gang members [of *Le Emi]* reportedly traffic multi-kilogram quantities of powder cocaine, heroin, and methamphetamine; and multi-ton quantities of marijuana from Mexico into the United States for distribution inside and outside prison.

Gang members obtain drugs from associates or members of the Osiel Cárdenas-Guíllen, and/or Vicente Carrillo-Fuentes Mexican DTOs. In addition, Mexikanemi members possibly maintain a relationship with Los Zetas [paramilitary enforcers], which is associated with a Gulf Cartel.[83]
— *Attorney General's Report,* April 2008

What Is *Le Eme's* Protege Doing in the Northeastern U.S.?

Outside L.A., MS-13 has its largest concentrations in Northern Virginia, Maryland, and New York. Intelligence officials indicate that in 2002, MS-13 members moved "multi-kilogram quantities of powdered cocaine, crack cocaine, and marijuana throughout the greater New York City metropolitan area and New Jersey." In the Northeast, *Mara Salvatrucha* distributes cocaine at the wholesale level. It is probable that other gangs do all the street selling while MS-13 provides the product and supervision. On Long Island, local cliques convene for large meetings—called "universals"—according to Michael Bolitho, a gang investigator with the Nassau County police department.[84]

Intelligence reports from 2002 also indicated that MS-13 members trafficked in powdered cocaine, marijuana, heroin, and methamphetamine throughout the Mid-Atlantic.[85]

More Questions about M-13's Sponsorship

Though MS-13 is closely aligned with the Mexican Mafia, it has not been hierarchically structured like the Mexican Mafia.[86] It operates more like a triad gang federation, with all procedural guidelines being disseminated piecemeal to its cliques.

Triad societies . . . are in fact loose cartels . . . of independent gangs that adopt a similar organizational structure and ritual to bind their members together. . . . The triads' organizational structure has become flexible and decentralized.[87]

MS-13 has also been far too friendly with Asian factions to be completely disassociated from them in the U.S. drug market. Accord-

41

ing to the FBI, Asian criminal enterprises more commonly cooperate across lines of racial and ethnic heritage. Those Asian enterprises have been identified in some 50 American cities and are most prevalent in the following: (1) Boston; (2) Chicago; (3) Honolulu; (4) Las Vegas; (5) Los Angeles; (6) New Orleans; (7) New York; (8) Newark; (9) Philadelphia; (10) Portland; (11) San Francisco; (12) Seattle; and (13) Washington, D.C.[88] Most of the Oriental factions just happen to be in the cities that lie along MS-13 operated drug routes from Texas. (Refer back to Map 2.2.) Chinese triads are also active in Sacramento, Houston, Dallas, Denver, Beaumont (Texas), Miami, Atlanta, Vancouver, Calgary, and Toronto.[89] Of particular note, 14-K's "transpo" contractors, Wah Ching, and the Mexican DTOs all use L.A. and Houston as hubs.[90] From where else would one manage two of the most active drug conduits into the U.S.—those from Tijuana and Laredo?

The Triads Also Have Diverse Gang Affiliations

The West Coast has long been recognized as the "stronghold of Asian organized crime activity" within the U.S. Deeply involved in the smuggling of both people and drugs, the Wah Ching undoubtedly involves other street gangs in its distribution network. It is known to protect its brothels with Black Dragons and Koolboyz.[91] Within Los Angeles County, Asian and Hispanic gangs often share the same neighborhoods. Why couldn't they also get their drugs from the same supplier? If the triads now have to sell most U.S.-bound drugs to the Mexican cartels, then the Wah Ching will have to repurchase those drugs from the Mexican cartels. Why couldn't the Wah Ching also hire Mexican-Mafia-affiliated MS-13 to handle its transport? For cover, such a multi-ethnic arrangement would make perfect sense.

The 14-K is the fastest growing triad in Canada and maintains a considerable presence in New York and other East Coast cities.[92] Its parent society in Hong Kong has strong connections to the following U.S.-based Asian gangs: (1) the Wah Ching; (2) Black Dragons; (3) Tiny Rascal Gangsters; and (4) Black Star. Those gangs operate in Detroit, Los Angeles, New York, San Francisco, and Seattle.[93] Some, if not all, appear to be active on both coasts. The Tiny Rascal Gangsters are also linked to the Wo Hop To triad.[94]

Tiny Rascal Gangsters is one of the largest and most violent Asian street gang associations in the United States. It is composed of at least 60 structured and unstructured gangs, commonly referred to as sets, with an estimated 5,000 to 10,000 members and associates active in at least 16 states. Most members are Asian American males. The sets are most active in the Southwest, Pacific, and New England Regions. The retail-level distribution of powder cocaine, marijuana, MDMA, and methamphetamine is a primary source of income for the sets.[95]

— *Attorney General's Report*, April 2008

After the Golden Dragon Massacre of 1977, the Jackson Street Boys were supposedly "dismantled" by San Francisco's police department. If they have since made a comeback, they would be in the same city and affiliated with Wo Hop To.[96]

New York's Tung On "gang" has been linked to Sun Yee On.[97] However, Tung On is more likely a tong-like triad within the Tung Group.[98] In China, the Tung Group is considered disloyal, dishonorable, and ruthless. After a bloody battle in 2007 between Shui Fong and the Tung Group (also known as the Kowloon Tong), the latter was disbanded.[99] Thus, the number of business contacts between Tung On and Sun Yee On are probably minimal.

Members of Sun Yee On also have connections with New York City's Fuk (or Fu) Ching gang.[100] The Fuk Ching is regarded as one of the most powerful, and transnationally active, Chinese organized crime groups in the U.S.[101] It smuggles people across national borders, so it probably sneaks in dope as well. As a tong-affiliated gang, it may function as Sun Yee On's northeastern middleman, while the Big Circle Boys help 14-K. Other Chinese gangs in New York are the Flying Dragons, Ghost Shadows, Tung On, and Born to Kill.[102] Only the Flying Dragons and Tung On are known to affiliate with Asian DTOs.[103]

There will be those who say that no assemblage of Chinese youth in America has anything to do with the PRC. One of the best recognized authorities on that subject begs to differ.

Ko-lin Chin concludes that many crimes in Chinese-American communities—especially drug trafficking, money laundering, and human trafficking—are linked to China. He says

43

that Chinese gang members flee to China when sought by American law enforcement.[104]
— United Nations Activities Report

The PLA-Affiliated Triads Want More Than Just Money

The Big Circle Boys have been identified as 14-K's main contact for narcotics sales in the northeastern United States. The same Big Circle Boys have also been distributing dope for the Colombian cartels.

Big Circle includes substantial numbers of triad members (Huston, 108-109).

The Big Circle Gang is primarily responsible for much of the exportation of Southeast Asian heroin that enters the United States, although its members also have been involved in the trafficking of . . . South American cocaine.[105]
— Library of Congress Report, July 2003

Because Big Circle deals in both Asian heroin and Colombian cocaine, one can reasonably conclude that its PLA triad parent is attempting to do more than just make money in the United States. And that parent's presence—along with Sun Yee On—in Paraguay's TBA suggests the same subversive design on the entire Western Hemisphere.[106]

Hard Times Ahead

Almost 92% of the world's supply of heroin now comes from Afghan opium.[107] While the white heroin from Colombia and Mexico are currently sufficient for the U.S. market,[108] a huge influx of Southwest Asian product may drastically change that dynamic. It could be easily pumped into America through Mexico's new Hutchison Whampoa ports and increasingly porous northern border.[109] If Asian heroin were freely to flow up the ever-expanding NAFTA corridor from Mexico, it could very possibly implode U.S. society. At many places along the Mexican border, the stream of manufactured goods has been increasing.[110] Many of those goods come from Asia. That creates a perfect opportunity for the drug smuggler. When this Asian/Mexican DTO partnership no longer experiences any shortages of product inside the U.S., it will expand and harden its distribution networks. This should pose quite a challenge for local police departments. (Read the following closely; a highly credible agency has identified the ultimate source of the problem.)

> [M]any law enforcement challenges remain, particularly the danger posed by the growing strength and organization of *Mexico-[based] . . . Asian DTOs* [italics added].[111]
> — *NDIC Drug Threat Assessment for 2008*

Chapter One has proven it is the Hong Kong triads that have been bringing most Southeast Asian heroin into the U.S. (through Canada). With that "connection" now largely interdicted, those Hong Kong triads (to include PLA proxies) would be looking for a new way into the U.S. and possibly even a new source of supply. The former would most logically be through Mexico, and the latter from Afghanistan. To see what such an arrangement might do to U.S. society, one must review the accomplishments to date of the American criminal-justice system.

3 ___ Too Much for U.S. Police to Handle?

- How much more prevalent are youth gangs in America?
- What role will they play in the drug deluge?

Gangs account for only part of every town's crime.

(Source: Correl Gallery Clipart, Totem Graphics, Man, Business, #28S009)

The Biggest Challenge to Further Research

If such an onslaught were beyond the U.S. law enforcement community's capabilities, its national agencies would never admit it. All "budget-dependent" bureaucracies nurture statistics to suggest that every previous challenge has been met. After "partial glimpses" into the past, most voters and Congressmen then assume overall success in the future. This little bureaucratic game will make it much harder to show that the U.S. military must now get involved to defend America against a "crime-like" 4GW offensive. Whether statistically hard to substantiate or not, the immediate need for more U.S. military assistance must somehow be communicated. Once the border dike has too many holes, there will be no stopping what is to follow.

Other evidence must be found of the unanticipated load about to be placed on local police departments and state penal systems. If everything has been going so well, why are so many residents of inner-city neighborhoods now resigned to the violence? And, why is the area around the nation's capitol one of the most dangerous in the country? Whatever the scope of undisclosed setbacks, Americans still owe a debt of gratitude to their state and federal agents. Counter-narcotics is the most dangerous of all law enforcement endeavors.

Extent of the Surface Problem

The expanse of America's drug-trafficking network is mind boggling. Just identifying its most active participants was tough. Though the DEA claims drug use has declined among teenagers and "workers" over the last few years,[1] it says nothing about adult nonworkers. They're the ones who commit most of the offenses. U.S.-bound cocaine production is up 27% in Colombia over last year,[2] and 92% of the world's heroin is now made from Afghan opium.[3] So, as the world's largest drug market, the U.S. is still very much "in play." Wherever there are drugs, there will be street gangs to share in the profits. According to the *National Youth Gang Survey for 2002,* "approximately 731,500 gang members and 21,500 gangs were active [then] in the United States."[4] The same survey for 2006 shows 785,000 gang members and 26,500 gangs.[5] That's a 23% increase in the number of gangs over four years. The *National Gang Threat Assessment for 2009* shows 1,000,000 gang members active as of September 2008.[6] That's a further rise of 27% in just two years. The problem is clearly getting worse.

In response to this increase in gangs, the Department of Justice has a launched an expanded program.[7] But will that program be enough if the new "gangbangers" are all part of an emerging superpower's coordinated effort to mire its only remaining opposition in drugs?

China Ocean Shipping Company (COSCO)—a PLA-owned business enterprise—has already been accused of international drug trafficking. And Chinese triads are known to be smuggling human contraband into Panama.[8] Those things make likely the cooperation/participation of other known PLA extensions, like Hutchison Whampoa, Sun Yee On, and (almost certainly) 14-K. Hutchison Whampoa already controls five separate port facilities along the most-often-used (Pacific) smuggling corridor to the U.S.—Manta (Ecuador), Balboa (Panama), and three more in Mexico (Lazaro Cardenas, Manzanillo, and Ensenada). On the Atlantic approaches, it controls port facilities at Cristobal (Panama), Veracruz (Mexico), and Freeport (Bahamas).[9] Put all of those facts together, and one starts to see the immense magnitude of the interdiction problem.

> "The activities of transnational and national organized criminal enterprises are increasing in scope and magnitude as these groups continue to strengthen their networking with each other to expand their operations," said FBI Deputy Director John S. Pistole.[10]
> — FBI News Release, April 2008

Many of the "free-trade-agreement" provisions don't make that interdiction any easier. The pilot program that allowed Mexican trucks to deliver goods to American cities was allowed to run out in March 2009, but it may not be entirely dead. According to Associated Press (AP), "The [new] administration . . . has asked the office of the U.S. Trade Representative to work with the Department of Transportation, State Department, and Congress to create a new trucking program."[11]

The Secondary Threat

When the streets are no longer safe to walk, "freedom" becomes more of a philosophy than a way of life. Revolution can only grow out of internal discord. That's why the Communists regularly destabilize targeted nations. Nothing short of chaos would result from too many drugs, street gangs to sell it, and underfunded police departments to combat it. Much of that chaos would come from secondary, drug-related crime.

National Drug Threat Survey (NDTS) data for 2007 show that . . . the percentage of state and local [law enforcement] agencies . . . identified cocaine as the drug that most contributed to violent crime (46.9%) and property crime (40.9%).[12]

— *NDIC Drug Threat Assessment for 2008*

If America were to experience a massive influx of Asian heroin from Mexico, those other types of crime would drastically increase throughout the country. At the end of 2006, one out of every 31 U.S. adults was already in prison, on probation, or on parole.[13] In fact, America had the highest incarceration rate of any country in the world.[14] Any soldier, Marine, or policeman who doesn't see the danger in this has no business in charge. A badly overstretched criminal justice system can't handle many more perpetrators without dire consequences. Those consequences would range from early release of large numbers of inmates to complete abandonment of any rehabilitation for those still incarcerated. Those two things have already happened in California's grossly overcrowded penal system, and only the Federal Bureau of Prisons is any bigger. California also has the nation's highest recidivism rate of 70%.[15] Perhaps other states would also like whole counties that resemble active war zones after dark.

That is not the extent of the repercussions. America already has a problem with prescription drugs. Many of its citizens now ingest unnatural chemicals at the first sign of discomfort despite serious side-effect warnings. To imagine the worst-case scenario from too much cocaine and heroin on the streets of Milwaukee, one must only look for trends in an assortment of near-narco-states (like Afghanistan, Colombia, Mexico, and Venezuela). While each has its own political affiliations, all share several symptoms. All have corruption at every level of their internal security apparatus. All are beset by street gangs and/or organized-crime syndicates. All suffer from rampant crime to include kidnapping. All pose an extreme risk to investigative journalists. And all have exercised varying degrees of extrajudicial punishment.[16] In such an environment, open revolution easily thrives.

A Terrifying Prospect

What if the distribution of all dope coming into the United States were consolidated, and then gangs of every ethnicity were to participate in its sale? Mexican DTOs have already taken over the transportation and wholesale distribution of illegal narcotics to every part of the country. And there is disturbing proof they have no intention of limiting their retail distribution to Hispanic and Asian gangs.

> In Florida . . . , they [Mexican DTOs] have gained a greater share of the drug market by forcing African-American street gangs out of mid-level drug distribution and relegating them to lower-level retail distribution.[17]
> — NDIC Drug Threat Assessment for 2008

The Bloods, Crips, Gangster Disciples, and many other African-American U.S.-based gangs already get their drugs from Mexican cartels. (Those named are in 37, 41, and 33 States, respectively.) So too are the Puerto Rican Latin Kings and Caucasian Hell's Angels supplied with drugs from Mexico. And they are in 33 and 28 States, respectively.[18] The combined coverage of the market would be considerable. (See Figure 3.1.)

Gangs Affiliated with the Sinaloa Gulf, Juarez, or Tijuana Cartels	
18th Street	Latin Kings
Bandidos	Mara Salvatrucha (MS-13)
Bario Azteca	Mexican Mafia
Black Guerilla Family	Mexikanemi
Bloods	Mongols
Crips	Nortenos
Florencia 13	Surenos
Gangster Disciples	Tango Blast
Hells Angels	Texas Syndicate
Hermanos de Pistoleros Latinos	Vagos

Source: State, Federal, and local law enforcement reporting

Figure 3.1: Gangs Already Distributing Mexican Cartel Dope
(Source: Table 8, National Drug Threat Assessment [for] 2009, "Gangs.")

Then, not only would wholesale distribution be consolidated, but most street sales would be by multiple chapters of the same gangs.

At least 23 gangs have been identified by law enforcement officials as national-level gangs, operating in multiple states and/or numerous major drug markets. . . . Moreover, . . . [there are] connections between transnational DTOs and 11 national-level street gangs, 6 national-level prison gangs, 4 national-level OMGs [outlaw motorcycle gangs], 2 regional-level street gangs, 1 regional-level prison gang, and 3 local prison gangs.[19]
— *Attorney General's Report,* April 2008

The Unfortunate Model for Other Cities

The Mexican Mafia and MS-13 both originated in L.A. And L.A. is where the Wah Ching now holds sway over many of the Asian gangs. Here, one can see the results of too many gangs and an increasing supply of drugs.[20] Eastern cities should take note.

"We in law enforcement are committed locally and internationally to suppressing violence in all its forms," said Sheriff of Los Angeles County, Leroy Baca. "The high number of deaths from gang activity has reached a crisis point. Over the last decade, in Los Angeles County, we've lost more than 5,800 people to gang violence in comparison to less than 500 people to natural disasters. The growing gang violence is not just a policing issue. . . . Whether it is a gang problem at the local level or the international level, the result is the same. We are facing a public health crisis. It is a crisis that needs to be treated with the same intensity and coordination of efforts that we would treat a major health crisis."[21]
— DEA Press Release, 3 March 2008

There are about 500 *"Sureno"* Hispanic gangs in Los Angeles County representing over 50% of its total gang population. Those Hispanic gangs are fairly evenly distributed throughout the region with significant numbers in the San Fernando Valley, San Gabriel Valley, Beach communities, Long Beach, Compton, and South Los

Alhambra [2 gangs]	Lakewood
Antelope Valley [former listing]	Lancaster
Artesia [3 gangs]	Lawndale
Atwater [former listing]	Lomita
Azusa [2 gangs]	Long Beach [13 gangs]
Baldwin Park [2 gangs]	L.A. County [34 gangs]
Bell [7 gangs]	Los Angeles [167 gangs]
Bell Gardens [5 gangs]	Lynwood [11 gangs]
Bellflower [2 gangs]	Maywood
Burbank [4 gangs]	Monrovia
Canyon Country [4 gangs]	Montebello
Carson [5 gangs]	Monterey Park
City of Commerce	Newhall
City of Industry	Norwalk [4 gangs]
Claremont	Paramount [7 gangs]
Compton [22 gangs]	Pasadena [6 gangs]
Covina	Pico Rivera [4 gangs]
Cudahy [2 gangs]	Pomona [4 gangs]
Culver City	Redondo Beach
Downey [6 gangs]	Rosemead [3 gangs]
Duarte	San Dimas
El Monte [12 gangs]	San Fernando [2 gangs]
El Sereno [former listing]	Santa Clarita [5 gangs]
Gardena	Santa Fe Springs
Glendale	Santa Monica
Hacienda Heights	South Gate [6 gangs]
Hawaiian Gardens	Temple
Hawthorne	Torrance [3 gangs]
Huntington Park [7 gangs]	Walnut
Inglewood [6 gangs]	West Covina
Irwindale	West Whittier
La Mirada	Whittier [7 gangs]
La Puente	

Figure 3.2: Places with Hispanic Gangs in Los Angeles County
(Source: Courtesy of streetgangs.com, "Hispanic Gangs in Los Angeles County")

Angeles.[22] Figure 3.2 shows a complete list (updated in May 2009) of the cities within Los Angeles County where Hispanic gangs are active.

Antelope Valley [3 gangs]	L.A.—South & Central Region
Arcadia [5 gangs]	[30 gangs]
Carson [7 gangs]	L.A.—San Fernando Valley
Cerritos [8 gangs]	[17 gangs]
Diamond Bar [2 gangs]	Monterey Park [3 gangs]
Gardena	Pomona [4 gangs]
Glendale [4 gangs]	Rowland Heights [5 gangs]
Eagle Rock [2 gangs]	San Gabriel Valley [15 gangs]
Hawthorne [2 gangs]	Torrance [5 gangs]
Long Beach [10 gangs]	West Covina [7 gangs]

Figure 3.3: Places with Asian Gangs in Los Angeles County
(Source: Courtesy of streetgangs.com, "Asian Gangs in Los Angeles County")

Some 20,000 Asian-gang members—with a diverse array of backgrounds and affiliations—also reside in Los Angeles County. As some affiliate with Bloods and Crips,[23] others may cooperate with *Surenos*. Figure 3.3 lists the locations in the county where Asian gangs were active in May 2009. There are also Asian Gangs in Garden Grove, Fullerton, and Santa Ana. That's to be expected because the Orange County communities of Santa Ana and Garden Grove have long been considered the "stronghold of Asian organized crime activity" in the U.S. Among the Asian gangs in Santa Ana are the Satanas, Natomas Boys, Black Dragons, and White Dragons.[24]

The Same Syndrome Elsewhere

Whatever drugs the Hong Kong triads cannot hide in the glut of manufactured goods now headed to the U.S. from Asia, they will sell to the Mexican cartels for further distribution in the north. NDIC's "Drug Threat Assessment for 2008" alludes to Mexican DTOs taking over transport and distribution of drugs to every part of America. That means trouble for all cities with a Mexican cartel presence. There are two recent sources of this information. One is

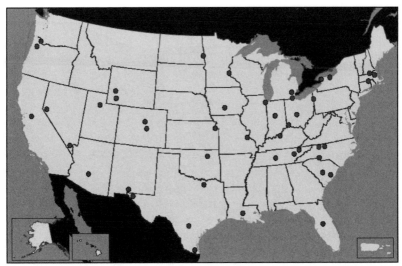

Map 3.1: Most Mexican Cartel Presence in the United States
(Source: "Mexico's Drug Cartels," by Colleen W. Cook, CRS Report for Congress, Order Code RL34215, 25 February 2008)

a Congressional Research Service study (Map 3.1) from February 2008 and the other is an NDIC situation report from April 2008 (Figure 3.4). When combined, they show the biggest presence in the following locations: (1) Brownsville and San Antonio, Texas; (2) New Orleans, Louisiana; (3) Charlotte, Greensboro, and Winston-Salem, North Carolina; (4) north of New London, Connecticut, near where I-395 leaves the state going north; (5) Boston and Fitchburg, Massachusetts; and finally (6) Greenville, New Hampshire (north of Fitchburg). What happened in L.A. may be about to happen here and in other East Coast cities as MS-13 takes greater control over their sale of heroin and cocaine. That sale is predicated on an abundance of other street gangs to do the selling. (See Map 3.2.)

55

Alabama
　　(Unidentified cartel—Albertville, Birmingham, Decatur, Dothan, Huntsville, Mobile, Montgomery)
Alaska
　　Anchorage　　　　　　　　　　Tijuana
Arizona
　　Douglas　　　　　　　　　　　Federation, Juárez
　　Glendale　　　　　　　　　　　Federation
　　Naco　　　　　　　　　　　　　Federation
　　Nogales　　　　　　　　　　　Federation, Gulf
　　Peoria　　　　　　　　　　　　Federation
　　Phoenix　　　　　　　　　　　Federation, Juárez
　　Sasabe　　　　　　　　　　　　Federation
　　Sierra Vista　　　　　　　　　　Federation
　　Tucson　　　　　　　　　　　　Federation, Juárez
　　Yuma　　　　　　　　　　　　　Federation
Arkansas
　　Little Rock　　　　　　　　　　Federation
　　(Unidentified cartel—Fayetteville, Fort Smith)
California
　　Calexico　　　　　　　　　　　Federation, Tijuana
　　El Centro　　　　　　　　　　　Federation
　　Goshen　　　　　　　　　　　Tijuana
　　Los Angeles　　　　　　　　　Federation, Tijuana
　　Oakland　　　　　　　　　　　Federation
　　Otay Mesa　　　　　　　　　　Federation
　　Porterville　　　　　　　　　　Tijuana
　　Riverside　　　　　　　　　　　Federation
　　Sacramento　　　　　　　　　Tijuana
　　San Diego　　　　　　　　　　Federation, Tijuana
　　San Francisco　　　　　　　　Federation
　　San Ysidro　　　　　　　　　　Federation
　　Stockton　　　　　　　　　　　Tijuana
　　Tulare　　　　　　　　　　　　Tijuana
　　(Unidentified cartel—Alameda, Bakersfield, Elk Grove, Fresno, Garden Grove, Hacienda Heights, Hayward, Oxnard, Perris, San Bernardino, San Jose, Santa Ana, Temecula, Westminister)
Colorado
　　Aurora　　　　　　　　　　　Juárez
　　Colorado Springs　　　　　　Federation, Juárez
　　Denver　　　　　　　　　　　Federation, Juárez
　　(Unidentified cartel—Greely, Olathe, Pueblo)
Connecticut
　　(Unidentified cartel—Hartford)
Delaware
　　(Unidentified cartel—Wilmington)
District of Columbia
　　Washington　　　　　　　　　Federation
Florida
　　Jacksonville　　　　　　　　　Gulf
　　Lakeland　　　　　　　　　　Gulf
　　Miami　　　　　　　　　　　　Federation, Gulf
　　Orlando　　　　　　　　　　　Federation, Gulf

Figure 3.4: Cities in which Mexican DTOs Operate
(Source: Federal, state, and local law enforcement reporting, in NDIC, "Cities in Which Mexican DTOs Operate . . . ," Situation Report #2008-S0787-005, 11 April 2008)

Tampa	Federation, Gulf
West Palm Beach	Gulf
Georgia	
Atlanta	Federation, Gulf, Juárez
Hawaii	
(Unidentified cartel—Honolulu)	
Idaho	
(Unidentified cartel—Boise)	
Illinois	
Chicago	Federation, Gulf, Juárez
East St. Louis	Gulf
Joliet	Federation
Indiana	
Fort Wayne	Federation
Indianapolis	Federation, Juárez
Iowa	
Des Moines	Federation
Kansas	
Dodge	Juárez
Kansas City	Juárez
Liberal	Juárez
Wichita	Juárez
Kentucky	
Lexington	Federation
Louisville	Gulf
Louisiana	
Lafayette	Gulf
New Orleans	Federation, Gulf
Shreveport	Federation
(Unidentified cartel—Baton Rouge)	
Maine	
(Unidentified cartel—Portland)	
Maryland	
Baltimore	Federation
Greenbelt	Gulf
(Unidentified cartel—Frederick)	
Massachusetts	
Boston	Federation, Gulf, Juárez, Tijuana
(Unidentified cartel—Fitchburg)	
Michigan	
Detroit	Federation
(Unidentified cartel—Kalamazoo)	
Minnesota	
Minneapolis	Tijuana, Juárez
St. Paul	Tijuana
(Unidentified cartel—St. Cloud)	
Mississippi	
Hattiesburg	Federation
Jackson	Federation
Missouri	
Kansas City	Juárez
St. Louis	Federation, Gulf

Figure 3.4 (Continued): Cities in Which Mexican DTOs Operate
(Source: Federal, state, and local law enforcement reporting, in NDIC, "Cities in Which Mexican DTOs Operate . . . ," Situation Report #2008-S0787-005, 11 April 2008)

57

Montana
    (Unidentified cartel—Billings, Helena)
Nebraska
    Omaha   Federation, Gulf, Tijuana
Nevada
    Las Vegas   Tijuana, Juárez
    (Unidentified cartel—Reno)
New Hampshire
    (Unidentified cartel—Greenville)
New Jersey
    Atlantic City   Federation, Juárez
    Camden   Tijuana
    Newark   Federation, Juárez
New Mexico
    Columbus   Federation
    Deming   Federation
    Las Cruces   Federation
    (Unidentified cartel—Albuquerque)
New York
    Buffalo   Gulf
    New York City   Federation, Gulf, Tijuana
    (Unidentified cartel—Albany)
North Carolina
    Charlotte   Federation, Juárez
    Greensboro   Gulf
    Raleigh   Federation, Gulf, Juárez
    Wilmington   Gulf
    Wilson   Gulf
    (Unidentified cartel—Asheville, Burlington, Durham, Hendersonville, Winston-Salem)
North Dakota
    (Unidentified cartel—Bismarck)
Ohio
    Akron   Federation
    Cincinnati   Federation, Gulf, Juárez
    Cleveland   Federation, Tijuana
    Columbus   Federation
    Dayton   Federation
    Hamilton   Juárez
    Toledo   Federation, Juárez
Oklahoma
    Oklahoma City   Federation, Gulf, Juárez
    Ponca City   Juárez
    Tulsa   Federation
Oregon
    Eugene   Federation
    Klamath Falls   Federation
    Portland   Federation, Juárez
    (Unidentified cartel—Medford, Roseburg, Salem)
Pennsylvania
    Philadelphia   Federation, Gulf, Juárez, Tijuana
    Pittsburgh   Federation, Juárez
Rhode Island

Figure 3.4 (Continued): Cities in Which Mexican DTOs Operate
(Source: Federal, state, and local law enforcement reporting, in NDIC, "Cities in Which Mexican DTOs Operate . . . ," Situation Report #2008-S0787-005, 11 April 2008)

Providence	Federation
South Carolina	
Greenville	Gulf
(Unidentified cartel—Charleston, Colombia, Florence, Myrtle Beach)	
South Dakota	
Sioux Falls	Gulf, Tijuana
Tennessee	
Knoxville	Gulf
Memphis	Federation, Gulf
Nashville	Federation
Texas	
Alpine	Juárez
Beaumont	Federation
Big Springs	Juárez
Brownsville	Federation, Gulf
Corpus Christi	Gulf
Dallas	Federation, Gulf
Eagle Pass	Gulf
Edinburg	Gulf
El Paso	Federation, Gulf, Juárez
Fabens	Federation
Fort Hancock	Federation
Fort Stockton	Juárez
Fort Worth	Federation, Gulf
Hidalgo	Juárez
Houston	Federation, Gulf, Juárez
Laredo	Federation, Gulf
Lubbock	Juárez
McAllen	Gulf
Midland	Juárez
Midway	Federation
Mission	Juárez
Odessa	Juárez
Pecos	Juárez
Presidio	Juárez
Rio Grande City	Federation, Gulf
Roma	Federation, Gulf
San Antonio	Federation, Gulf
Tyler	Federation, Juárez
Waco	Juárez
(Unidentified cartel—Austin)	
Utah	
(Unidentified cartel—Ogden, Salt Lake City)	
Virginia	
Arlington	Federation
Galax	Federation
Washington	
Seattle	Tijuana
(Unidentified cartel—Spokane, Tacoma, Vancouve, Yakima)	
Wisconsin	
(Unidentified cartel—Milwaukee, Sheboygan)	
Wyoming	
Rock Springs	Juárez

Figure 3.4 (Continued): Cities in Which Mexican DTOs Operate
(Source: Federal, state, and local law enforcement reporting, in NDIC, "Cities in Which Mexican DTOs Operate . . .," Situation Report #2008-S0787-005, 11 April 2008)

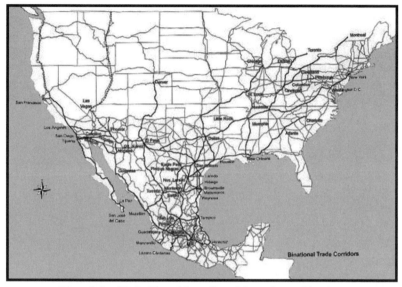

Map 3.2: Main Trucking Corridors from Mexico
(Source: U.S. Dept. of Transportation map "mexico_usa_trade_corridors.jpg," by Barton Aschman & La Empressa, 1997, based on information from McCray Research)

MS-13's Expansion into Northern Virginia

The MS-13 presence in Northern Virginia was initiated in 1993 when three members of *Mara Salvatrucha* traveled there from Los Angeles to begin a whole new branch of the gang. Those three members had the goal of uniting all Latino gangs in Northern Virginia (over 20 separate groups at that time). Since this first migration to Fairfax County in 1993, MS-13 has spread to the following Virginia counties: Arlington, Loudoun, Prince William, Clarke, Frederick, Shenandoah, Stafford, Spotsylvania, Rockingham (Harrisonburg), Albemarle (Charlottesville), Hanover, Henrico, Chesterfield (Richmond), Chesapeake (Norfolk), Lynchburg City, and possibly Roanoke City.[25]

The Drug Route to the Mid-Atlantic

It's not too hard to figure out the route over which drugs are transported to the Middle Atlantic from South Texas. There are several known "storage and distribution points" along the way. Those points are the same at which southbound bulk cash is consolidated: Charlotte, Atlanta, and San Antonio. San Antonio is not only a known distribution point, but also a known headquarters of the Mexican Mafia.[26] (Having a heavy presence of *Le Eme* in *Le Emi's* backyard now makes more sense.)

Mexican DTOs transport illicit drugs to the Mid-Atlantic Region from southwestern states and Mexico as well as from major U.S. drug distribution centers, including Atlanta, Charlotte, Chicago, and New York City.[27]
— *NDIC Drug Threat Assessment for 2008*

That makes the most probable northern conduit as follows: (1) I-35 from Nuevo Laredo to San Antonio; (2) I-10 via a Houston way-station to Mobile; (3) I-85 to Montgomery, Atlanta, and Charlotte; then (4) either US 29 to Washington (D.C.) and I-95 north or I-85 to Petersburg and I-95 north. At least that's the route the trucks were taking in 1998. (See Maps 3.2 through 3.5.) The Norfolk Southern Railroad just happens to parallel US 29. The geographical record of MS-13 activity in Virginia fully supports the two-route hypothesis. (Compare Maps 3.3 and 3.5.) It's clear that the gang has become most active along the US 29 and I-95 corridors. Within North Carolina, *Mara Salvatrucha* has been active in both Charlotte and Greensboro on the US 29 corridor,[28] and Durham on the I-85 corridor.[29] (See Map 3.4.)

New England's MS-13 Activity Also Defines Its Drug Route

From October 2005 to October 2008, much of the MS-13 activity in the Northeastern U.S. occurred in Massachusetts. Local news media reported ten separate incidents in Boston alone. There were others in the Boston suburbs of Abington, Lynn, and Somerville. Along I-95 south from Boston, the L.A.-born gang was also reported in New Haven, Connecticut. Within the entire state of New York, only New York City (in Nassau County) and four of its suburbs—Greenport,

61

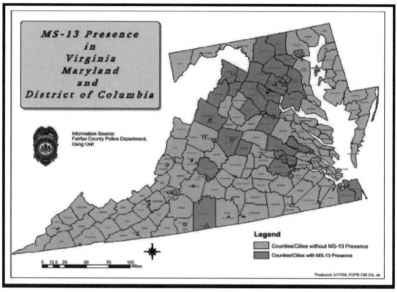

Map 3.3: MS-13 Activity in Virginia
(Source: Courtesy of www.policefoundation.org, "Crime Mapping News," vol. 6, issue 3, summer 2004)

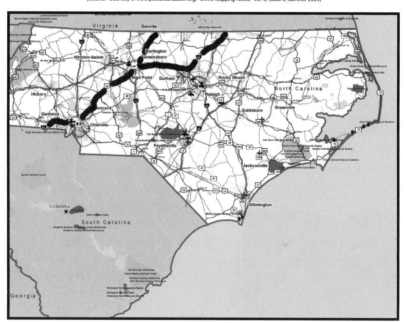

Map 3.4: US 29 and I-85 Corridors in North Carolina
(Source: Courtesy of U.S. Dept. of Transportation, from Federal Highway Administration website, www.fhwa.dot.gov, for map designator "nc-northcarolina.pdf")

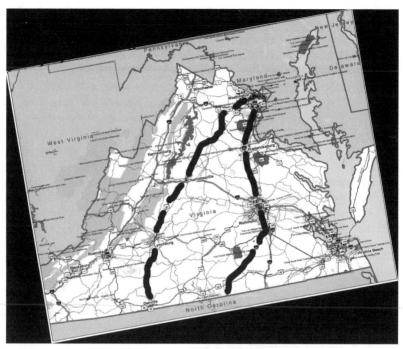

Map 3.5: US 29 and I-85/95 Corridors in Virginia
(Source: Courtesy of U.S. Dept. of Transportation, from Federal Highway Administration website, www.fhwa.dot.gov, for map designator "va-virginia.pdf")

Huntington, Central Islip, and Port Chester—experienced *Mara Sal-vatrucha* related disturbances during that same three-year period. New Jersey also had trouble in Princeton, Elizabeth, and Newark. The last two cities lie side by side along I-95 as it passes New York City. As for Pennsylvania, the Salvadorian gang was reported only in Mt. Pocono and Hazleton. Neither is near Philadelphia or I-95. Within Delaware, news articles about MS-13 appeared only in Wilmington (which lies on I-95 south of Philadelphia).[30] (See Map 3.6.)

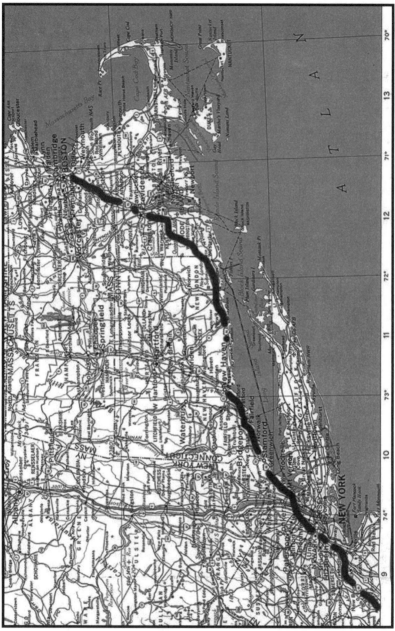

Map 3.6: Main Route As It Reaches New Market
(Source: Courtesy of General Libraries, University of Texas at Austin, from their website for map designator "ca000015.jpg")

Because many of the Boston incidents involved arrests of gang members, it is not clear whether that metropolitan area experienced more criminal activity or law enforcement. Either way, the Mexican cartels appear to have made Boston a major distribution hub.[31] As I-95 obviously constitutes the main drug conduit, both Philadelphia (Pennsylvania) and Providence (Rhode Island) should brace for more Asian heroin and Colombian cocaine deliveries. Along with the increased supply of drugs will come the violent extortion of the street clubs that do the selling.

MS-13's West Coast Route

While much of the illicit product comes into California from across (or under) its immediate border with Mexico, some undoubtedly comes by way of entry points in Arizona, New Mexico, and Texas. Again I-10 is its most likely route, with waystation/depots in El Paso and Phoenix.

Mexican DTOs smuggle significant quantities of illicit drugs through and between ports of entry (POEs) along the Southwest Border and store them in communities throughout the region. Most of the region's principal metropolitan areas, including Dallas, El Paso, Houston, Los Angeles, Phoenix, San Antonio, and San Diego, are significant storage locations as well as regional and national transportation and distribution centers. Mexican DTOs and criminal groups transport drug shipments from these locations to destinations throughout the country.[32]
— NDIC Drug Threat Assessment for 2008

Map 3.1 shows a Mexican cartel presence in the following locations: (1) El Paso; (2) Las Cruces (New Mexico); (3) Phoenix; (4) Las Vegas and Reno; (5) Sacramento; (6) Portland; and (7) Vancouver (Washington). That would make I-10, I-5, and the highway along the eastern edge of the Sierra Nevada the most likely smuggling conduits.

The *Maras'* Midwest Conduit

Texas' controversial new I-69 North-South Toll Road will

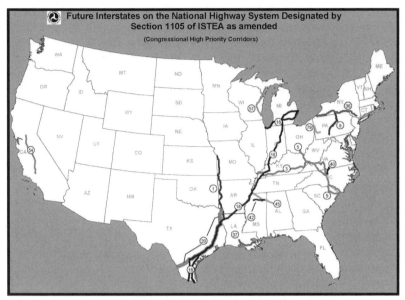

Map 3.7: The New Midwest Corridor from Mexico
(Source: Courtesy of U.S. Dept. of Transportation, from Federal Highway Administration website, www.fhwa.dot.gov, for map designator "hpcfi.pdf")

undoubtedly play a tremendous role in the future distribution of drugs to the Midwest.[33] Dubbed the NAFTA superhighway, it originates in South Texas and parallels I-35 north. At the Louisiana line, it connects to other new roads that will eventually lead to Indiana. (See Map 3.7.) It's clear that the Mexican cartels have already chosen Chicago as their regional distribution center.[34] The current route to Chicago undoubtedly runs through the known depot/waystation at Dallas. According to Map 3.1, there is a Mexican cartel presence in St. Louis. That might make I-44 and I-55 the preferred way from Texas to Chicago, but there are other possibilities (like through Indianapolis). Map 3.1 also shows several areas of Mexican cartel presence along a straight line from South Texas to Minneapolis. That track includes the following urban centers along I-35: (1) Tulsa; (2) Kansas City; and (3) Des Moines.

Not So Fast

While Mexican DTOs have been reported in many U.S. cities, their cartel affiliation matters because not all cartels get along. Upon closer examination, NDIC's report (Figure 3.4) reveals some interesting trends. To properly interpret them, one must remember that the Tijuana and Gulf Cartels are allied, and so too are the Sinaloa Federation and Juarez Cartel. Maps in the same report show the Gulf Cartel catering to the eastern half of the U.S., while the Tijuana Cartel concentrates on the Far West. It also shows the Sinaloa Federation distributing to both coasts, while the Juarez Cartel covers the south center of the country.[36]

Unfortunately, it is not possible to link MS-13 or M-18 to any location through its DTO cartel affiliation. While MS-13 is most often associated with Juarez and Gulf Cartels, it has also worked with the Sinaloa Federation and Tijuana Cartel.[37] The DEA agrees with the Attorney General that MS-13 is most closely connected to the Juarez and Gulf Cartels, but goes on to say that M-18 has associated with the Tijuana and Sinaloa Cartels.[38] Thus, one can only surmise that all four cartels have subcontracted through the Mexican Mafia for both "transportation protection" and "collections muscle." Wherever competing factions appear in the same location, one must assume an active (and often bloody) competition for the drug trade. The most populous locations with both cartel alliances present are as follows: Los Angeles, San Diego, Dallas, Houston, San Antonio, El Paso, Fort Worth, Oklahoma City, Omaha, St. Louis, Minneapolis, Chicago, Cleveland, Cincinnati, Philadelphia, New York City, Boston, Raleigh, Atlanta, Memphis, New Orleans, Miami, Orlando, and Tampa.

By plotting (on a map) all Figure 3.4 cities that are serviced by the same cartel, one may still be able to locate the alternate drug routes that run through any particular part of the country.

MS-13's Most Probable "Transpo" Method

Unlike military and police detachments, MS-13 cliques have no doctrine or policy to restrict their degree of flexibility and initiative. As such, they can more easily manage assigned sectors along a resupply conduit. The U.S. government threat assessments talk repeatedly of Mexican DTOs taking over the transportation and distribution of drugs throughout the country, but fail to mention MS-13's specific role in either endeavor. In Central America, MS-13 just protects the routes over which the drugs travel. Those routes are mostly railroads. Here, they may be mostly trucking conduits. That would explain the apparent spread of cliques along certain interstates. Each clique must be responsible for its sector of highway, much as the local Viet Cong (VC) were for their sector of infiltration trail in Vietnam. The VC would follow all American ambush patrols into position and then mark occupied paths. They would also lead any North Vietnamese Army (NVA) force in transit through the maze. The 21st-Century Stateside equivalent would be more technologically sophisticated. Automobile-borne MS-13 scouts would patrol the interstates and use cell phones to report too much law enforcement activity. If they spotted trouble, they could alert a Mexican Mafia contact who would, in turn, divert the container load into an intermediate stop. If that load were then shifted into specially outfitted cars that took parallel roads, it could still get through. That's what appears to have happened at Walpole, Massachusetts (a suburb along I-95 south of Boston) in mid-November 2008. Along US 1, local police intercepted a "high-tech" and cleverly compartmentalized automobile that was packed with drugs.[35] Equally unpleasant is the thought of *Mara Salvatrucha* follow vehicles. That would mean any law enforcement element that intercepted a truck for whatever reason might be suddenly outgunned from the rear.

MS-13 is a bottom-up organization in which each clique thinks for itself. As such, it may use several "transpo" alternatives. In most of the country, its cliques might just monitor the progress of legitimate freight loads and stand ready to off-load them early. In others, they may patrol interstates and personally transport the contraband. But, there are any number of other possibilities—like the use of public or camouflaged conveyances. Then, any train, bus, taxi, community service vehicle, delivery truck, or motorcycle becomes suspect.

Dope can be so easily hidden in other manufactured goods that legitimate trucking firms almost certainly carry the vast majority of its tonnage into the Northeast. Their loads could be most safely unloaded at Mexican-DTO-controlled loading docks. Such facilities exist at the waystation/depot cities of San Antonio, Atlanta, and Charlotte. Why shouldn't they also exist near the most lucrative destination—New York City? That might be something for the

Newark, Providence, and Boston police departments to look into. The same holds true for the sheriff's deputies and policemen who share the freeway corridors with MS-13 guards/scouts. After all, every clique will need someplace to shift a legitimate freight load into private vehicles. Local law enforcement officials should also start mapping the roads driven by known gang members. Of particular interest would be the time spent on known drug conduits and parallel highways. The combined effort of several departments might come up with the boundaries between each clique's zone of responsibility.

MS-13 cliques have also been trying to influence local politics. Whenever arrested, their members quickly summon attorneys and then are too often let out on bail. Thus, the political influence they seek must be within the criminal justice system. It would include both law enforcement and court system favors. Just to get the drugs into the U.S. from Mexico, MS-13 has already played every game there is—from blackmail to assassination—with public officials. Those same pressures will almost certainly be applied along their Stateside drug conduits.

> Like Al Qaeda . . . , [3rd-generation gangs] seek to create a shadow government or influence targeted states that are unable to provide security within their borders and whose officials are susceptible to recruitment.[39]
> —U.S. Army War College Strategic Studies Inst.

MS-13's Perverted Role in the Distribution of Drugs

MS-13 undoubtedly extorts money from the street gangs that do the selling as it handles collections for the Mexican DTOs. To maintain control, it depends heavily on the "never show weakness" or "tolerate disrespect" *mantras* that the Mexican Mafia has developed in prison. Should any street gang member not cooperate with MS-13 and then end up in prison, his life expectancy would not be long.

What Inevitably Accompanies Illicit Drugs

If the U.S. is now under a growing deluge of drugs, then one of the least-talked-about aspects of narcotics enforcement will also increase. That is official corruption. And such matters easily transcend national boundaries.

In November 2008, several high ranking Mexican officials were arrested for taking drug cartel bribes. Among them were the ex-head of Mexico's Anti-Organized Crime Agency and current head of its Interpol Office. The ex-crime chief had been additionally offered a monthly stipend for information.[40] These were not isolated incidents. They came on the heels of Mexico's Federal Police Commissioner having to resign after an aide was accused of working for one of the cartels. While that aide had allegedly offered protection to Sinaloa cartel members, the Mexican press claimed the commissioner's office had been allowing Sinaloa to smuggle drugs through Mexico City's international airport.[41] With that much infiltration at the highest levels of the criminal justice system, its lower echelons must be rife with corruption. While U.S. border officials are the most likely targets for similar bribes and intimidation, any justice system worker along America's main drug conduits is at risk. Much of the intimidation will come from MS-13.

The U.S. Law Enforcement Successes So Far

MS-13 plays a key role in the wholesale distribution of drugs, but other gangs do the street selling. The "Violent Gang Safe Streets Task Force" is the "vehicle" through which federal, state and local law enforcement agencies have banded together to confront the problem. The FBI's Safe Streets and Gang Unit administers 144 such task forces nationwide.[42]

Joint task forces are an admirable way for national law enforcement authorities to try to deal with the growing gang and drug problem. They promote the sharing of both information and assets. And they certainly give the impression of progress. But like multinational peacekeeping forces, they have their limitations. When it comes to narcotics work, too much coordination can often lead to an untimely tip-off. Then, what should have been a good arrest ends up being just another missed opportunity. This growing gang and drug problem is not the random product of criminal opportunism. It is well coordinated, fully supported by organized crime, and very possibly orchestrated by an unfriendly foreign power. That means plenty of political clout from official payoffs. In the many suburbs that surround each of America's big cities, no amount of coordination will make up for too few adequately paid police officers. It is they who—for the time being—must man the front lines of what looks very much like the main offensive in a 4GW assault. In most places, those police officers already have enough to do. In 2007, gang membership in San Antonio increased 130% over the previous year (from 1,989 to 4,543).[43] For the same period in Charlotte (where one would not expect much gang activity), no fewer than 167 separate gangs (many of them Hispanic) were reported to have up to 2,500 members.[44] That many new gangs would not be happening without a reason. One could blame it on the breakdown of the traditional family structure or the profits to be made from a larger drug supply. But the U.S. Army's Strategic Studies Institute likens it to "urban insurgency."[45] What if the 21st-Century variant of Maoist expansionism were to involve the softening up of targeted countries through transnational gangs? Either way, a national emergency is in progress, and the PRC is peripherally involved.

Americans have never liked U.S. soldiers or Marines helping with the day-to-day functioning of their civilian infrastructure. This latent mistrust of the military must come from an inherited aversion to martial law. That has not happened on a wide scale in this country since the War between the States. Many developing nations use troops for everything from road building to traffic control, but their troops have not come to depend almost entirely upon firepower.

To make a good case for the Pentagon's greater involvement in what may well be the drug deluge portion of a 4GW attack, one must revisit the Mexican border.

4 Border Crisis Too Big for Govt. Agencies

- Across what part of the Canadian border do drugs come?
- Which Mexican border towns see the most drug activity?

America's southern border is two thousand miles long.

(Source: Correl Gallery Clipart, "Totem Graphics," People #42P004)

Too Extensive a Boundary to Fully Protect

The combined length of the U.S. border with Canada and Mexico is almost 5,000 miles. Add to that another 5,000 miles of shoreline, and one can readily see why Prohibition smuggling was so difficult to stop.

Through the dedicated efforts of U.S. and Canadian law enforcement agencies, the flow of heroin through Canada has now been largely abated. The Hong Kong triads are still getting some product through, but they are undoubtedly shifting their focus to the Mexican border.

Canadian Border Entry Points for Smuggled Drugs

Since 1997, most of the Asian heroin has come into Canada through Vancouver, somehow made its way to Toronto, and then filtered south into the United States. While the flow has been greatly reduced in recent years, it still occurs.

Heroin moves from the source in Southeast Asia through China's Guangdong Province to Vancouver, which is a central distribution point for North American sales. Big Circle [Boys] and Hong Kong-based triads regularly have used commercial transport to move large shipments of heroin into Canada (Criminal Intelligence Service of Canada, "Annual Report 1998").
. . . The Akwesasne Mohawk Territory in northern New York, Walpole Island, Ontario at the west end of Lake Erie, and the Niagara frontier region at the east end of Lake Erie have been transit points into the United States from Canada for trafficking migrants and goods.[1]
— Library of Congress Research Paper, April 2003

The St. Regis Mohawk Indian Reservation is a primary entry point for drugs, principally marijuana and cocaine, and other illicit goods smuggled from Canada into New York. This reservation straddles the border between northern New York and the Canadian Provinces of Quebec and Ontario and includes portions of the St. Lawrence Seaway. There are no border checkpoints on the reservation. Most drugs are smuggled through an isolated area of the reservation known as Snye. Members of the Hells Angels outlaw motorcycle gang (OMG) frequently smuggle marijuana, and Asian heroin distributors occasionally smuggle heroin from Canada through the reservation into and through New York. Cocaine and MDMA also are smuggled through the reservation.[2]
— NDIC New York Drug Threat Assessment 2002

Most New York Drug Shipments Now Come from the South

The U.S. and Canadian authorities have so greatly slowed the flow of drugs into New York from Toronto that the Hong Kong triads have had to find another route. They must now be sending more of their product through their traditional port of entry—Acapulco. That's where the Gulf Cartel and Sinaloa Federation first vie for its ownership.[3] Then, most is shipped overland to the U.S. via Nuevo Laredo, Juarez, and Tijuana.

To summarize in one chapter what goes on at the U.S./Mexico border is an almost impossible task. According to the NDIC, no fewer than six cartels, 129 mid-level organizations, and 606 local groups engage in drug trafficking there.[4] And that number does not include all the Mexican manufacturers, freight handlers, and police departments that are unwittingly involved. It is precisely this decentralization of control that makes the process so hard to stop on the U.S. side of the border. Whenever one conduit dries up, ten others spring up to handle the load. While U.S. law enforcement agencies of every description have dedicated considerable resources to the problem, it appears to be growing. Drug traffickers deal in percentages. If only 20% of their product gets through, they stand to make a huge profit. By every indication, a much higher percentage than that makes it across. And all too often, it is the unsuspecting or coerced "mule" who must pay the price for what doesn't.

> [M]ore than 90 percent of the cocaine and heroin entering the U.S. . . . is smuggled through the ports of entry. The remaining stashes are packed across by "mules," who work for their bosses using an arrangement . . . between share-cropping and slavery.[5]

In terms of sheer quantity of drugs entering this country, the most efficient means of smuggling appears to be via the trucking industry's handling of NAFTA-related goods. But there are also indicators of an insidious backup. At El Paso, not only do untold numbers of trucks from hundreds of assembly plants cross every day carrying manufactured goods, but also 200,000 people in cars or on foot. Within that big a crowd, a considerable quantity of drugs could be concealed piecemeal (with or without the carrier's knowledge). While 1,500 human "mules" and six tons of narcotics have been seized since 2006, one can only guess at how much more got through. As a corollary to this Asian-style "coolie" assault are the El Paso stash houses where tiny loads are consolidated before forwarding.[6]

75

The Vehicular Part of the Onslaught

Laredo is the busiest port of entry for truck-borne cargo in the world, and the second-busiest for all types of cargo in the U.S. Add to that the fact that most drugs are now reaching the U.S. through South Texas, and one starts to see the problem. It has less to do with "infiltrators" sneaking through bushes, and more to do with the sheer volume of imported goods. The really sad part is that Laredo is the southern hub of freight logistics and international commerce with the U.S. Any company or country that considers narcotics to be legitimate trade goods can ship them through Laredo under the auspices of NAFTA. Somewhere within the 20,000 vehicles that daily make their way north through the Laredo crossing,[7] most of the drugs are being hidden.

Once a Mexican truck with a Chinese or Colombian shipping container is approved by U.S. Customs at Laredo, that container is probably not opened until it reaches its ultimate destination. That could mean little, if any, inspection before arriving at a private loading dock in New Jersey. And it might help to explain why certain interstate highways are the principal drug conduits. While the NAFTA provision allowing Mexican trucks to enter the U.S. was not funded in March 2009, so many had already done so that the pattern was set. That means the conduits will likely remain the same. (See Map 4.1.)

The Mexican Truck Fiasco

According to Mexico's Economy Secretary, no fewer than 46,000 Mexican trucks made it onto U.S. soil before the pilot program that allowed them was suspended in March 2009.[8] The extent to which they may have been inspected for drugs or aliens is disturbing. Here's what that program looked like at its inception. While its acronyms are impressive, its logic isn't.

> Mexican trucks carrying loads of consumer goods into the United States under a test program could be across the border in as little as 15 seconds, according to government officials setting up the procedures.
> A spokesman for the Federal Motor Carrier Safety Administration [FMCSA] has confirmed . . . [that] Mexican

trucks participating in the cross-border program would be eligible to participate in the U.S. Customs and Border Protection's Free and Secure Trade [FAST] system.

Participation in the FAST program would keep physical inspections of truck trailers or shipment containers to a minimum, and speed their processing on lanes specially designated for the shipments. . . .

Truckers using the high-speed border crossing procedures also will be given access to electronically-cleared [radio frequency identification] RFID programs, a special driver registration for the speedy crossings, and access to B-1 visas, qualifying them to deliver Mexican cargoes in the United States and to pick up U.S. cargoes for delivery to Mexico, officials reported. . . .

The FMSCA spokesman confirmed that electronic measures . . . would be the primary check made by law enforcement as the Mexican trucks in the program cross the border.

FAST operates in specially designated border-crossing highway lanes designed to allow Mexican and Canadian trucks entry into the United States with minimal delay.

At the border, the electronic FAST lanes will operate as follows:

* RFID . . . transponders built into truck registration certificates posted on the cab windshield feed C-TPAT [Customs Trade Partnership against Terrorism] and FAST data into the border agent's computer.

* A second transponder built into the FAST ID card issued to accompany a driver's commercial license is also read electronically.

* RFID transponders with the shipment must correspond with the e-manifest data the C-TPAT data shipper has pre-processed to U.S. border patrol through an electronic ACE (Automated Customs Environment) shipment processing system.

The Customs and Border Patrol officer at the booth in the FAST lane can then request to physically inspect the driver's B-1 visa.

Mexican trucking companies can participate in FAST provided they are enrolled in the [C-TPAT program].[9]

— *World Net Daily* (Washington, D.C.), April 2007

A Closer Look at the Laredo Crossing

Across from Laredo, Texas, lies Nuevo Laredo, Mexico. There are six permanent checkpoints between them. Some 10,000 freight trucks and 10,000 more cars cross into the U.S. daily. Sniffer dogs inspect them, but full searches are random and rare. According to one researcher's poll of both U.S. Customs and U.S. Border Patrol agents, 90% to 95% are never searched at all.[10] That researcher is David J. Danelo, a former Marine turned investigative reporter. Much of this chapter has been based on his 2008 research in *The Border.*

The Texas side of the frontier (Laredo) is relatively peaceful compared to the ongoing turf war between Gulf and Sinaloa Cartels on the Mexican side (Nuevo Laredo). Still, there have been troubling discoveries on U.S. soil. On 27 January 2006, the Laredo Police Department discovered two Improvised Explosive Devices (IEDs) and enough wherewithal to make 33 more, along with 15 AK-47 assault rifles and quantities of cocaine, methamphetamines, and cash.[11] One hates to think of what might happen if the Mexican cartels or MS-13 started using IEDs to get their way.

What Are Plazas?

The drug cartels call portal cities (like Nuevo Laredo) "plazas." These are border exchange areas in which black-market commerce flows in both directions. Unfortunately, plazas consist of more than just concrete and asphalt.

> More than just a city, a plaza is a network of operatives that consists of a few people at the right places or times: an agent that looks the other way, a customs inspector inside your camp, a freight forwarder to clear your cargo for travel north into America, a crooked police chief. . . .
> Some plazas don't need any double agents. All it takes is the right pedimento [customs form], the correct cargo container, or the proper deception ploys to fool the dogs. A fence wouldn't eliminate the Laredo plaza; after all, the vehicles carrying their illicit cargo drive unmolested over the bridge and legally through the port of entry.[12]

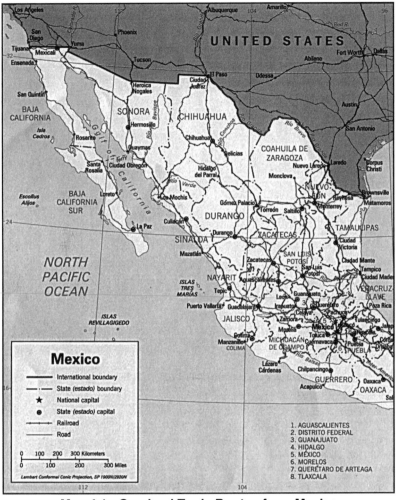

Map 4.1: Overland Trade Routes from Mexico
(Source: Courtesy of General Libraries, University of Texas at Austin, from their website for map designator "mexico_pol97.pdf)

Drug smuggling is hard to stop because of the huge sums of money involved. The street gangs want a cut, and so will an occasional inspector. But not all lapses in responsibility are caused by greed. They can just as easily grow out of financial hardship. An official with a terminally ill child or variable-rate home loan is just as likely to be tempted. The Mexican cartels know that. They also know that married border guards will sometimes fall for another woman. In other words, they have more ways to cultivate leaks than policemen do to develop "snitches." Four U.S. agencies mostly manage the border: (1) the Border Patrol; (2) Immigration; (3) Customs; and (4) Alcohol, Tobacco, and Firearms (ATF). To preclude leaks, all would have to rotate their agents every six months. This would be no problem for the U.S. military. Its turnover rate is so high that replacement happens automatically.

Smuggling is difficult to stop, because—like gambling—it is based on the law of averages. For the drug runner to make a profit, he has only to get a small fraction of his product through. If that product is so carefully hidden in legitimate freight that its original owner can no longer be traced, then what's the harm in a certain percentage getting seized?

To see how important it may be to reduce the flow of "free trade" through Laredo, one must look at the entire length of the U.S.-Mexico border—from Brownsville to San Diego.

The Daunting Size of the Problem

Vehicular and pedestrian crossings are not the only way into Texas. There are also Mexican rail lines that pass through Del Rio, Eagle Pass, Laredo, and McAllen. As MS-13 controls enough of Mexico's rail network to provide protection to the smugglers who use it,[13] any NAFTA trade goods entering the U.S. via train need to be carefully inspected. Texas also has a world-class port, 400 miles of coastline with several smaller ports, and a very busy international airport. Houston's Bush Intercontinental has to be where most air travelers from Latin America arrive in the U.S. In 2006, it was named the fastest growing of America's big airports by the U.S. Department of Transportation. In 2007, it served 43 million passengers. For the U.S. carrier with most Latin American routes, this airport handles 700 departures a day.[14] What one frequent traveler experienced there in August 2008 should shed some light on the lesser-known challenges of drug interdiction.

Having recently been through U.S. customs at New York, New Jersey, Detroit, Los Angeles, Chicago, and Atlanta, this particular traveler was awed by the much greater size of the Houston reception hall. As he was moving toward the only U.S. official inspecting claimed baggage as it left the hall, he noticed a Latino woman and two children nearby. They were dressed as if from Venezuela or Central America, but the woman spoke some English. Between them, they had no fewer than 25 suitcases and bundles on two oversize baggage carts. The woman was in front of the observer with one cart and a customs declaration. The boy was behind him with the other cart and another customs declaration. (Only one form is required per family.) The observer asked if they were together and, after a nod from the mother, let the boy pass. As their two overloaded carts reached the checkpoint, the seated official made no attempt to inspect any piece of luggage and fairly ripped the extra customs form out of the boy's hand. As did all other passengers in line at that time, the observer was cursorily waved through this uncharacteristically casual checkpoint without having to unzip one bag or answer one question. Afterwards, he wondered how much the woman had paid her airline for all that excess baggage (normally $50 per item). He also wondered what was wrong with what he had just witnessed. Perhaps all the items had been sniffed and x-rayed before ever reaching their owners. Still, the observer had worked a while in drug law enforcement and felt a little uneasy with all the inconsistencies.[15]

Within Texas, what happens at Laredo's truck crossing should still be everyone's greatest concern—simply because of the larger quantities of drugs that could potentially slip through. Within the Laredo phone book, there are several hundred logistics companies and freight forwarders listed. Also advertised are transport companies, trucking associations, and truck drivers. Most exist only to carry freight out of Mexico, and all seem to be gainfully employed. Among the loads of Mexican-made goods handled by one jobber, there were overseas shipping containers requiring expensive 48-hour delivery to New Jersey.[16]

Logistics companies are different from trucking agencies. They act as middlemen between trains, ships, or airplanes and the eighteen-wheelers or courier vans that finally deliver the load to its destination. That normally entails the pickup and delivery of international cargo. Such a logistics company normally subcontracts a foreign shipment to three people: (1) a Mexican trucker; (2) a freight forwarder; and (3) an American trucker. The Mexican truck hauls the container to the freight forwarder who fills out a customs form detailing its contents. All containers are subject to inspection while the freight forwarder processes his paperwork. Such an inspection happens randomly, and many containers are shipped without their seals ever being broken. Once the cargo has been cleared, the American trucker links up with the container and delivers it to its destination. Much less attention is paid to the container that gets hauled all the way to its final U.S. destination by a Mexican truck.[17]

Of course, there are many other overland passages into the United States besides Laredo. The most prominent are described below.

Elsewhere between the Gulf of Mexico and Eagle Pass

Between the Gulf of Mexico and Eagle Pass, there are Browns-ville and McAllen as well as Laredo. Across from Brownsville is Matamoros, and just to the west of McAllen is Reynosa. Both sit astride highways to the Mexican interior. Eagle Pass and its Mexi-can sister Piedras Negras are also on a road leading south. Along this "Eastern corridor between countries," the Rio Grande forms a shallow moat. Its banks are covered with so much carrizo cane that any fence would be easily circumvented.[18]

Shortly after 9/11 at Eagle Pass, the people smugglers discovered a bureaucratic loophole. Residents of Nicaragua, Venezuela, and Uruguay could request asylum. The closest Federal Courthouse was two hours away in Del Rio. By February 2005, 7,000 aliens were being captured per month at Eagle Pass. Because that town didn't have the cell space for that many detainees, many were issued a 30-day U.S. travel visa along with a notice to appear on a certain date in front of an immigration judge. Mixed in with the hordes of migrants were members of MS-13. While Operation Streamline II has since fixed this particular problem, it still stands as a warning of what can happen with too little logistics and an opportunistic foe.[19]

The Expanse between Del Rio and El Paso

While Del Rio and its cross-border counterpart Ciudad Acuna are not large, they still rate their own road into Mexico. So do Big Bend National Park and Presidio.

Before recently leaving Del Rio, a resident noted a much younger, louder, and tougher Hispanic crowd than had been there previously.[20] For 50 miles to the northwest of Del Rio lies a reservoir from damming up the Pecos River. Then, over the huge stretch of sagebrush between that reservoir and El Paso, the Texas Border Sheriff's Coalition pretty much keeps the lid on things. However, lone drug "mules" still get through. They may be paying off a debt or making amends for a family member. Or they may have just been kidnapped from a destitute village and effectively enslaved. Then, any failure at their assigned task may mean death to a loved one. Either way, their reward for evading capture and delivering their load is often higher than the Border Patrol's incentive for catching them.[21]

From Presidio, a road leads south to Olinga—the former citadel of Pablo Acosta, a smuggling affiliate of the Juarez Cartel.[22] While Acosta was killed by U.S. authorities in 1987, strange things still happen 75 miles to the northwest of Presidio at a place called Neely's Crossing. There, in January 2006, Hudspeth County Sheriff's Deputies learned of a drug run and chased two SUVs back down to the ford. They were met by a dozen people with Mexican Army uniforms and leveled AK-47's. The deputies could only watch as a military humvee with Mexican Army markings escorted the smugglers back across the Rio Grande.[23]

At Redford, some 16 miles southeast of Presidio, another event occurred in 1997 that would doom a governmental decision to use regular Marine and Special Forces units to help the Border Patrol. That decision was first made in 1989 with the formation of Joint Task Force Six (JTF-6), based in El Paso. Its mission was to support local, state, and federal agencies in their efforts to stop the cross-border smuggling. For several years JTF-6 had few actual troops. Then, in the fall of 1992, the Pentagon asked regular Army and Marine units to perform counter-drug and border security missions. Those units did so successfully for several years. Then, late in the afternoon of 20 May 1997, a few heavily camouflaged Marines from an artillery headquarters battery were moving into a nighttime outpost overlooking the Polvo Crossing. Without their knowledge, a young American sheepherder had taken his goats down to the river to graze. On his way back, there was an unfortunate accident. Seeing movement in the brush and thinking his herd threatened by wild animals, the teenager fired at the Marines. Thinking him to be a smuggler, the Marines shot back with more accuracy. Then, what

83

had been a no-fault, though tragic, misunderstanding escalated into a national incident. That incident would mark the last of 3,300 U.S. military counterdrug missions on the border. There are still U.S. National Guard units on watch at various places behind that border, but none are allowed an active role in its defense.[24]

El Paso

Across from El Paso is Ciudad Juarez. It lies along one of the three major highways leading south into Mexico (the others are at Laredo and Nogales).

There are four bridges over the river at El Paso. Only Laredo rates any higher in Mexican imports entering Texas. In fact, two major Mexican rail lines merge before reaching the U.S. at Ciudad Juarez. From the El Paso Intelligence Center at Fort Bliss, what is left of JTF-6 operates. It is now called JTF North.[25]

What has happened of late in El Paso may be an unpleasant glimpse into the future. Despite several thousand Mexican Army troops deployed to the host State of Chihuahua, things in Juarez are getting worse. Last year some 1,400 people were killed there, as opposed to only 316 the year before. Its "plaza," or drug-smuggling corridor, is being hotly contested by the Juarez, Sinaloa, and Gulf Cartels. As such, the Juarez Cartel may or may not still be an integral part of the Sinaloa Federation, as previously claimed by NDIC.[26]

Douglas, Nogales, and San Luis

There are no roads into Old Mexico through New Mexico. The first occurs at Douglas, Arizona. Across from Douglas lies Agua Prieta. And farther west is Nogales, Arizona. Here, the cities on both sides of the border have the same name. Both Douglas and Nogales have roadways leading south, but that through Douglas quickly intersects with a much larger thoroughfare from Nogales. South of Yuma is San Luis, and across the border from it lies San Luis Rio Colorado. It has no direct link to the Mexican heartland but lies only 25 linear miles from both highway and railroad. It is also only 40 linear miles from the northern end of the Gulf of California.

The Border Patrol's Tucson sector covers 262 miles of Arizona desert. Every year since 2000, half of all the illegal aliens caught sneaking into the United States were apprehended here. And last year, as many as 300,000 of the 350,000 arrested along the border were picked up in the Tucson sector. That's a 20% increase over the previous year. According to a Border Patrol spokesman, 45,000 people enter the U.S. through the Nogales port of entry every day, and $18 billion worth of cargo each year. While U.S. Customs watches the official border crossings, the Border Patrol watches everything else. Of the two, Customs may have the harder job. It must check for irregularities while still allowing all legitimate NAFTA traffic to flow. Of course, most of the illegal aliens walk around the official port of entry. In addition to watershed drainage tunnels, the Border Patrol discovered 14 homemade excavations beneath the boundary in 2007 alone. Those tunnels were being used for both migrants and drugs. Unlike Texas, most of Arizona's borderlands are federally owned. They consist of wildlife preserves, Native American reservations, and military training grounds. Despite hundreds of agents in Nogales and Douglas, much of that human smuggling occurs nearby. And the court system in Douglas has a somewhat checkered history.[27]

When visiting a retirement community south of Tucson several years ago, the same observer as in the Houston airport noticed an eighteen-wheeler headed north (presumably out of Nogales or Mexico) on I-19. It was well after dark, and the truck was traveling a good 15 miles over the posted speed limit. Right behind it was a sedan that was carrying so much something that its rear bumper barely cleared the road's surface. In 1960's Alabama, that would have been a moonshine runner with a full load. But here, it was obviously a follow car with enough gas to make it to L.A. The observer followed the truck and its escort for about 10 miles through the heart of Tucson and then broke away as it turned onto I-10 heading west. At no time, did any law enforcement agency—city, state, or federal—say "boo" to what was obviously a contraband load.[28]

Calexico and San Diego

Across from Calexico lies Mexicali, and adjacent to San Diego is Tijuana. Both have roads leading south, but Mexicali's highway connects to the mainland. A major Mexican rail line also crosses the border at Mexicali. As in San Luis, Arizona, there are street gangs in Calexico.[29]

In 2007, the California sector was the only one to show an increase in both apprehensions and violence against Border Patrol agents.[30] Here, the drug flow has increased despite a fence built in 1994.

Of course, the most dangerous of the two Mexican cities is Tijuana. During the first week of December 2008 alone, almost 40 people were killed (of which four were children and nine beheaded).[31] The streets are no longer awash with fun-seeking tourists. In fact, the whole place now more closely resembles a war zone under martial law. That's because of the official corruption that too often accompanies drug trafficking.

> At one point, the military briefly disarmed the local police force . . . [in Tijuana] and asked residents to report crimes directly to them. . . . [L]ast month . . . federal troops fanned [out] . . . after 500 cops were removed and sent . . . for retraining. . . .
>
> The military is considered less corruptible than police for a number of reasons: they undergo constant training in a way that local law enforcement does not. They are also deployed far from their homes, and often rotated, so that they find less opportunity for collusion. . . . [T]hey are also less susceptible to intimidation by drug traffickers.[32]
> — *Christian Science Monitor,* 5 December 2008

The person who used to handle border-issue liaison between Tijuana police and U.S. law enforcement agencies claims that deporting felons straight out of U.S. prisons to Tijuana was fueling gang violence. He and 18 others were later accused of working for the cartels, but gangs do undoubtedly play a big part in the smuggling.[33]

> An estimated 25 to 30 gangs with a total membership of between 2,000 and 3,000 reportedly operate within . . . San Diego County. . . . [G]ang-related crime . . . is estimated to account for 50 percent of all crime. . . . Hispanic gangs dominate the distribution of drugs. . . . These gangs main-

tain long-standing associations with the Mexican Mafia (la Eme) . . . and major Mexican DTOs, which have resulted in . . . increasing levels of drug trafficking. . . .

Street and prison gangs such as Surenos 13, 18th Street, and Mexican Mafia (La Eme) maintain significant influence over most of the local suburban and rural gangs in these areas. They work very closely with Mexican DTOs located in Tijuana, Mexico, to smuggle drugs and illegal aliens into the United States.[34]

— *Attorney General's Report*, April 2008

Like Juarez, Tijuana has many export factories. Their shipments to the U.S. create a number of smuggling opportunities. In fact, the border checkpoint between Tijuana and the San Diego suburb of San Ysidro is now the busiest land portal into the U.S. Up to 65,000 vehicles and 35,000 pedestrians cross every day in each direction.[35]

China's U.S. Border Coordination Center?

Mexicali has historically been the "hub" for sneaking Chinese nationals across the U.S.-Mexico border. (See Map 4.2.) American officials admit that Mexicali/Calexico is one of the most active por-

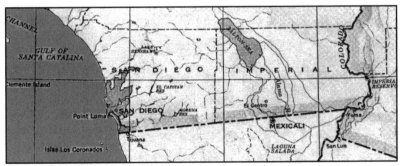

Map 4.2: China's U.S. Border "Hub" at Mexicali
(Source: Courtesy of General Libraries, University of Texas at Austin, from their website for map designator "California_South_90.jpg")

tals through which hundreds of thousands of ethnic Chinese have illegally entered this country since the late 1980's. (The others are Los Angeles, New York, and Seattle.) However, the real problem is that as many as 35,000 one-time PRC citizens now make Mexicali their permanent place of residence.[36] In one of the world's most inhospitable climates, they must be doing more than just selling fried rice.

> U.S. officials believe the community is used for Chinese intelligence-gathering activities. . . . The alien smugglers use the Chinese community in Mexicali as a base from which to launch operations to get illegal immigrants into the United States. Intelligence officials also believe China uses the Mexicali Chinese community for logistics for intelligence operations in the United States.[37]
> — *Geostrategy-Direct,* February 2005

Considering the ongoing deterioration in U.S. border security, much more than intelligence gathering may be happening at Mexicali. All types of contraband come into the U.S. through Mexico. Perhaps the U.S. border is more important strategically to the ruling party of China than anyone dared to imagine. That it plans to economically and politically dominate the world is blatantly obvious to anyone who regularly follows events in Africa, South America, and South Asia. Then, in terms of criminal activity coordination, Mexicali may be the North American equivalent of Ciudad del Este, Paraguay. Chinese people smugglers (or "snakeheads") are known to be triad gangs.[38] To accomplish this much infiltration at Mexicali, they would need the endorsement of the Tijuana Cartel. That might mean a slightly closer relationship with the Gulf Cartel in Laredo than with its Sinaloa competitor. But that's where the stream of affiliations gets murky. The Mexican Mafia, MS-13, and M-18 have all (at one time or another) interacted with both cartel alliances. The Chinese snakeheads probably do as well. Should any work for Hong Kong's biggest triad, then the all-elusive link to the PLA has been established. There have been tunnels between Mexicali and "the opium dens of Calexico" since Prohibition days.[39] Hopefully, that is not an indicator of what is now to come. That so much tunneling has occurred in the California sector of the border recently should come as no surprise to those who still realize how much PRC soldiers love to burrow.[40] (See Map 4.3.)

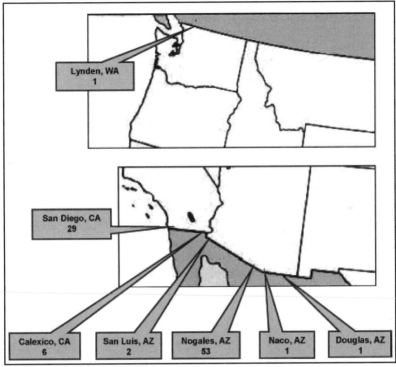

Map 4.3: Tunnels beneath U.S. Border as of November 2008
(Source: U.S. Northern Command Briefing, as retrieved from fas.org on 23 February 2009)

The People Smuggling Comparison

The flow of illegal aliens into the U.S. does not carry with it as much risk as drugs, but it helps to highlight the flaws in the border defenses. By the Border Patrol union president's own admission, "Thousands of people jump the border every day."[41] And Mexican passenger trains run regularly to Nuevo Laredo, Ciudad Juarez, Nogales, and Mexicali.

Most of the ambulatory-people smuggling occurs from Nogales west. At an ancient volcanic dome 40 miles north of Nogales, smugglers man an observation post to monitor all law enforcement activity in the desert below. Whenever overflown by a helicopter, they hide in caves. Further north within view of Tucson, walkers drop their incriminating packs on the ground and move to $250,000 houses that function as waystations.[42]

The Latest Tunneling Trend

Tunnels are still being constructed beneath America's borders to transport drugs and illegal aliens, according to a recent U.S. Northern Command Task Force briefing. (Refer again to Map 4.3.) Between 1990 and November 2008, no fewer than 93 cross-border tunnels have been discovered. And there is no telling how many more remain undetected. Of those found, 35 were in California, 57 in Arizona, and one in Washington State.[43] (Refer back to Map 4.3.)

Of note, all excavations are from the Tucson Sector west. That means the Texas smugglers are doing just fine without any tunnels. The ones around Nogales handle people, whereas those in California are for drugs. The most impressive of the latter variety was found in January 2006. It starts at the bottom of an 80-foot shaft in a warehouse near Tijuana's international airport. Then, it gradually slopes upward for half a mile to some vacant industrial building in Otay Mesa, California (about 20 miles southeast of downtown San Diego). Sometimes dubbed the "Grand Tunnel," this passageway was built with a sophistication that surprised officials. It was outfitted with a concrete floor, electricity, lights, forced ventilation, and a groundwater pumping system.[44]

The U.S. Border Patrol makes mention of another "Grand Tunnel" near Nogales, Arizona.[45] It's near a veritable rash of more recent excavations. Either people smuggling has become more lucrative, or there is something else to be gained from flooding America with illegal aliens. Might it be that someone is trying very hard to keep 4GW infiltration routes open?

Between fiscal years 2003 and 2008, 34 separate tunnels have been identified and filled within the Tucson Sector. So far during fiscal year 2009 [since 1 October 2008], six tun-

nels have been discovered [of which three were in downtown Nogales during the second week of December].[46]
— Border Patrol News Release, 16 December 2008

Border Protection Is More Properly a Military Function

Long forgotten is what happened some 70 miles west of El Paso at Colombus, NM, on the morning of 9 March 1916. That was when a Mexican rebel by the name of Pancho Villa took his revenge for a perceived breach of promise from the U.S. government to provide his band with arms. He and 500 of his men crossed the border, surrounded Colombus, and proceeded to steal most of its token Army garrison's supply of weapons and horses. In the process, they robbed businesses, torched buildings, and shot residents. In their wake, they left ten U.S. soldiers and eight civilians dead.[47] Unfortunately, the Mexican cartels still rely on America for their source of ordnance. In many places, there are almost as many weapons being smuggled south as there are drugs coming north. That means another Pancho Villa type raid is not completely out of the question.

There have been more recent Mexican army incidents on U.S. soil. One researcher accounted for 226 reported incursions by the Mexican military from 1996 to 2005. Of those, 180 took place from El Paso west.[48] So, while there may be little need for a U.S. military presence in Brownsville, McAllen, or Eagle Pass,[49] the Laredo crossing and everything west of Eagle Pass could use one. Here, pistol-packing Border Patrol agents stand little chance against narcotics runners with AK-47's and light-infantry instruction.

MS-13 and Mexican Cartels Now Getting Military Training

There are now FARC operatives in Mexico. They have been showing the cartels and *maras* how better to protect the Colombian cocaine on its way to market.[50] That's tantamount to providing them with light-infantry instruction.

Unfortunately, FARC is now being trained by Vietnamese contractors expert at sapper tactics [51]—the same short-range infiltration skills that were able to defeat the U.S. phalanx piecemeal in Vietnam. Hopefully, the unabated flow of U.S. small arms into

91

Mexico will seduce those cartels and *maras* into instead using the same "surprise-free" 2nd-Generation Warfare (2GW) maneuvers that are stock in trade with other rich armies.

Best Strategy at the Mexican Border

American leaders must choose between a flood of society-destroying drugs and unlimited free trade across the Mexican border. One cannot be curtailed without limiting the other. Only the most porous and compromised parts of that border must now be taken over by the U.S. military. That means the road/rail entry points at Tijuana, Nogales, Juarez, and Laredo. Only the U.S. Army has the assets to fully search hundreds of vehicles at a time. At any other border town with an overburdened criminal justice system (like possibly Douglas), limited military assistance might also prove worthwhile.

All along the border, the situation is quickly spiraling out of control. With 60,000 Mexican troops already committed, drug traffickers heavily armed, civilian control over Juarez and Tijuana crumbling, and the death toll doubled since last year,[52] a greater U.S. military presence is definitely in order.

But, any Pentagon takeover of border control must be made in full partnership with the Mexican military establishment.[53] No combination of physical barriers and surveillance devices along the U.S. side of the border will work without manned outposts on the Mexican side. While Combined-Action Platoons (CAPS, like those with which American forces combatted police corruption in Iraq) would be appropriate for that role, they might more effectively be manned by Mexican Army troops. If those platoons were comprised of one squad each of national army, federal police, and local police, then those three elements would soon sort out their differences. That would leave most U.S. forces free to continue their crucial interdiction of Afghan heroin. If necessary, a few could contribute to CAPS—consisting one squad each of U.S. infantry, local police, and local militia—in some of the more threatened U.S. border communities.

The immediate danger is that the violence and anarchy that now pervades northern Mexico will somehow jump the border. According to *Newsweek* and NDIC, "the increased bloodshed in Juarez 'could spill into the [West Texas] region,' since . . . drug-trafficking organizations will 'confront law enforcement officers . . . who seek to disrupt . . . [their] smuggling operations'."[54] Of course, there will be more corruption as well.

Before tactical techniques can be designed for situations involving people and drug smuggling, one must see which parts of U.S. police procedure might usefully be copied by the U.S. military. As has already become apparent in Iraq and Afghanistan, 4GW is more like high-intensity police work than traditional combat.

Part Two

As Military and Police Missions Merge

"An eye for an eye makes the whole world blind."
— Mahatma Gandhi

(Source: Attributed to Mahatma Gandhi)

5 The 4GW Policing Requirement

● Why is it more important to convert a 4GW opponent?

● Could smuggling routes be found more easily this way?

Public safety is harder to provide than military defense.

(Source: *Corel Gallery* Clipart, "Totem Graphics," Man #28V024)

Why 4GW Is More Like Police Work

To win simultaneously in the martial, political, psychological, and economic arenas, one cannot assassinate enemy leaders or measure progress through body counts. Only by processing those leaders through a civilian court system will they not become martyrs. And only when their soldiers are converted instead of killed, will vendettas not perpetuate the cycle of violence.

[T]he key connection between police work and what the military needs to do in 4GW . . . [is] de-escalate. De-escala-

tion is what police strive to do in almost all conflict situations. Their main tool is talking.[1]
— William S. Lind
father of 4th-Generation Warfare theory

Just as policemen regularly protect suspect, bystander, and property, so too must 4GW warriors accomplish their missions with less force (and no more standoff bombardment).

Public Safety Is an Inherent Part of National Defense

Whether America is now under low-intensity 4GW attack from China or just being randomly plundered by international crime factions, it's clear that the U.S. law enforcement community could use some help. Either way, the Mexican cartels are now flooding this country with aliens and drugs. To determine how the U.S. military might help, the reader need not agree that the PLA has added Sun Yee On and 14-K to its growing list of civilian business enterprises. Nor must he or she see COSCO's huge container fleet and Hutchison Whampoa's four Mexican port facilities as supporting the smuggling. Only necessary is the realization that international organized crime has now become as big a threat to the U.S. as is Islamic militancy. With almost all the world's cocaine coming from Colombia, and 92% of its heroin-producing opium from Afghanistan, the damage its criminal syndicates could do must now be acknowledged.[2]

However large, criminal activity requires a law-enforcement-like solution. The U.S. military has spent most of its illustrious history defending against conventional attack. To be of much help with a drug onslaught, it must add a completely new dimension to its already impressive portfolio. But neither will all of America's police departments be up to the challenge. To whatever extent their field procedures have been based on U.S. military tactics, those procedures will be too obvious and predictable. To safely attack an objective or arrest a criminal, one must achieve complete surprise. Instead, the U.S. military has generally opted for a firepower-based (albeit "high-tech") solution to almost every circumstance. In police work, that much collateral damage is never acceptable. A law enforcement agency cannot "whack" a drug lord from long distance unless he poses an immediate and lethal threat to someone else nearby. Nor can it blow up or burn down the building he shares with other people. In essence, the laws of civilized society are more strict than those of war. And the differences between policing and defense go even deeper.

A Stateside military operation would tend to make too little provision for the corruption that routinely accompanies narcotics trafficking. To preclude embarrassing mistakes, a U.S. military commander would apprise all cooperating agencies of every action and not be surprised if that action failed to produce results. His closest comparison to corruption would be the terror that Communists and Islamists have often inflicted upon neighborhood leaders.

Law Enforcement Is Not Like Traditional Combat

Crime fighting requires something that the U.S. military has tried hard to avoid—decentralization of control. The internal war on drugs can only be won by tiny, highly opportunistic elements that cooperate at the local level (as in police task forces) to keep a lid on local trafficking. However well intended, overly centralized control will simply sap the initiative that the small units need to win.

Police work is also about continual research and purely objective record keeping. Every detail—however small—of each crime is painstakingly collected and then carefully saved for comparison to other crimes. Possible suspects are then investigated. Once their whereabouts (alibi) at the time of the incident and any past *modus operandi* have been determined, most are cleared of any wrongdoing. And before any legal action can be taken against the most likely perpetrator, enough hard evidence has to exist. In essence, small-unit "research" has been occurring with no preconceived notions as to its outcome. That's quite different from always having to do what one's division commander thinks right. And all his reams of electronic intelligence can't make up for the inevitable lack of frontline reconnaissance.

Though the American military has been lately trying better to disseminate lessons learned, it still mostly ignores what squads discover in combat. It neither applies their collective experience to the next operation, nor institutionalizes it for the next war. That's why the squad tactics manuals contain so little surprise-oriented detail. Without it, their procedures do not qualify as maneuver techniques. And without it, American commanders have little choice but to revert to the collateral damage of overwhelming fire-power. The bottom line is that what happens at the squad level within the U.S. infantry, whether in training or combat, has never looked anything like research. That must change. Then, commanders will be able to delegate sufficient authority to their non-commissioned officers (NCOs). When accidents happen (as they did at Polvo Crossing), the American public must be finally told that—against a well-dispersed and exceptionally clever foe—over-control produces too much inertia and predictability. While the past implications of such an admission are immense, there is no time like the present to catch up with tactical evolution. Perhaps that's the hidden blessing in a steady diet of irregular warfare.

Border-Crossing Method Confirmed

Many of Part One's conclusions come from drug syndicate *modus operandi*—current predictions based upon past behavior. On 16 April 2009, ABC's prestigious "Nightly News" confirmed that the vast majority of drugs being smuggled into the U.S. are coming in through hidden compartments in "container trucks." By container trucks, one normally means trucks that carry to market what were formerly ocean-borne shipping containers. It is no secret where the vast majority of those shipping containers originated. The report goes on to say that fewer than 5% of those trucks are being inspected at the U.S.-Mexico border. It finally asserts that Atlanta, Houston, Phoenix, Denver, and Los Angeles are some of the biggest distribution hubs for truck-delivered drugs.[3]

Four days later, a front-page Associated Press article further affirmed that "tractor-trailers have become a transportation mode of choice among [drug] traffickers." It went on to claim that "4.9 million trucks" cross into the United States from Mexico every year, and that "close to 1,000 [Phoenix] kidnappings over the last three years [have been] tied to border smugglers." While these two statistics are not easily confirmed, the exact numbers are probably just as shocking. The article goes on to claim that the Mexican cartels are now establishing "sub-hubs" along America's major highways. In one such location just south of Birmingham, it suggests that the Atlanta-dominating Gulf Cartel just made an example of five potential competitors. That would make Birmingham a sub-hub on the way to Chicago.[4]

How Drug Traffickers View the Situation

Before discussing how U.S. military and police organizations might adapt to the new situation, one must make every effort to view it from the drug traffickers' standpoint. This can't be done without alluding to possible weaknesses in the drug-interdiction system. Those weaknesses may or may not exist, so the next few paragraphs must be taken with a grain of salt. One can only be sure that the average drug trafficker does not view the world in the same way as a Western leader does. His organization has little if any structure, and he is not noticeably restricted by its rules. His view is from the "bottom-up" of a huge and unwieldy "restrainer" of what he perceives to be a legitimate business opportunity. He has closely studied that restrainer and knows of every chink in its armor. Here is what he may see.

Most of the white heroin used to come through Canada to New York, but U.S. and Canadian law enforcement agencies have since constricted that flow. Now, almost all the cocaine and heroin enter America through South Texas. By selling them to Mexican cartels, the Colombian and Asian producers cannot only mask their identities, but also lower their work load. That's why both are now abandoning their distribution apparatus in the Northeastern U.S., so that the Mexican cartels can take over all marketing. With 92% of the world's opium now coming from lawless Afghanistan and Colombian cocaine production up 27% over last year, those cartels are assured of plenty of product.[5]

The Mexican cartels most highly value the high-volume border crossings. They know enough vehicle traffic in response to NAFTA will make thorough inspection impossible. Their most important subcontractor is the Mexican Mafia and its MS-13 and M-18 extensions. MS-13 protects rail conduits through Mexico and sometimes helps with the border smuggling. It further guards the trucking routes to the Northeast and provides alternative "transpo" wherever those routes are blocked. Finally, it keeps the street gangs in line that do the selling. M-18 is being groomed to provide a similar service in other locales.

The U.S. Military Must Alter Certain Procedures

Both U.S. infantry branches have a distinguished heritage. All who have served with them consider that time to be the most pride-filled of their lives. Still, most agree that those branches tend to fight defensively and in a reactionary manner (i.e., primarily responding to enemy initiatives). That tendency may have initially grown out of WWII. In the Pacific, Marine units more easily secured an isolated island by seizing its beach and then allowing its defenders to launch a costly *bonzai* attack. And in Europe, Army units more easily stopped *blitzkrieg* attacks by pinching off or bombing their supply lines. Unfortunately, this preference for defensive action persisted. To shift the momentum in Korea during Operations Killer and Ripper, Ridgway's 8th Army moved forward very slowly and in tight formation so as to steam roll everything in its path.[6] Then during the Vietnam War, as long as a helicopter-borne expeditionary force could occupy a place for a few weeks and kill enough enemy soldiers, it claimed tactical victory.[7]

A drug war cannot be won that way. It must be offensively waged, and enemy initiatives effectively predicted. Thus, anyone who would try to help (whether police or military) cannot disdain the "bottom-up" thought process simply because it contradicts their own "top-down" background. Thinking like the enemy is not tantamount to being the enemy. All low-ranking police and military personnel also think "bottom-up." That is what makes them best qualified to combat the problem.

Higher-level staff personnel can still help. But their assistance must be more in the way of support than of direction. And their most effective tools will be satellite and computer technology. For example, if one were to spot a few drug-filled containers in Acapulco and then monitor their movement north from satellites, he might come up with some very interesting leads. First, there would be the question of which Customs official was on watch when all made their way through the Laredo checkpoint at approximately the same time. Then of interest would be any correlations in logistics companies, freight forwarders, transport companies, or truck drivers. If all vehicles for two miles behind and 10 miles in front of each container were somehow recorded in Texas, and then rechecked in Georgia, follow or lead cars might become apparent. Or if satellite imaging showed different vehicles at approximately the same distance from the containers for long distances, alternating protection vehicles may be present. But at this point "big daddy" must play it cool. The whole idea in fighting a thinking adversary is not to alter that adversary's habits. Once he thinks his methods compromised, he will change them. Thus, coincidently discovering his drugs during a random safety check of a loading dock can be much more productive than seizing them on the open road. But there will be more chance for deception, if the commander and his staff will properly delegate this final-decision-making authority.

The Freight Part of the Equation

The Chinese have so flooded developing nations with cheap goods that many of those nations' manufacturers have been forced out of business. They consider drugs to be legitimate trade goods, so the Hong Kong triads would first try to move them to America through normal freight channels. But even if those triads have not been stuffing manufactured goods with hidden drugs, the sheer volume of freight containers crossing the U.S. border would make them the obvious conveyance of choice.

The Corruption Factor

The Chinese may not be trying to turn the U.S. into a narco-state or even overload its criminal justice system. But, drug trafficking involves such large sums of money that corruption at every level will still result. That corruption may surface in any form—from less regulation on trade to scheduled laxity at a border inspection station.

Once the Biggest Conduits Are Identified

It's much easier to smuggle guns and money south than to smuggle narcotics and aliens north. That's because Mexican authorities seldom check trucks headed south through the Laredo crossing.[8] Still, both sets of contraband probably share the same facilitators. So, by shipping guns or money south after carefully rigging them with state-of-the art homing devices, one might come up with some very interesting details about how the border is being breached. Then, instead of settling for one corrupt official or a temporary block to the conduit, U.S. police and military must think in terms of "strategic offense." As long as they know where the conduit is, they have a decided edge over their opposition. When that cargo is sufficiently away from the border and no longer in transit, they can "coincidently discover" it without causing the drug traffickers to alter their smuggling arrangements. There are hundreds of ways of discreetly sabotaging an infiltration route. One has only to use a little imagination. Unfortunately, U.S. military strategists have more often depended on massively destroying whatever they could catch.

6 Law Enforcement Not _ Military's Job in Past

- How much "policing" did U.S. forces do in Korea?
- Do Muslim rebels use a criminal-justice system?

There's little time for police work in firepower-oriented war.

(Source: "Self-Propelled 155", file #03c-01a.gif, at http://www.au.af.mil/au/awc/awcgate/cliparmy.htm)

U.S. Military to Be Congratulated on Its Progress in Iraq

In a last desperate try to stabilize Baghdad, U.S. commanders finally decided in late 2007 to take back the only strategically important ground for this type of conflict—its neighborhoods. To do so, they used a variation of the Marine CAP concept from the Vietnam War (wherein GIs and Iraqis would serve together in district police stations). With citizen support far from certain, those commanders also walled off many neighborhoods and jailed huge numbers of suspects.[1] In places where GIs could only occasionally visit, they formed Concerned Local Citizens (CLC) groups to act as armed community watch elements.[2] By 1 March 2008, Baghdad's level of violence had fallen off dramatically. A tenuous cease fire with al-Sadr was partially responsible, but the Surge and its police augment plan were obviously working as well. Then, there was more trouble with the Mahdi Army in both Basra and Sadr City. In late May, a deal was struck with al-Sadr through Iran, in which Iraqi Army troops alone could enter the center of either urban area without encountering any resistance.[3]

There is no guarantee that what U.S. expeditionary forces have recently learned about 4GW will ever make it into their organizational memory (i.e., doctrine, manuals, and formal schools). Once peace breaks out again, their more doctrinally oriented Stateside headquarters may well return to preparing for a more traditional type of conflict. That which is "traditional" within a well-established military bureaucracy is not what happened last. It is how U.S. forces have handled the last few decades. That's why one must review history to predict its "emphasis."

The Pentagon's Last "Police Action"

For U.S. forces, the Korean War of 1950 was a "police action" in name only. (See Map 6.1.) While technically committed to the Geneva Conventions of 1949, they made little attempt to enforce any host-nation civil-rights statute. Their job was simply to kill any North Korean invader who refused to surrender.

When the U.S. 8th Army counterattacked during February of 1951 to retake Seoul, it blew down everything in its way. Because U.S. infantry squads were not as tactically adept as their Communist counterparts, their parent units had little choice but to blaze a trail with supporting-arms fire. History records what happened as a veritable meat grinder.[4]

The advance of the seven American divisions now in the line was the twentieth century successor to the Roman "tortoise": instead of long columns, exposed to surprise attack, Ridgway's units now deployed at every stage for all-around defense in depth, securing themselves against infiltration while they waited for the massed artillery and air strikes to do their work upon the Chinese positions. On March 7, Killer

Map 6.1: Juxtaposition of Seoul and Cheju Island
(Source: Courtesy of General Libraries, University of Texas at Austin, from their website for map designator "korean_peninsula_pol_1993.pdf")

was succeeded by Ripper. . . . The envelopment of Seoul by the success of Ripper made the Communist evacuation of the capital inevitable. On March 14 the victors recovered a devastated city, a metropolis of ruins and corrugated iron in which, of the principal buildings, only the Capitol and the railway station survived.[5]

[Some] 40 million gallons of napalm were used in Korea.[6]
          — PBS Special, *Korea — the Unknown War*

For the South Korean civilians being liberated, Ridgway's method must have left something to be desired. They were used to military offensives, but this was nothing like those of the Communists.

The North Koreans were like ghosts. They passed over the countryside and left no mark on it in many ways. But when you use the rock crusher techniques of an American army you hurt your friends. And that was true in Vietnam as well as in Korea.[7]
          — Brig.Gen. Edwin Simmons USMC (Ret.)
           former Director of USMC History & Museums
           PBS Special, *Korea — the Unknown War*

The U.S. military had emerged from its WWII struggle with the world's best light infantry as an addict of 2GW's overwhelming firepower. (See Figure 6.1.) To handle Cold War flare-ups, its commanders relied more on massive bombardment than surprise-oriented maneuver. Where civilians were present, that meant collateral damage. It also meant a less-than-humanitarian example for their riflemen.

Chinese and North Korean units had little trouble sneaking through, and operating behind, U.S. lines. By decentralizing control, they had harnessed the collective wisdom of their foot soldiers. In American rear areas, those foot soldiers looked a lot like impromptu rebels and enemy sympathizers. With the distinction between combatant and noncombatant thus blurred, Allied commanders were often tempted to overlook the physical welfare of adjacent civilians. Instead, they assumed all noncombatants would be smart enough to get out of their way. Unfortunately, not all could. Instead, they took refuge in cellars or tried to flee at the last moment.

Figure 6.1: Stand-Off Warfare Holds Great Allure
(Source: Ft. Sill Military Clipart Library, www.hqda.mil/aoguide/clipart, #CDRBINO4.jpg)

Suddenly, in trying to get away from a firefight in their neighborhood, hundreds of women and children would mob into our area, blocking us off.[8]
— PFC Win Scott
(during a previous recapture of Seoul)

To make matters worse, the Marines were fighting a 3rd-Generation Warfare (3GW)—surprise-oriented—foe who intentionally shifted his defensive strongpoints rearward.[9] To escape encirclement, other Oriental soldiers had already demonstrated a willingness to hide among relocating civilians.[10] So, the Marines had trouble telling combatant from refugee. After seeing civilian-occupied buildings leveled, a few may have even started shooting at anything that moved. Only certain is that South Korean citizens in the path of Operations Killer and Ripper had mixed emotions about being "saved."

> The thing that shook me more than anything was to see
> people—in extreme danger certainly—just shooting indis-
> criminately and even shooting civilians.[11]
> — Rt.Hon. George Younger M.P.
>   Future British Defense Minister
>   Then Argyll & Southern Highlander
>   PBS Special, *Korea—the Unknown War*

Of course, Seoul was no stranger to bombardment. During its
first recapture in September 1950, U.S. forces had also resorted to
plenty of artillery and air strikes. "The slightest resistance brought
down a deluge of destruction blotting out the area," wrote an eye-
witness R.W. Thompson of the *Daily Telegraph*.[12] Then, when the
Chinese entered the war in November, the stakes became higher
as Seoul fell again to the Communists. After Operations Killer and
Ripper, that city's rubbling was much worse than before.[13]

Problems with Host Country Police

If those deployed Americans had tried to cooperate with South
Korean police, they would have faced a whole new set of problems.
South Korea's residents had limited experience with excess bom-
bardment, but they knew all too well about surplus small-arms fire.
More than a few had been summarily shot after being suspected of
Communist sympathies on Cheju Island in 1948.

> The [prewar] South was in trouble. The economy was hurt
> by high inflation and discontent was widespread. Order was
> maintained by the police.[14]
> — PBS Special, *Korea—the Unknown War*

> The [South Korean] police were very cruel. They defended
> where they would. They arrested frequently without war-
> rant. The kind of justice that was dispensed relied very little
> on rules of evidence. It was not very just, and people were
> tortured to provide statements for the prosecutors.[15]
> — Gregory Henderson
>   U.S. Vice Counsel to Korea 1948—1950
>   PBS Special, *Korea—the Unknown War*

All Communism poses a threat to freedom, but not all popular discontent is Communist inspired. It's difficult to tell how much of the Cheju problem was North Korean in origin. Only certain is that it was brutally suppressed.

On the island of Cheju, guerrilla activity was intense. In May 1948, the U.S. military governor General William Dean flew in to supervise [the] counterinsurgency operations. The guerrillas were mainly poor peasants who had taken to arms. Their weapons were often crude but could be lethal. A cycle of revolutionary violence and reprisal was under way. Some 30,000 people were killed on Cheju. In October 1948, a constabulary unit at Yoshu refused to go there and mutinied.[16]

    — PBS Special, *Korea — the Unknown War*

Though Kim Je-Hue—the Yoshu rebels battalion commander—had been my student while I was principal of the military academy, I volunteered to command the expedition to suppress the guerrillas in the South Chiri Mountains. It hurt and broke my heart when I shot him and the whole battalion, but they were enemies that wanted our country to become communist and were therefore unforgivable, so I annihilated them before returning to Seoul.[17]

    — Chung Il-Wan
     South Korean Constabulary
     PBS Special, *Korea — the Unknown War*

Constabulary are paramilitary police. In a 4GW environment, host-nation soldiers can also pose a problem. Collocated GIs might be tempted to ignore their roommates' excesses. That's why U.S. CAP platoon members must immediately report any extrajudicial activity by indigenous security personnel.

Problems with Host-Country Soldiers

South Korea's newly formed 11th Constabulary Regiment was tasked with ending the rebellion on Cheju Island. With only a brief heritage of law enforcement, it was more like a national army unit.

111

One of the first tasks undertaken by American occupation forces when they arrived beginning 8 September 1945 was to train and replace existing Japanese police and security forces. This took the form of a police academy to train policemen and the establishment of police constabulary regiments patterned on the U.S. infantry regiment of that time. . . .
. . . [O]n 10 March 1948, the U.S. Joint Chiefs of Staff approved plans to increase the Korean Constabulary to 50,000 men and arming the constabulary with U.S. weapons including artillery up to 105mm howitzers plus armored cars and M24 tanks. . . .
. . . [O]n 15 December 1948 . . . the 1st, 2nd, 3rd, 5th, 6th, and 7th Constabulary Regiments became the 1st, 2nd, 3rd, 5th, 6th, and 7th Republic of Korea Infantry Divisions. Two months later . . . the 8th and 11th Infantry Divisions were formed from the two remaining constabulary regiments.[18]

Seeking a speedy resolution to the insurrection, the South Korean government sent 3,000 soldiers of the South Korean 11th Constabulary Regiment to reinforce local police, but on April 29 several hundred [11th Constabulary] soldiers mutinied, handing over large small arms caches to the rebels. . . .
By spring of 1949, however, four South Korean army battalions arrived and joined the local constabulary, police forces and Youth Association partisans. The combined forces quickly finished off most of the remaining rebel forces.[19]

There is no guilt by association inferred here, only challenges associated with helping obsessively rightist regimes. After the North Koreans attacked in 1950, many of Syngman Rhee's soldiers continued to view anyone who had allowed him- or herself to be overrun as a Communist sympathizer. This created a severe moral quandary for their more idealistic Western allies.

I took lots of pictures. Inchon was just a sea of rubble. . . . Now don't forget that all of these civilians are being liberated by the South Koreans. I think the South Korean soldiers were mad because they shot at everything that moved. And all these kids and old ladies are walking along with their

hands up because they are terrified of these South Korean soldiers.[20]
— Bert Hardy
Picture Post Photographer
PBS Special, *Korea — the Unknown War*

That Was Long Ago

Despite the arms manufacturers claims to the contrary, short-range combat in urban areas has not changed all that much since 1950. Under similar circumstances, today's forces would have just as much difficulty.

There was no "law enforcement" aspect of the U.S. infantry company's mission in Vietnam either. Most commanders didn't even know the name of their local Viet Cong (VC) leader. There were only rumors about what happened to VC suspects after being turned over to the South Vietnamese Army.[21]

During the Communist uprisings of the 1980's in Central America, the U.S. military was so displeased with Guatemala's human-rights record that it twice disowned the Guatemalan security establishment.[22] That country's National Police had so bad a reputation that it had to be disbanded as part of the 1996 peace settlement.[23]

A definite trend had started to appear. Many of the rightist-regimes with which the U.S. had affiliated were prone to extrajudicial excesses. Within Central America, those excesses led to the same *maras* that now terrorize U.S. streets. With the current upswing in drug trafficking, many of those foreign regimes have been further corrupted. When next asked for troops to confront Islamist or Communist subversion abroad, Washington must now strictly stipulate that the host government refrain from any further indiscretions.

How America's Foes Have Dealt with Similar Dilemmas

Communist forces have encountered similar challenges over the years. Instead of gaining a foothold in a city and then slogging forward, they will attack it from the inside out with the "blooming lotus" maneuver.[24] This permits less collateral damage and immediate access to opposition leaders. Though most are summarily executed, this integral part of a Communist invasion still constitutes an elementary (albeit brutal) form of "police work."

The Islamists also combine law enforcement with battlefield maneuver. The Mahdi Army has had its own police and courts in Sadr City and Basra for years.[25] Similarly, the Taliban has its own *sharia* courts in much of Afghanistan.[26] Thus, it now seems clear that—to defeat either foe—deployed U.S. forces must take more interest in local law enforcement. To do so, their "ground pounders" will need additional training.

7 _ Modern Infantrymen Need Police Training

- Do enemy combatants have legal status?
- Then why not treat them like crime suspects?

In 4GW, Too Much Shooting Creates More Opponents.

(Source: "Squad Attacking Forward", file #1-14b.gif, at http://www.au.af.mil/au/awc/awcgate/cliparmy.htm)

Like "Crime Fighting," Wars Are Regulated

The laws of war are far too complicated to rehash here, but everyone knows they exist. By following the "rules of engagement" published for every conflict, GIs implicitly obey their provisions. In a 4GW environment, insurgents are most productively handled like local-legal-statute violators. It would make perfect sense, then, to train all U.S. counterinsurgents in law enforcement procedure. In Iraq and Afghanistan, American infantrymen could make good use of police apprehension methods. Why would their service branches withhold such training?

The Geneva Convention Amendment Protocols

The United States has yet to ratify two 1977 amendment protocols to the original Geneva Conventions of 1949. One applies to "international" armed conflicts, and the other to "non-international" armed conflicts (civil wars). Therein may lie the root of the problem. Perhaps the U.S. military's ongoing attempts to evolve into a 4GW-capable force have been impeded by politicians who have yet to realize that war has changed. That would explain why America was so easily persuaded by China to add the legitimately separatist Uighurs to its official list of terrorist groups.[1]

By not ratifying these Geneva Convention amendments, the U.S. government may have further encouraged the 2GW type of intervention that so nurtures Communist and Islamist 4GW victory. That intervention is so standoffish, all-inclusive, and heavy handed that it effectively cedes popular support to the enemy. It also separates every liberator from the very person he is trying to rescue. From recent successes in Iraq, it's clear that deployed GIs and host-country civilians must now coexist in the same tiny communities to get the better of an insurgency. By living and working together, they are better able to detect and remove enemy infiltrators. Then only targeted is that small part of the population that is actually culpable. Each case must be considered on its own merits. And the U.S. CAP platoon members could better function if trained in criminal investigative procedure.

Amendment Protocol I

Amendment Protocol I relates to the protection of victims of *international* armed conflicts. As of 14 January 2007, it had been ratified by 167 countries, with the U.S., Israel, Iran, Pakistan, Turkey, Afghanistan, and Iraq being the notable exceptions. Three paragraphs of its Article 44 appear to be the sticking point. They cover the treatment of captured insurgents and guerrillas. While U.S. leaders admit that most of Protocol I's provisions have already been added to customary international law, they worry that some might legitimize groups waging illicit wars of "national liberation." The main U.S. objection is that the protocol extends Geneva Convention protection to those it regards as "unlawful combatants" and "terrorists." Though Amendment Protocol I has yet to be officially ratified in Washington, the U.S. Army has already added many of its central precepts to its "Law of Land Warfare" field manual.[2] Below is the first of the three paragraphs in question. It apparently draws too little distinction between combatant and civilian to suit U.S. political leaders. That may help to explain why American troops have never attempted to match their Eastern counterparts in infiltration skills.

In order to promote the protection of the civilian population from the effects of hostilities, combatants are obliged to distinguish themselves from the civilian population while they are engaged in an attack or in a military operation preparatory to an attack. Recognizing, however, that there are situations in armed conflicts where, owing to the nature of the hostilities an armed combatant cannot so distinguish himself, he shall retain his status as a combatant, provided that, in such situations, he carries his arms openly:

(a) During each military engagement, and
(b) During such time as he is visible to the adversary while he is engaged in a military deployment preceding the launching of an attack in which he is to participate.[3]

All insurgents and guerrillas are afforded prisoner of war status by the original Third Geneva Convention providing they carry arms openly, are responsible to superiors, and somehow distinguish themselves from civilians (like with an armband). Amendment Protocol I would give them prisoner of war status even if they didn't follow the last provision. More specifically, Article 4 of the Third Geneva Convention requires combatants to have a "fixed distinctive sign recognizable at a distance." Amendment Protocol I would release lawful combatants from this obligation. Without such distinctive identification, U.S. troops could come under attack from enemies posing as civilians without those enemies violating their combat legitimacy. This would be especially relevant to peacekeeping operations. Whereas civilian police forces are trained only to shoot if certain of their targets' hostile intent, Western militaries are trained to shoot any time their target is in view. Therein lies the dilemma. Militaries wishing to become proficient at 4GW can no longer count on their adversaries being recognizable from civilians, and must therefore treat every person they see as having civilian rights.[4]

117

Amendment Protocol II

As of January 2007, the U.S. had also to ratify Amendment Protocol II—the one dealing with the "protection of victims of *non-international* armed conflicts" or civil wars. By not ratifying this protocol, the U.S. has not only forgotten how it threw off the British yoke, but also implicitly endorsed every dictatorial regime in the world. America's political leaders must have worried that this protocol would enhance the status of rebels, even though the U.S. military had little objection to the ratification. Part II of this second amendment protocol includes articles on the following topics: (1) humane treatment; (2) persons whose liberty has been restricted; and (3) penal prosecutions. And the articles of Part IV deal with these additional protections: (1) of the civilian population; (2) of objects indispensable to the survival of the civilian population; (3) of works and installations containing dangerous forces (like dikes or nuclear generating stations); (4) of cultural objects and places of worship; and (5) of civilians being forcefully displaced.[5] Other countries not ratifying Amendment Protocol II are Israel, Iran, Pakistan, and Afghanistan.[6]

Summation

Not ratifying these Amendment Protocols may have been intended to protect civilian populations from harm (in the form of subversive activity). But, it has also exposed them to harm (in the form of occupier error). Once they are ratified, the U.S. military may have more of a reason—during counterinsurgency operations—to function as part of the local criminal justice system. Until that happens, its deployed units will be too easily accused of human-rights abuses. After being "sensationalistically" photographed, even a fairly legitimate airstrike will damage public opinion. That's why policemen would never even consider an airstrike against a house full of escaped felons.

Counterinsurgency Is All About Civilian Alliances

As U.S. forces so brilliantly discovered in Iraq, there was no "Sunni insurgency" *per se* (as their political leaders and news media kept telling them). By having the courage to act on this discovery, those wonderful Marines and soldiers have established a proud new heritage of counterinsurgency excellence.

The Communist and Islamic extremists swim through a peace-loving population like sociopaths through a crowd. They terrorize everyone in their way and then take what they want. That in no way detracts from the basic goodness of their victims. It is only through those civilian populations that insurgents can be eliminated. And it is only through a civil court system that those insurgents can be eliminated without encouraging their replacement.

GIs Have Too Little Experience with Civilian Populations

In many parts of the world, national armies play a much more active role in everyday life than do American forces at home. Of course, their dual-role is not always welcomed by the local populace. In Communist countries, those armies outpost the cities to prevent a popular uprising. But in many free countries, soldiers also help out with everything from traffic control to road maintenance. That gives them more exposure to a civilian (4GW-like) setting than GIs normally receive. For counterinsurgency work, such experience can prove invaluable. Of late, the U.S. military has invested a lot of time and money in role-playing exercises. But such exercises tend to emphasize societal differences more than common bonds. The civilians of every nationality are primarily interested in one thing—their families. They simply want to provide for, and protect, those families. As such, they are no different from one's neighbors of some other ethnicity down the street. For 4GW, more time on overseas "shore patrol" would do the troops more good than role-playing exercises. (See Figure 7.1.) Then, at least, they would come to realize they are dealing with irrational elements within basically friendly societies. They would also come to see themselves as protecting the weak from unruly elements within their own military units and those of host countries.

To function alone, 4GW-qualified CAP platoon members must be highly self-disciplined. Whatever they demand of themselves, they will also demand of their fellow squad members and host-country counterparts. They are not allowed, nor will they tolerate, any extrajudicial excess. Fully to appreciate what that means,

Figure 7.1: "Shore Patrol" Duty Good Training for 4GW
(Source: FM 19-95B1/2 [1978], cover; DA Pam 550-175 [1989]. p. xxxvii)

most will need the same amount of legal-statute instruction that a novice policeman receives. They will also need more tactical skill, because minimal force takes total surprise. Within Part Three are some advanced 4GW techniques for intelligence gathering and active combat.

Part Three

Shared Experience in Tactics

"Instead of death and sorrow, let us bring peace and joy to the world." — Mother Theresa

(Source: Attributed to Mother Theresa)

8 Foiling Foe's Resupply ___ and Reinforcement

- How might an insurgent openly replace his expenditures?
- What can be done to stop this?

Rebel Replenishment Masked As Normal Civilian Activity

(Source: Courtesy of Sorman Information and Media, from Soldf: Soldaten i falt, ©2001 by Forsvarsmakten and Wolfgang Bartsch, Stockholm, p. 144)

The Need to View Things Differently

In the most volatile parts of the world, there can be no peace without some initial sacrifice. Afghanistan promises to be a far greater challenge to the U.S. defense establishment than was Iraq. The Taliban largely supports itself through drugs.[1] Routes of communication and commerce are easier to sever in mountainous terrain. And Afghan tribes have more guerrilla experience. To be the first invader to successfully occupy this place, the U.S. military must consider every option.

The Pentagon has been attempting to halt Communist and Islamist expansion for quite some time. It considers most insurgents to be reinforced and resupplied from outside their parent nation along well-hidden infiltration conduits. Over the years, many an aerial-bombing run and ground operation have been dedicated to that premise. Along today's Ho Chi Minh Trails, American soldiers and Marines look for obscure paths, camouflaged waystations, and clever tunnels.

Yet, modern 4GW revolutionaries can get most of what they need from inside their own borders. Whatever they can't steal or inherit from a well-supplied and bombardment happy occupier, they extort from fellow countrymen. If they have too few fighters or laborers, they abduct some. If they lack funding, they grow and sell drugs. Everything else, they buy. Those resources then come to them inconspicuously through the normal ebb and flow of everyday travel and commerce. That's why a better (4GW) model for enemy support conduit might now be that of a long-established smuggling route. Much of what the smuggler does occurs within plain sight of local residents, not in some remote vine-covered tunnel. Thus—within the drug and people traffickers' assault on America—may lie vital lessons for U.S. expeditionary forces. And how U.S. law enforcement has tried to impede that flow may hold the clues to better military interdiction.

The Border Comparison

Most of the places in which U.S. troops now fight have too little vegetation to support a Vietnam style infiltration trail. Yet, their foes still receive plenty of support from foreign sources. That support has not always been in the form of manpower or materiel. Right before the January 2005 presidential election in Iraq, the king of Jordan warned that over a million Iranians had crossed the border to participate. Other estimates ran as high as four million.[2] Before Iraq's Parliamentary election of December 2005, ABC News reported a truckload of counterfeit ballots being intercepted at the Iranian border.[3] Thus, any of the instruments of political, economic, or psychological 4GW may be in transit. They could run the gamut from specialized advisors to monetary hoards. For either the economic or psychological categories of 4GW, banned narcotics would certainly qualify.

Of course, arms can also be smuggled. Some 90% of the automatic weapons, rocket launchers, and .50-caliber sniper rifles with which Mexico's drug cartels are currently fighting its army have come from the U.S.[4] Some ordnance can even be camouflaged. Within Southern Lebanon and Israel, *Hezbollah* proxies ship irregularly shaped pieces of explosive as if it were landfill rock.

Inside-the-Country Parallels

As guerrillas do not always require exterior support, one must eventually consider how they might generate enough fighters and war materiel locally. In the case of the latter, thousands of tiny increments would be progressively accumulated. Their production and transport would look like the normal processes of routine business. And then, over time, the insurgents would amass as much wherewithal as an accomplished smuggler might. Much of what a North Vietnamese Army (NVA) infantry division would need to hold Hue City for 30 days in 1968 was brought in ahead of time. All Perfume River, Phu Cam Canal, and highway approaches to the city had been clogged with Tet traffic throughout the month of January. This elevated level of activity must have provided ample opportunity for the prestaging of supplies. Very possibly, no one bothered to check all the tiny boats.

Hundreds of infantry weapons — including .51 caliber heavy machineguns and perhaps hundreds of tons of ammunition, demolitions, and supplies—had been smuggled into Hue disguised as civilian goods.[5]

Interrupting the Process

Many things have been attempted over the years to keep rebels from acquiring support from their own populations. Most—like the resettlement.camps—have only served to further alienate those populations from their legitimate governments. Whatever is now done must look to the average civilian like an aid to his or her individual security without concurrently disrupting his or her lifestyle. In essence, it must fit the definition of legitimate police protection.

Whatever U.S. police currently do to capture felons or drugs

125

would qualify. In the latter, they already have a way to watch highways without disrupting vehicular flow. They do so by being extra vigilant while enforcing traffic laws. As they request the driver's registration, they take a cursory look into his vehicle with their flashlight. If the driver must open his glove compartment to retrieve that registration, they glance in there as well. Then, under certain circumstances, they can search the vehicle further. While the legal parameters for this additional search are well beyond the scope of this book, here is an example of each.

This is in response to your request for a brief description of the Fourth Amendment's probable cause, reasonable suspicion, and reasonableness standards. In over simplified terms, probable cause "exist[s] where the known facts and circumstances are sufficient to warrant a man of reasonable prudence in the belief that contraband or evidence of a crime will be found." . . .

[R]easonable suspicion is a standard, more than a hunch but considerably below preponderance of the evidence, which justifies an officer's investigative stop of an individual upon the articulable and particularized belief that criminal activity is afoot. . . .

And Fourth Amendment reasonableness is that point at which the government's interest advanced by a particular search or seizure outweighs the loss of individual privacy or freedom of movement. . . .

. . . [The] *Pringle* [case] found probable cause to arrest the passenger in a small car on a charge of possessing the five "baggies" of cocaine [that were] found in the back seat of the car. . . . An officer had stopped the car for speeding at 3 [A.M.] in the morning. . . . Pringle was the front seat passenger and the officer saw a large roll of cash in the glove compartment when it was opened to retrieve the car's registration. . . . To these the Court added the inference that a trained, experienced officer might draw: "Here we think it was reasonable for the officer to infer a common enterprise among the three men [traveling together]. The quantity of drugs and cash in the car indicated the likelihood of drug dealing. . . .

[The] *Brignoni-Ponce* [case] explained . . .that "[a]ny

number of factors may be taken into account in deciding whether there is reasonable suspicion to stop a car in the border area. Officers may consider the characteristics of the area in which they encounter a vehicle. Its proximity to the border, the usual patterns of traffic on the particular road, and previous experience with alien traffic are all relevant. They also may consider information about recent illegal border crossings in the area. The driver's behavior may be relevant, as erratic driving or obvious attempts to evade officers can support a reasonable suspicion. Aspects of the vehicle itself may justify suspicion. For instance, officers say that certain station wagons, with large compartments for fold-down seats or spare tires are frequently used for transporting concealed aliens. The vehicle may appear to be heavily loaded, it may have an extraordinary number of passengers, or trying to hide [something]." . . .

In highway checkpoint cases, [the] *Martinez-Fuerte* and *Sitz* [cases] apply a Fourth Amendment reasonable balancing test. . . . *Martinez-Fuerte* balanced the substantial public interest served in terms of smuggling and illegal entry by permanent highway checkpoints located proximate to the border against the reduced expectation of privacy associated with automobile use and the "quite limited" and "minimal" intrusion upon private interests. . . . *Sitz* uses a similar standard for highway drunk-driving checkpoints – "balanc[ing] the state's interest in preventing drunken driving, the extent to which this system [of highway checkpoints] can reasonably be said to advance that interest, [against] the degree of intrusion upon individual motorists who are briefly stopped."[6]

— Congressional Research Service Memorandum

Not all roadside opportunities to spot drugs may have been exploited. For example, why couldn't there be drug-sniffing dogs at the truck weigh stations and agricultural inspection stops? Stateside, that may violate somebody's privacy rights. But, overseas, U.S. forces would only have the host-country statutes to worry about. Any replacement fighters or military contraband that they coincidentally found while ostensibly doing some public service would be less to confront on the battlefield. Such seizures are most usefully turned over to local police. Then, those GIs will be more closely associated with civil justice than martial excess. That's one of the best ways to appear more peacekeeper than occupier. Where hearts and minds are in play, appearances are everything.

With Which "Public Services" Could GIs Spot Rebels?

There are many ways to check for infiltrators and contraband that look to the average passerby like some other public service. In pairs, GIs could man checkpoints or walk "beats" in high-crime areas. Or they could check the undersides of all vehicles entering public markets for bombs. Either way, their vigilance would eventually be rewarded with a sighting of guerrillas or war materiel. Then, they would only have to discreetly identify the suspects or conveyance to local officials. Those officials could then—at a slightly later time and place—look into the matter further under the pretext of a routine administrative check. All the while, the GIs would be foreign-aid workers in the law enforcement sector, and never personally involved in any counterinsurgency operation.

Simply assuming a different attitude on patrol can sometimes net big gains. One afternoon late in 1966, a young Marine lieutenant was leading a platoon-sized patrol around the Vietnamese border outpost of Gio Linh. As Gio Linh was under imminent threat of North Vietnamese attack, the last thing on his mind was refugees. Upon encountering an unexpected column of civilian travelers on an otherwise deserted landscape, he noticed one man with a bulldog jaw and a well-endowed lady behind him. That lieutenant and his patrol kept on walking. If they had stopped and searched that supposed column of refugees, they would have minimally come up with an NVA sergeant major, his main squeeze, and a large quantity of hand grenades.[7] Like everything in war, it is all in one's perspective of his assignment in relation to the foe's agenda.

U.S. forces have a common and likeable tendency to follow through on high-level strategy at the expense of local opportunity. A month or two later and several miles to the west, members of that same U.S. platoon discovered the grass crushed at one-meter intervals along a vine-covered and cobblestone-paved road leading north. When their lieutenant called in the sighting, he was told that helicopters were inbound to shift the company to a different operation. That time, the proper follow-through might have netted an anti-aircraft gun (or gotten the whole platoon killed). Several months earlier within 100 yards of this very spot, another company had lost the battalion's most talented and popular young officer— Jack Cox. He had been trying to outflank an NVA battalion with a single platoon.[8] But any on-site trepidation notwithstanding, the unfortunate truth is that by operating from the "top-down," U.S. forces had just missed another golden opportunity.

How NVA's Infiltration Routes Could Have Been Spotted

The Ho Chi Minh Trail originated in North Vietnam. Its most famous parts ran down the 1,000-kilometer Truong Son mountain range that separated South Vietnam from Laos and Cambodia. (Map 8.1 shows how the road network looked in 1968.) From that time until the war's end in 1973, this network was considerably expanded. It eventually included a string of underground (subsurface) roadways that stretched all the way from Ben Tat, North Vietnam to Po La Khoc, South Vietnam (near Kontum in its Central Highlands).[9]

As the North Vietnamese troops and supplies veered off the Truong Son road network, they entered onto progressively smaller trails that headed toward South Vietnam's coastal plain. Most ran through heavily vegetated and mountainous terrain that was otherwise inaccessible. Others led through sparsely populated valleys in which U.S. forces seldom operated. As those many smaller trails reached the heavily cultivated low lands, they split into hundreds of micro-filament ends. Those ends were so well hidden as to virtually disappear into the background. Running through the hamlet-dotted rice fields, each consisted of a foot-wide track that indirectly connected a series of obscure waystations. The average waystation was on a tiny islet amidst the seemingly endless sea of rice paddy. It containing a single farmer's hut and vegetable garden. But the hut's original owner was no longer there, and the furrows in his cultivated plot were now rows of camouflaged rice bags. Nearby were underground stores of medical supplies and ordnance. Like most patches of dry ground in this part of Vietnam, this one was surrounded by bunkers and a trench system. Its neighbors were all part of a wide band of strategic hamlets that protected the infiltration trail and its various waystations. To preclude discovery, local bands of VC continually shifted their "operational headquarters" between the "underground hide facilities" of ten or so hamlets. The

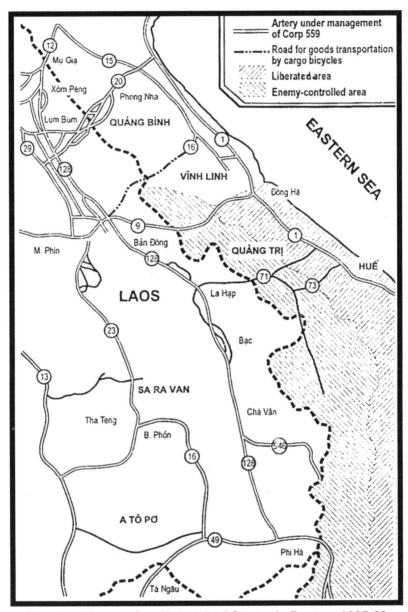

Map 8.1: Truong Son Network of Strategic Routes, 1965-68
(Source: Courtesy of The Gioi Publishers, from The Ho Chi Minh Trail, © 2001 by Hoàng Khôi and The Gioi, p. 26)

waystation also had such a retreat, but it was bigger and harder to find than the others. Its points of access were often below water level. Its entrance was through the submerged wall of a well, and its exit was below the surface of a deep and fully flowing irrigation ditch.[10] (See Map 8.2.)

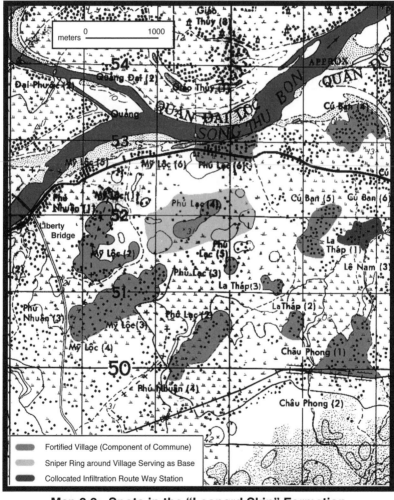

Map 8.2: Spots in the "Leopard Skin" Formation
(Source: 1:50,000 map of area northeast of An Hoa Marine Base)

Whenever a U.S. sweep spent any time crossing one of these lowland infiltration trails, it would find caches of weapons, rice, and medical supplies. Occasionally, it would encounter an enemy unit in transit and a big firefight would ensue. Other times, U.S. patrols saw enemy soldiers on the move. Or an American outpost spied (through long-range binoculars) a slowing running column of bushes at sundown.[11] Once one understood how the infiltration trails operated, those three types of sightings told a story.

What That Story Was in Vietnam

NVA units regularly came in from the mountains to attack U.S. bases and Vietnamese cities. Most of what they would need in the way of supplies and equipment had to be prestaged. That means it probably came in along one of the above-mentioned infiltration trails.

While on the approach march, those NVA units did not carry much so as to be able to move more quickly than U.S. artillery spotters could get clearances to target them. Instead of slogging cross-country through the endless muck, they jogged in column along pre-existing dikes and hamlet pathways. That means they must have again taken advantage of the prestocked infiltration conduits. Thus, every sighting of a unit on the move could be reasonably inferred to be along such a conduit. And, every uncovered cache was in its immediate vicinity.

These hidden, lowland infiltration trails were of tremendous strategic value to the North Vietnamese. Their maneuver forces would fight until nightfall when surprised along one. And, the VC tasked with defending one would divert (often through sniping from a different location) any inquisitive trespasser.

Thus, if a GI were to plot all the caches found, enemy columns sighted, and chance firefights recorded on a map of his tactical area of responsibility, he could find the approximate trace of the hidden routes. He only had to connect all three types of dots (without any deference to variety) as they occurred outboard of his base in any radial sector. He would then end up with several jagged lines that resembled the shattered spokes of a wheel. The one leading to the mountains would be his most promising, but as with Hue City, the others would also deserve a closer look. If there had been any U.S. mantrackers in that conflict, they could have then established the

Figure 8.1: City Roads Also Look Like Wagon Spokes
(Source: FM 90-10 [1979], p. 1-9)

exact trace of each route. To do so, they would have only had to patrol back and forth across it. Wherever there was evidence of more human passage than the local residents could create, they would have a confirmed trail segment. A similar thought process might help to locate modern-day smuggling conduits.

Finding a Contemporary Infiltration Route

These days, rebels resupply themselves in the same way that smugglers move their wares, namely by road. From any category of smuggler, one could therefore learn how to interdict guerrilla wherewithal. But, the drug runner is the most sophisticated of the bunch, so his activity will serve as the model for the new route-finding method. Then, both police and military can find utility in it. (See Figures 8.1 and 8.2.)

Cities are the drug smugglers' biggest market. As should have been evident from Chapter Three, they send most of their product to that market over public roadways. At various places along those roadways, they have intermediate warehouse facilities. When a rolling load gets too much unwanted attention, its guards object

133

Figure 8.2: Mapping the Smuggling Routes in Afghanistan
(Source: U.S. military website within the *http://www.usafns.com/art.shtml listing, image #1-07ab.gif*)

or the load gets seized. Thus, we again have three indicators of a smuggling route's approximate trace: (1) a materiel stash; (2) a roadway disturbance; and (3) a confiscated load. On any map of a "greater metropolitan area," plotting those indicators also tells a story. When every dot is indiscriminately connected while moving outboard in any particular direction from the city's center, they define such a trace. (See Maps 8.3 and 8.4.)

Obviously, there must be some qualifiers in the "roadway disturbance" category, or too many entries would cloud the picture. In late 2008, there was a running automatic-weapon fight along one of Houston's peripheral freeways. As no police were involved,[12] one can reasonably assume that drugs were. Perhaps someone had tried

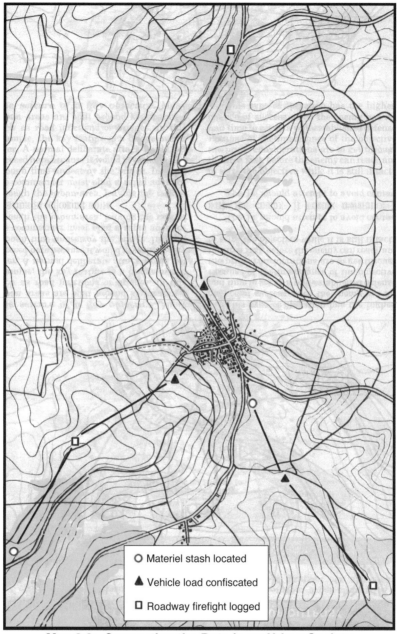

Map 8.3: Connecting the Dots in an Urban Society
(Source: *FM 90-10-1* [1982], p. 3-23)

Legend:
- ○ Materiel stash located
- ▲ Vehicle load confiscated
- ☐ Roadway firefight logged

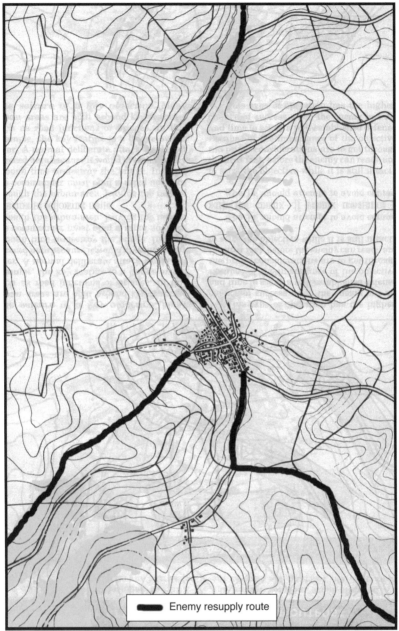

Enemy resupply route

Map 8.4: Precisely Locating Drug or Resupply Routes
(Source: *FM 90-10-1* [1982], p. 3-23)

to "boost" a load, or the local gangs were fighting over sales "turf." Sadly, a more common incident along public roads is the killing of a policeman by the multiple occupants of some car during a routine traffic stop. In that case, one can reasonably assume that those occupants are either all fleeing felons or responsible for a drug load. Thus, by limiting the roadway incidents to running gunfights and police ambushes, one might have a valid third indicator of a drug route. A possible fourth would be the sighting of a known MS-13 member. He is not out on a Sunday drive. He is more probably doing one of the following: (1) transporting drugs; (2) running interference for a load; or (3) performing advance reconnaissance of law enforcement activity. In any given city, the vehicle types and license numbers of all MS-13 members are well known to the local police department and could be easily forwarded to the state patrol. Finally, any MS-13 incident in a city suburb might also serve as an indicator. It would most likely occur in the general vicinity of a warehouse or route. Unfortunately, then finding the exact trace of that route within an asphalt road system will not be as easy as it would have been in Vietnam's dirt trail network.

Perhaps, the opposition guerrilla army also depends upon a readily recognizable element to handle its resupply. Some of its members might even be known smugglers. Then, one would only have to monitor their activity to find the parent organization's infiltration conduits.

Other Opportunities

The FARC has—on several occasions—traded drugs for guns with parties outside of Colombia.[13] Those guns must be coming in along the same routes that carry the cocaine out. If one were to secretly hide a nondetectable "space-age" locator in a bogus load of outbound drugs, he might very well discover the exact path of the inbound weapons. Where weapons travel, so do replacement fighters.

To then interdict those routes, one must be able to take down a contested enemy strongpoint without doing any harm to its civilian occupants. This is, by far, the hardest of all tactical maneuvers. As such, the next chapter should be of particular interest to America's most elite special-operations and SWAT teams.

Civilian-Saving Attack
_____ on a Building

● Will terrorists and drug traffickers take more hostages?

● Can civilians be spared during an urban infantry assault?

To win at 4GW, fewer civilians must die in urban offense.

(Source: Courtesy of Sorman Information and Media, from Soldf: Soldaten i falt, @2001 by Forsvarsmakten and Wolfgang Bartsch, Stockholm, p. 307)

The Next Round of Terrorist Attacks

In late November 2008, 15 to 20 Lashkar-e-Toiba (LET) militants launched a series of ground attacks from Karachi, Pakistan, against civilian targets in Mumbai, India. While LET was heavily reported in the U.S. to be a creation of the Pakistani Interservice Intelligence (ISI), it may have been only its Kashmir proxy. In 2003, the U.S. State Department identified LET as "the armed wing of _Markaz-ud-Dawa-wal-Irshad_ (MDI)," a Sunni anti-U.S.-missionary faction formed in 1989 from Wahhabi roots. Of late, MDI has gone by the name of _Jamaat ul Dawa,_ and LET by _Khairus Naas._[1] LET is also affiliated with *al-Qaeda* and the Dawood Ibrahim crime syndicate. Among other things, that syndicate coordinates the shipment of Afghan heroin. Though originally from Mumbai, Dawood is now the godfather of the Karachi underworld. There is evidence his organization lent material support to the perpetrators of this latest Mumbai ground assault, as well as to those of its 1993 bombings.[2] Whether he had anything to do with that city's 2006 train detonations is not known. But to acquire funding, Muslim extremists will sometimes sell their services to "dissimilar entities." (*Hezbollah* did to the Communist rebels or drug cartels in Mexico in 2001.[3]) With Dawood as intermediary, that dissimilar entity with which LET was dealing need not have been from Pakistan or Afghanistan. According to *Newsweek,* India's Maoist rebels are also interested in Mumbai.[4] If the attack did have a strategic purpose, it was to create enough of an Indian-Pakistani border confrontation to take the pressure off some other region. That region could have been Eastern India, Pakistan's Taliban and *al-Qaeda* infested North-West Frontier Province (NWFP) and Federally Administered Tribal Areas (FATA), or Pakistan's southern drug route.

In other words, a terrorist attack can be of great help to either drug syndicate or nonaffiliated expansionist player. Because the November event achieved much greater media attention than the previous bombings, more "commando-style" hostage seizures will undoubtedly occur elsewhere. To successfully counter them, one must first review every detail of the Mumbai assault.

Specifics of the 2008 Assault on India's West Coast City

Among the targets of the Mumbai attack were several luxury hotels, a restaurant, a train station, a Jewish community center, a cinema, two hospitals, and a police headquarters. Though the assaults against the Marriott and Ramada were unsuccessful and only briefly reported, those against the Taj Mahal Palace and Oberoi Trident may have achieved their intended purpose. There, the attackers took hundreds of hostages and thereby got worldwide media attention during an extended siege. Only after 60 hours of on-and-off battle was the massive and historic Taj retaken. Indian policing, intelligence, and counter-terrorism agencies were soon being heavily criticized for too little foresight and speed.[5]

While the details of the Taj fight were never fully disclosed, some things are known. The raiders had AK-47's, grenades, and cell phones. They were high on drugs and having their every action coordinated by satellite phone from Pakistani territory. Well aware of the hotel's floor plan and security arrangements, they easily moved throughout the immense structure, firing at erstwhile rescuers from several different stories. To bottle them up, Indian authorities were forced to commit 900 personnel. While there is no hard evidence of an escape route being used, it may have still existed. Later, it was divulged that the Indian authorities and Taj security personnel had been forewarned of an attack from the sea.[6]

According to Fox News, it took the Indian commandos a full seven hours to reach the two luxury hotels. By that time, the gunmen had fully established their defenses and trapped hundreds of people. Rata Tata, head of the Taj conglomerate, had been warned of a possible attack, but he said that no security arrangements could have completely stymied the highly skilled militants. "They did not go through the front entrance; all our security arrangements are in the front," he said. "They planned everything. . . . [T]he first thing they did . . . [was to shoot] a sniffer dog and his handler." The sole militant captive told police he was trained in Pakistan and that the terror strikes were intended to kill as many as 5,000 people with whites – especially Britons and Americans—being specifically targeted.[7]

After the tragedy, it was determined that 195 people had been killed and 295 wounded. Among the dead were 18 foreigners, including six Americans.[8]

The Extent of the Terrorists' Planning at Mumbai

An obscure Indian organization (the *Deccan Mujahideen)* later tried to take credit for the operation,[9] but it was more probably the multinational Dawood Ibrahim syndicate that provided LET with support.[10] That support may have included help with reconnaissance and escape. One event stands out among all the others. After shooting over 50 people in the train station, the gunmen just happened to ambush (and hijack) the police van carrying Mumbai's counterterrorism chief.[11] While ambushing response routes is an integral part of all raid tactics, planning to kill the most proficient response leader is not. That smacks of Asian Communist method. The terror commandos also dropped 10-pound RDX (nitroamine) bombs on extended timers along their attack routes. While all were found and defused, these bombs had been intended to impede pursuit.[12] That suggests something other than strictly suicidal intent. And the bottom line is this—after terrorizing an entire city for three full days, almost half of the minuscule assault force may have gotten away.[13]

What Mumbai's Responders Could Have Done Differently

The Mumbai police did not have the Special-Weapon Assault Team (SWAT) assets to immediately take back the Taj and Oberoi. When India's special counterterrorist commandos finally reached the city, the deranged gunmen had enjoyed ample time to seize hostages and consolidate positions.[14] Once a building contains both defenders and hostages, capturing it becomes a much more challenging proposition. That "proposition" is the focus of this chapter. In recent years, the most successful urban hostage rescue occurred in Lima, Peru.

The Model Rescue Was at a Japanese Ambassador's Home

On 17 December 1996, 14 members of the Tupac Amaru Revolutionary Movement (MRTA) took more than 400 high-level diplomats, government officials, and business executives captive. Those newly appointed victims had done nothing more risky than attending a party at an ambassador's residence. That structure had been converted into a veritable fortress by the Japanese government. It was surrounded by a 12-foot-high wall and had doors that could withstand a grenade explosion. All of its windows were covered by grates, and some had bulletproof glass. Once inside, the Marxist rebels had little trouble defending the place. Their principal demand was that the 450 MRTA prisoners in Peru's prisons be freed. Without giving in to the rebels, Peruvian authorities finally won the release of all but 72 of the hostages. Then, at the request of Fujimori (Peru's president of Nipponese descent), they made a thorough study of how safely to rescue the remainder. Within their findings may lie the key to "hostage-friendly assault"—a topic with which both U.S. military and police communities have long struggled. That key has probably to do with non-Western tactics.

After being held captive for 126 days, the 72 dignitaries were finally rescued on 22 April 1997 by Peruvian commandos. During the raid, 25 hostages were superficially wounded, and one died of a heart attack. Two of the commandos were killed by enemy fire, and all 14 MRTA militants subsequently died. When the militants' bodies were later exhumed, it became evident that a few had been executed.[15] Whether in law enforcement or 4GW, all extrajudicial activity is counterproductive. Still, that any of the militants were captured alive is further proof of the assault's initial effectiveness. And everything up to those unwise executions can usefully serve as a model for future operations.

Preparations for the Peruvian Attack

As in most hostage rescues, Lima's commandos would attempt to neutralize all kidnappers before they could hurt their victims. Their success would depend on how well everyone's whereabouts at the time of the assault could be pre-ascertained. As such, the guerrillas' daily schedule became the first order of business. Much would be learned from surveillance devices throughout the ambassador's residence, but little is known about how they were placed. The Peruvian Red Cross functioned as intermediary, and a few journalists were allowed inside. There was also a two-way communication link between the authorities and one of the captives. It may have been facilitated by the pager he was carrying.

> [R]etired naval officer Admiral Luis Giampietri Rojas . . . had been able to hide a radio receiver from the . . . (MRTA) terrorists for the entire four months of his captivity.[16]
> — Emergency Net News Intel. Rpt., 24 April 1997

[S]ophisticated miniature microphones and video cameras had been smuggled into the residence, concealed in books, water bottles, and table games. Giampetri and other military officers among the hostages were given the responsibility for placing these devices in secure locations around the house. Eavesdropping on the MRTA commandos with the

143

help of these high-tech devices, military planners observed that the insurgents had organized their security carefully, and were particularly alert during the night hours. However, early every afternoon, eight of the MRTA members, including the four leaders, played indoor football for about one hour.[17]

The rescue planners could thus monitor most of the terrorists' discussions and movements within the residence. From released hostages, they subsequently learned how to turn the kidnappers' own methods against them.

Rooms in the building, he said, were wired with explosives, as well as the roof. He added that the terrorists had anti-tank weapons and wore backpacks that were filled with explosives that could be detonated by pulling a cord on their chest.[18]

Many facets of the final rescue were handled during the siege. Light-colored clothing was ferried to the hostages, so they could be easily distinguished from dark-clad militants. To stall for time, Fujimori used an Asian trick—working toward peaceful resolution while planning assault.[19]

All the while, the rescuers were doing something U.S. police and military have not attempted since the Civil War—tunneling. The Peruvians covered the sound of their digging with psychological-warfare-like music and noisy tank maneuvers. But the guerrillas still heard it coming, and their commander unwittingly helped by moving all hostages to the second floor. The local press then published a military official's assessment that the tunnels were for anti-personnel gas. They were never used for gas, but they did facilitate the installation of more listening devices beneath the floors. Fujimori had a scale model that showed where the tunnels were. And his commandos may have also had a building mock-up above an ancient labyrinth of catacombs. Normally, an assault rehearsal that realistic only happens in Asia.[20]

Overall Dynamics of the Lima Assault

Roughly 140 Peruvian army and navy commandos took part

in the final rescue attempt. Many had hidden for a whole day in the tunnels and adjacent houses. Just before jump-off, there was a last-minute try to keep the hostages away from their captors.

In preparation for the raid, . . . Giampietri . . . was secretly provided with a miniature two-way radio set and given encrypted instructions instructing him to warn the hostages ten minutes before the military operation began, telling them to stay as far as possible away from the MRTA members.[21]

Then, it was time to go. The commandos had already practiced crawling in tight formation through subterranean passageways to preclude any accordion effect as they emerged from the tunnels. The signal to assault would be the initial explosions. Of all the events that day, one of those explosions would contribute more than any other step in the attack sequence. It was to pave the way for further maneuver.

Three explosive charges exploded almost simultaneously in three different rooms on the first floor. The first . . . hit in the middle of the room where the soccer game was taking place, killing three insurgents immediately . . . . Through the hole created by that blast and the other two explosions, 30 commandos stormed into the building, chasing the surviving MRTA members . . . before they could reach the second floor.

Two other moves were made simultaneously with the explosions. In the first, 20 commandos launched a direct assault at the front door in order to join their comrades inside the waiting room, where the main staircase to the second floor was located. On their way in, they found the two other female MRTA insurgents guarding the front door. Behind the first wave of commandos storming the door came another group of soldiers carrying ladders, which they placed against the rear walls of the building.

In the final prong of the coordinated attack, another group of commandos emerged from two tunnels that had reached the back yard of the residence. These soldiers quickly scaled the ladders that had been placed for them. Their tasks were to blow out a grenade-proof door on the second floor, through which the hostages would be evacuated, and to make two openings in the roof so that they could kill the MRTA members upstairs before they had time to execute the hostages.[22]

The first stage of the plan was to disorient or kill as many rebels as possible with detonations, and then appear everywhere at once on the ground floor to follow-up with gunfire. The planners hoped to pick a time when few, if any, of the terrorists would be with the hostages. With a little Divine help, they managed to do just that. Only one of the rebels must have been near the prisoners at the time of the assault, because two were guarding the front door and three more were at the top of the stairs watching an eight-man soccer game. Thus, all but one was somehow affected by the blasts under the front waiting area, stairwell, and connecting hallway. That gave the surface-level reinforcements the time they would need to get through the compound's gate and main-building entrance.

> Over the months, police had dug under the building and had been closely monitoring the discussions of the terrorists and their movements. Peruvian intelligence had painstakingly tracked the movements of the terrorists. They knew where they were, what they said, and how they were armed. Just as important, at the time of the raid, they knew where the hostages were.
>
> When the initial explosion took place, three terrorists who were watching the game from upstairs and another three, who were on guard, barely had time to react. A few of them tried to open fire on the dark-clad invaders. One terrorist did manage to throw a grenade and killed one of the two soldiers who died in the assault.
>
> The Peruvian commandos seemed to be everywhere at once. They blasted through the front door. They blew a hole into the roof. They seemed to pop out of the ground like jackrabbits.
>
> Unlike their captors, the hostages were ready for the assault. They knowingly sprawled onto the floor and covered their faces so the terrorists couldn't tell . . . the more important hostages to kill. Somebody threw a mattress over the Japanese ambassador's head to protect him.[23]
> — Emergency Net News Intel. Rpt., 24 April 1997

After the assault, the troops had trouble locating three of the terrorists. They found one trying to impersonate a hostage.[24] Such a ploy is common in police standoffs and Asian breakouts.

More on the Final Peruvian Maneuver

The Lima attack was launched at 3:23 P.M. (in mid-afternoon). Its initial thrusts were through tunnel openings in the building's floor. They must have come as quite a surprise to the militants after the Peruvian press had predicted a nighttime helicopter assault. That the guerrilla leader and building center had been first hit makes this much like the North Vietnamese "blooming lotus" maneuver. If it can work on a town, why couldn't it also work on a building?

This methodology was developed in 1952 in an assault on Phat Diem. Its key characteristic was to avoid enemy positions on the perimeter of the town. The striking columns move directly against the center . . . seeking out command-and-control centers. Only then were forces directed outward to systematically destroy the now leaderless units around the town. . .

This approach contrasts sharply with Western doctrine, which traditionally would isolate the town, gain a foothold, and systematically drive inward to clear the town. This sets up a series of attrition-based battles that historically make combat in built-up areas such a costly undertaking.[25]
— *Marine Corps Gazette,* April 1999

The Lima attack also had "swarm" characteristics. In fact, there may have been as many as 14 concurrently moving maneuver squads when the bell rang. It's possible that all attacked from different directions—four from beneath the ground inside and 10 more from outside the compound. Small groups of commandos were seen running along the tree-lined streets that surrounded it. Then one or more blasted their way through its front gate while others "swarmed" over its side and rear walls. Every tunnel contained 10-12 men, so each surface assault may have involved the same number of people. In some locations (like at the building's front entrance), there may have been a follow-on squad to shuttle out the wounded. It's not clear whether any of these troop movements were for diversionary purposes, but one of the exterior explosions may have been. The MRTA intruders had originally blown a hole in the garden wall, so such a ruse would certainly have been appropriate.

There was a detonation from each tunnel inside the building, so the men crawling through it must have first looked for dazed rebels. Some 40 men eventually emerged from those subterranean passageways. That leaves 100 for surface assaults. Almost all may have funneled through the front gate after a lead squad secured it. Then, while one squad and its backup assaulted the building's main entrance, two other pairs could have moved along the structure's sides to blow breaches at its right and rear. And a final pair could have followed with ladders to prop against its back side. But not that many people were seen at the front gate, so it is more likely that most of the remaining squads entered the compound by other routes. Climbing its walls at 10 different places would have created enough of a diversion to initially protect the two that were eventually to breach the building. Such a strategy is strictly Asian in origin. On a somewhat larger scale, it is often used in Afghanistan.

Commandos were seen at just before 3:30 p.m. running along the tree-lined streets surrounding the Japanese compound. Shooting began. A small team of special forces stormed through the double doors of the compound's outside wall. The shooting increased at the front of the building.

Two teams of commandos, each with 12 men, attacked the front and rear of the building. A loud explosion rocked the front of the house. The soldiers had blown open the front door and burst inside, guns blazing. Another explosion occurred on the right side of the building and then another from the rear. Soldiers attacked from the rear.

Within seconds, hostages began climbing out windows and down ladders. Inside of the building, gunfire could be heard. Soldiers had ordered the hostages to drop to the floor to avoid being shot. More explosions shook the building. Hostages began appearing on the roof. On hands and knees, they crawled along the flat roof to a side stairway where more soldiers escorted them to freedom.[26]

— Emergency Net News Intel. Rpt., 23 April 1997

The massing of guerrillas within full view of the front entrance is what gave the Peruvian authorities such a good chance at success. Whichever guerrilla was not killed by the main blast would then pose less danger to the frontal assault force. That Cerpa (the rebel leader) was one of the soccer players didn't hurt either. His demise would leave the group leaderless. As it turned out, all but three of the 14 terrorists were killed by the explosions and fighting that immediately followed. Then, those three could not be immediately found. After so decisive a first blow, some may have had second thoughts about being martyred. That's why the overall operation took 30 minutes.

After the ladders had been placed against the rear of the residence, one squad that had come up through the backyard tunnels climbed to the second floor to blow open the door that led to the hostages. The other ascended to the roof to blow open a hole through which any terrorist who came near the hostages could be shot. Some of its members must have dropped down into the building, because those originally kidnapped were soon seen exiting by way of its windows and roof. As waiting columns helped them down the ladders and out to ambulances, some of the 14 squads must have had that as their mission.

The Peruvian troops had used an encirclement variant of "swarm tactics"—something that is largely avoided by Western police and never attempted by Western infantry. That infantry has become so fond of overwhelming firepower that it must often sacrifice speed, surprise, and even mission accomplishment to prevent fratricide. Its doctrine makes no provision for multidirectional entry to any objective. Still, encirclement tactics are common in the Orient. All they require are a little natural cover, personnel positioning, and fire discipline. Of course, concussion grenades and low-velocity munitions also help. So does pointing all inactive muzzles away from fellow participants.

The Lima Tunnels

There are conflicting accounts of the number and destination of tunnels at Lima. One claims three reached the building, and a fourth the yard. Another claims two came up in the residence, and two more emerged from its grounds. Either way, all subterranean passageways were apparently excavated from houses adjacent to the compound. One may have extended the full length of the ambassador's first-floor corridor—to include front vestibule and stairwell-hosting hallway. Another came up in the kitchen. And one or two more terminated in obscure parts of the backyard. All were undoubtedly reinforced to preclude collapse.

> The key to the success of the mission was the tunnel that reportedly led to three points within the compound—the main reception area where the terrorists were playing soccer, the kitchen, and under the tent that had been set up way back in December.
> A Lima newspaper reported that professional miners had started building the tunnel in January. Four-man teams worked in four hour shifts.[27]
> — Emergency Net News Intel. Rpt., 24 April 1997

All original residents had been cleared from the immediate neighborhood, and police operatives taken their place. Reporters had also been restricted from the area, so that truck loads of dirt could be discreetly removed after dark.[28]

What Was Learned in Peru

The MRTA guerrillas made two mistakes: (1) establishing a regular routine; and (2) leaving all hostages in one place. The rescuers were then lucky to capitalize on these mistakes. Still, the final assault remained rife with danger. After several Western special operations commands had been consulted, the final approach to the problem had the unmistakable look of Asian tactics. It was a combination of encirclement, blooming lotus, and swarming into the center to reinforce it. After all, the Japanese ambassador's house was technically on Japanese soil, and the green light for the final assault was granted by the Japanese government. When Fujimori met with Japan's Prime Minister in Canada, the two leaders said they were in agreement on how to handle the hostage situation.[29] Thus, it is likely that the Japanese military also provided tactical advice. Its light infantry tactics had evolved from the same ancient Chinese formations as those from North Vietnam. And its forefathers had possessed enough tunneling know-how to allow 300 soldiers to assault an airfield on Iwo Jima two weeks after that island had been declared secure.[30]

That no hostage was killed by either commando or kidnapper during the rescue was more than just coincidence. The Peruvian assault had been so well designed that it should now serve as the model for attacking any contested building containing noncombatants. The key elements of that assault are as follows:

° Prepositioning surveillance devices to monitor activity.
° Killing or stunning most kidnappers in the initial blow.
° Confusing those left as to the direction of the assault.
° Moving immediately to protect hostages.
° Coming to close-quarters combat with every foe.

The Previous British Model

British Special Air Service (SAS) has long been considered the most authoritative Western source on hostage rescue. Its advice came into play at Lima. Prior to the Lima operation, the SAS's 1980 assault on the five-story Iranian Embassy in London (at Princes Gate) was the model to study. (See Figure 9.1.)

The Princes Gate siege began at 11:30 A.M. on 30 April 1980, when six armed Iranians overpowered a British police constable and forced their way into their own embassy, taking 26 hostages. The attackers were Iranian Arabs in search of autonomy (from Ayatollah Khomeini's new government) for their southwestern region of Khuzestan. They demanded the release of 91 political prisoners in Iran and a plane to fly themselves and their hostages out of Britain. And they promised to execute all hostages and blow up the embassy if those demands were not met. Through negotiations, six of the captives were released. Feigning a stomach ailment, British Broadcasting Company (BBC) journalist Chris Cramer was one of them. He then provided the rescue team with crucial information about the building's layout and numbers of gunmen and hostages. Early in the standoff, that team had already implanted listening devices in the embassy's walls and chimney. They had also located a loose skylight and shared wall with the Ethiopian Embassy. Once all of that wall's bricks had been removed, only a thin sheet of plaster separated the team from their objective. But Salim (the rebel

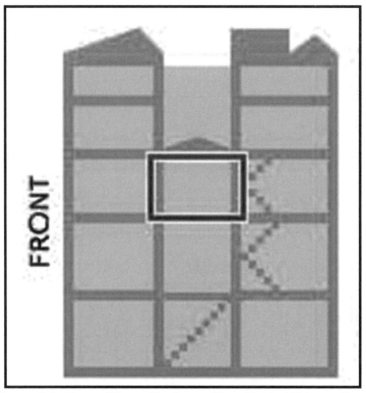

Figure 9.1: Room Where Hostages Were Held at Princes Gate
(Source: "SAS Storm the Embassy." BBC News, n.d.)

leader) noticed a bulge in that plaster and moved the hostages to an interior room. After negotiations broke down the sixth day, the gunmen executed a hostage at 7:10 P.M. SAS made their move 20 minutes later. At 7:23 P.M., they lowered an explosive charge into the embassy's stairwell from the loose skylight. As it was detonated a few minutes later, two four-man teams rappelled down the rear of the building on separate ropes. When one man got entangled, the others could not blow their window "frame charges" without endangering him. Instead, they hacked their way through the windows and tossed in stun grenades. At the same time, another assault team attacked at the front of the building. From a second-floor balcony, they blew open the heavy glass windows. Then, they must have also thrown in stun grenades because that room caught fire. Meanwhile, the hostage constable tackled Salim as he tried to shoot an SAS man at his window. This enabled that same SAS man to enter and to shoot Salim. Then, in the panic and confusion of all those explosions, the gunmen on the third floor (or possibly second) opened fire on the male hostages. One hostage was killed and two others injured. The gunmen then decided to surrender, throwing their guns (but not all grenades) out the window. SAS members soon burst into the room and shot three gunmen. When the hostages were taken to waiting ambulances, another gunman was identified among them and captured. The assault had taken less than 15 minutes. Five of the six gunmen were dead and 19 of the remaining 20 hostages saved.[31] Luckily, there is a good book on SAS procedure. Many of the following ideas come from it.

An Overview of SAS Methods

There is little margin for error in hostage rescue. It can only be accomplished through a "deliberate attack"—i.e., one that has been fully reconnoitered and rehearsed. If the kidnappers unexpectedly start to execute their captives, then a "quick deliberate" attack becomes necessary. That's what German Stormtroopers used against successive Allied trenchlines in the Spring Offensives of 1918. To determine their next objective's particulars, the lead squad relied on "recon-pull"—i.e., following the path of least resistance. On occasion, its members had to retrace their steps and try a different route. To this day, no other Western army allows its squads that much discretion.

From the SAS standpoint, there are two types of deliberate attacks against hostage-occupied buildings—"surreptitious entry" and "dynamic entry." The first is based on stealth or deception, while the second depends more on speed and overwhelming force. Sometimes the stealth variant is employed to get someone close enough to the hostages to protect them while a dynamic entry is made from a different direction. Other times, it is used until the latter becomes necessary. On occasion, the same team can transition from one to the other.[32]

Of note, the SAS book says that "during a dynamic entry, a 'swarm' . . . in which as many personnel enter as possible to dominate a site, is desirable."[33] That sounds a lot like what happened in Peru. That the two styles of assault involve different ways of moving forward is also of interest.

> During a crisis-entry when speed is critical, these sets of two men [each] may leapfrog each other, with the follow-on men becoming the first through the door to the next room. . . . [A] "snake entry," in which personnel enter in a line [column], may be more desirable during a stealth entry.[34]

During a dynamic entry, room clearers often carry shotguns with special munitions for blowing off door locks. And they toss concussion grenades or flash/bangs into each successive room. For a stealth entry, they have other options—like inspecting the path ahead with a folding-extension mirror or quietly neutralizing any opposition with a silenced weapon. For extinguishing lights during the initial approach, they have a suppressed .22 caliber pistol.[35]

SAS Intelligence Gathering

"Barricade" situations require careful study. There are three crucial categories of information: (1) kidnappers; (2) hostages; and (3) scene. For both groups of people, one must know their number, sex, complexion, and leader. Of equal importance are how they are dressed, armed, equipped (e.g., with gas masks or ballistic vests), and rigged for detonation. An adequate analysis of the scene includes the following: (1) number of entry points (doors, windows, sewers, vents); (2) entry-point specifics (composition, locks, hinges, opening direction); (3) building construction (wall composition, attics, cellars, roofs, eaves); (4) external lights or motion detectors; (5) alarms; (6) presence of flammable materials; (7) hostage locations; and (8) favorite kidnapper locations.[36]

There is now more technology for the acquisition of such information: (1) endoscopes and fiber optic lenses that fit through tiny holes or vents; (2) parabolic or laser microphones to pick up sounds off window glass; and (3) radar that can detect motion through nonmetallic walls.[37] Still, there is a limit to what can be electronically learned about the situation. Much must be left to "recon-pull."

SAS Isolation and Assault of the Objective

First, both inner and outer perimeters are formed around the occupied building.[38] Their purpose is twofold: (1) to limit media and bystander exposure; and (2) to prevent enemy exfiltration. Second, all utilities and phone lines are controlled. Finally, all entry movements, covering procedures, and reactionary responses are carefully planned and heavily rehearsed. That's because of the brief period available to get inside the objective.

Once an entry begins with the deployment of distraction devices, then the team normally has, at most, seven seconds in which to enter and neutralize the hostage-takers. After that, the odds that hostages will die increase dramatically.[39]

But, what if the kidnappers won't wait for all that preparation? That's when a decidedly Eastern style of attack might come in very handy—one from the inside out without any tunnels. If a pair of infiltrators could surreptitiously penetrate the building and hide within easy striking distance of the hostages' guards, then more time would be available to "dynamically" reinforce them. Where booby traps and barriers are likely, a few extra moments might make all the difference. But, whether or not there has been any "recon-pull," the follow-on forces must move quickly. To do so, they will need ways to confound their foes.

SAS Trojan Horses and Other Distractions

The idea of a hidden entrant to a barricade situation is so appealing that hostage rescuers have often tried "trojan horses"—the insertion of coincidental visitors. The most common variant is a delivery man with a package large enough to conceal a machinegun.[40]

There are many ways to divert the attention of kidnappers: (1) helicopters or planes overhead; (2) approaching sirens; and (3) road or building maintenance nearby. A clever telephone negotiator can even explain away breaching noises. At Princes Gate, one of the kidnappers was kept on the phone while the assault was in progress. That phone call not only distracted him, but also fixed his location.[41]

155

SAS Diversionary Devices

Distraction ordnance gives the entry team a few extra seconds to locate and engage any adversaries in a room. Hostage rescue "flash/bangs" are much more powerful than those used in U.S. military training exercises. They produce 165-185 decibels of sound, 2.5-7.5 million candle power of flash, and 3.0-5.0 pounds per square inch (psi) of overpressure. That much overpressure will cause ear damage to 1% of the population, so users wear ear protection. While most effective in darkened and enclosed areas, they should not be used around small children. There are also concussion grenades, multi-detonation devices, shotgun variants, and grenade launcher equivalents. There is even a strip device to slip under a door before using another point of entry.[42] The most convincing diversions are created by a distant cohort.

Anti-personnel gas is not used where hostages are present,[43] and care must be taken not to set the whole place on fire.

SAS Special-Movement Techniques

The SAS is quite partial to stealth entries. In urban terrain, utility service tunnels often allow a secret approach to the immediate proximity of the objective building. Then, SAS attempts as many concurrent entries as possible, while still going where least expected. Of course, the assault team's approach can always be compromised by motion-triggered security lights. For those, it carries a suppressed weapon. At Princes Gate, SAS personnel secretly acquired the objective's roof. (Such a thing can sometimes be accomplished from an adjoining building or by mechanical "cherry picker.") Three teams of commandos then rappelled down the objective's sides, but they did not swing through its windows as in the movies. Instead, they had to use frame charges.[44] Crashing through a window on the end of a rope requires a lightly constructed window, the right length of stretch-prone nylon, and considerable practice. A padded extension ladder is often a better option. And all buildings are easier to clear from the top down. Once the roof and top stories have been searched, someone must be left on each floor to prevent the suspects from moving upwards in the building.[45]

While darkness definitely facilitates a stealthful approach, night vision equipment can be more of a hindrance than a help. Not only does it create problems with depth perception and peripheral vision, but it also tends to override the other senses. And the red laser beams for target acquisition do little to enhance the element of surprise. A happy compromise would be to approach the objective before dawn, and then raid it from the sunrise side.

Once the building has been breached, hostage rescue personnel try to move between points of concealment/cover in three seconds or less (the time it takes someone to draw a good "bead" on them). Wherever that's not possible, their point men use ballistic shields.[46] All are careful not to silhouette themselves in any opening or cast a shadow beneath any door.[47] If fact, they avoid back-lit areas altogether. To minimize the noise, they turn knobs instead of breaking down doors. That gives them the option of a "limited entry," wherein they can take a quick peak at what awaits before passing through the opening. This should not be tried from behind thin interior walls. In a stealth entry, all stay in column but maintain enough of an interval to not all fall prey to an automatic-weapon burst. Where speed is critical during a crisis entry, pairs of men leapfrog each other to enter successive rooms. At the hostage enclosure, they try to come through two apertures at once.[48]

Finally, a last detailed search of the building may be necessary to ferret out hidden perpetrators. No stranger should be assumed to be a hostage.[49]

SAS Covering Techniques

Every aperture in the objective building must be carefully covered by fire. All must be mapped and codified.[50] Then, each sniper/observer team must have a radio and camera. That way, every sighting can be recorded and reported. Removing one of the hostages' closest guards might be the very edge needed for a successful assault. And eliminating a sentry by a long-range silenced shot is a good way to initiate a surprise entry.

Of course, all radio and telephone transmissions must be carefully muffled. And each sniper/observer team and their relief element must be able to secretly move in and out of their position. Once the building has been entered, they cannot shoot except to save a life.[51]

157

Do U.S. Infantry Tactics Allow for Noncombatant Rescue?

Most of the urban assault tactics published by the U.S. military assume that the objective has long since been vacated by civilians. They are therefore predicated on maximum force. Thus, little thought is given to whether breaching explosions or preparatory grenades might result in collateral damage. Military assault forces rarely resort to any kind of blinding, stunning, or gaseous munition to temporarily disorient defenders. Yet, its troops are still trained in various humanitarian procedures. One of the most productive is how to "pie off" a room from either side of its door or window. Potential entrants incrementally scan the space without ever exposing more than their rifle and eye socket. Should it contain civilians, the GIs can then easily withhold their fire.

The U.S. military is also very diligent about preventing fratricide within buildings. Its maneuver elements seldom attack without covering fire and never work toward one another. As a result, the enemy's avenue of escape is generally left open.

To What Extent Do U.S. Police Tactics Protect Civilians?

Most U.S. police raids are predicated on the possibility of a "barricade situation" with hostages. As such, they often involve fairly sophisticated maneuver and deception. Still, wherever a "Waco" can happen, one suspects room for improvement. Two areas, in particular, come to mind. First, all female and underage companions of besieged suspects must be treated as hostages. Then, all former U.S. military SWAT team members must realize that their previous training was more about firepower than surprise. That being said, the U.S. military could still learn a lot about 4GW assault tactics from their law enforcement contemporaries.

One of the biggest differences in a police assault is the amount of detailed intelligence that is collected by preliminary reconnaissance. U.S. infantry units spend far less time and effort reconnoitering their objectives. Often, they have only an aerial photograph and long-range-binocular assessment to go on. They pay little attention to where claymores or booby traps might be, and barely consider the possibility of barbed wire.[52] Police reconnaissance routinely looks for booby traps and barriers. It is so complete as to provide specifics on door latches/locks, window coverings, fence configurations, alarm/security systems, and hidden lookouts. This degree of detail undoubtedly springs from the police officer's constant struggle to collect nearly obscure evidence. During a contested assault, knowing whether the front door is made of metal or opens outward can make a tremendous difference. The police officer is often willing to imitate a pizza delivery man to figure this out. He will also use drive-bys, walk-bys, jog-bys, photo surveillance, bogus utility checks, and fake census or city-planning visits to get what he needs.[53] His other intelligence-gathering subterfuges include building inspector, repairman, United Parcel Service (UPS) man, and welfare, probation, or health inspector. Then, whenever possible, he will draw his suspects outside to make their takedown safer.[54] Of course, police also have technological ways to retrieve information. To rescue hostages, they sometimes use a tiny, cable-end video camera that will fit through a quietly drilled hole in the floor.

In other words, the police raider is at least carrying the right equipment when it's time to risk his life. Depending on the door configuration during a contested breach, that equipment can range from a door frame spreader, to a battering ram with hook, bolt cutters, or small ladder for window entry.[55] He has the option of disguises and routinely runs a diversion—like breaking a window that is nowhere near the planned point of entry. If the initial point of entry proves too difficult, he has an alternate already planned.[56] He does generally have more time to prepare than his military counterpart. But, there are such things as long-range digital cameras with which to instantaneously transmit high-resolution images for further assessment. So, U.S. infantry and special-operations units could easily adopt many police methods. Most helpful would be a few concussion grenades. All Eastern armies use them during almost every assault.

During the average police raid, the following details have been handled. Snipers have been positioned to cover the assault team's placement of a breaching charge, movement across open ground, or subsequent climb.[57] The raiders have a way to quietly neutralize guard dogs. They know in advance if there is anyone in the building besides suspects. They are carrying stun, and sometimes, gas grenades. They also have flash-bangs to temporarily blind their opponents. If chemicals are present, they wear fireproof hoods and goggles.[58] To the rear of the building are other police so that the

159

suspects cannot escape.[59] The entry teams have special equipment with which to inspect the premises and stay safe. For the former, they carry everything from pole-end mirrors to latent-fingerprint collectors. For the latter, they have lightweight armored vests and shields with bulletproof viewing ports (known as "body bunkers").[60] Yet, their expertise is not limited to the use of fancy equipment. To physically apprehend (as opposed to simply confront) bad guys, they require a considerable amount of "tactical" skill. For example, they know to quickly peek—at ground level—around all dangerous corners.

U.S. police have two basic techniques for room clearing: (1) dynamic entry for speed and surprise; and (2) the more deliberate entry and search. Both are conducted by four-man teams with a two-man augment for each additional room. In the dynamic entry, #3 opens the door and steps aside as #4 tosses in a stun munition. Then #1 and #2 enter and clear the room. They signal to #3 and #4 to move through to the next room (with the first two-man augment in tow). Two men are thus left behind in each cleared room. One stands in its doorway to create a communication link. In the deliberate version, #1 and #2 take supposed cover behind either side of the open door and systematically "pie off" the room. Once all threats are engaged, they enter the room while #3 and #4 move to the entrance of the next room. Unfortunately, thin interior walls seldom provide much cover.[61]

Narcotics agents have a different way to control more suspects simultaneously. It involves a six- or eight-man "snake." In the snake technique, #6 breaches the door while #1 and #2 enter the first room followed by everyone else in single file with weapons alternating outward and down. As #5 and #6 handcuff the occupants, #3 and #4 cover the next door. Then #1 and #2 move into the next room, and the file order is preserved as the process repeats itself. When confronted by two separate openings, each man in column covers the path not taken until the next man can take responsibility for it. Ultimately, #6 covers that area until #1 and #2 can return to enter and clear it. Additional agents follow as necessary to remove suspects.[62] On occasion, two stories of a building are cleared at the same time from separate points of entry.[63]

U.S. police can only kill their quarries under certain circumstances and must make every attempt to save noncombatants. As such, they never use gas where civilians are involved.[64] Russian commandos made that mistake after a Chechen-rebel takeover of

Moscow's central opera house several years ago. The images of lifeless novice opera-goers still haunt all who saw them. Law enforcement personnel also carefully avoid munitions that might lead to a conflagration. They will sometimes sacrifice the safety that comes from overlapping fields of fire.[65] Their lower-muzzle-velocity weapons help to decrease the risk, but pellet-spraying shotguns are best. Other types of rounds tend to penetrate thin inner walls and endanger other policemen. Still, for every urban assault, U.S. police design a unique "tactical technique."[66] GIs tend to use the same "standard procedure" for every situation.

Through continual practice, many big-city Special-Weapons Assault Teams (SWATs) have become quite proficient at building entry. Yet, they are by no means perfect. Like U.S. military assault teams, they unwittingly lower their natural senses and reaction times by carrying too much gear. Almost every law enforcement raid begins with a motorcade so lengthy that it would fully alert any world-class foe.[67] To keep drug busts from looking like rip-offs, police raiders will even announce their presence with a patrol car.[68] By shouting out accomplishments and commands,[69] their entry teams further telegraph all movements to still-hidden perpetrators. Still, the U.S. law enforcement community provides one of the best sources of tactical innovation. 4GW requires a more civilian-friendly (minimal-force) approach to adversarial relationships. That just happens to be the essence of good police work.

The Subtle Differences in U.S. Police Tactics

A big-city "beat" cop can encounter a "kidnapping" or "barricade situation" at any moment. He is therefore more adequately trained in hostage scenarios than the average U.S. infantryman. And the procedures of his SWAT counterparts during a hostage rescue are more advanced than standard infantry methods. All SWAT moves toward a building are routinely covered by snipers, while the U.S. military has too few snipers to use in this role. But the law enforcement community's most progressive methods are the precursors to "swarm tactics." First, it will loosely encircle a building so that no suspect can escape. Then, its ladder-carrying assault teams will often enter every floor at once so that risky stairs are avoided.[70] Though strictly opposed to multiple same-floor entries, it will sometimes allow one floor to be flooded with agents from the same direction. And those agents can hit several rooms at once along the same hallway or send people outside to cover subsequent rooms through windows.[71] While such people are technically within the frontal assault team's zone of fire, they are protected from accidental gunshot by the building's exterior walls. This amounts to "controlled" swarm tactics.[72]

Another maneuver of police origin is initially to gain entry to one's objective through the use of a disguise. That is not too different from first launching an infiltrator. And the first officers to enter a barricade situation intentionally draw fire away from the hostages.[73] That's as much risk as an infiltrator takes. Why couldn't an American infantry unit secretly gain entry? By limiting collateral damage, it would help them to win any 4GW or guerrilla conflict.

Mixing SAS and Police Tactics with Those of U.S. Military

One cannot strictly follow U.S. military doctrine and still minimize collateral damage. That doctrine disallows not only encirclement, but even double envelopment. It ostensibly does so to preclude fratricide. But if a single aspect of the standard U.S. assault were altered, its infantrymen could attack from more than one direction without committing fratricide. That aspect is the overwhelming firepower that is normally directed against the foe. The NVA used the encirclement maneuver all the time in Vietnam. When they did so, their quarry was normally up on a rise or down in a depression so that stray rounds would not hit any encirclers. If that quarry were on the same level, the NVA would climb trees and shoot downward. All the while, every member of their circular formation would stay behind cover and take well-aimed shots.[74] Within such parameters, it's doubtful that many NVA soldiers got accidentally shot. In fact, an over-reliance on close air support is far more likely to cause harm. By some estimates, 15 to 20 percent of all U.S. casualties in Vietnam were from friendly supporting arms.[75] Therefore, U.S. infantry doctrine could usefully allow encirclements under certain conditions—like when abundant cover and fire discipline make fratricide unlikely. U.S. military hostage-rescue specialists and (to a lesser extent) U.S. police already use "swarm tactics." To see if ordinary GIs might successfully accomplish something similar, one must first discover how their use of cover and rifle might be sufficiently controlled.

If the objective building were to be rushed by surprise from every direction at once, its construction alone would stop any assault fire from doing unintended damage. Normally, the enemy is so confused that little shooting is necessary. Then, at worst, there might be a few ricochets. If most assault elements were further to remain outside that building, they would be protected from booby traps and enemy gunshots by its exterior walls. By additionally standing at the sides of windows and doors, they could take well-aimed shots along crisscrossing diagonals (as in "pieing" off a room) without ever exposing their heads or torsos. Then, the only real chance for fratricide would be inside the building. If the building is small with several stories, the noncombatants/hostages will most likely be grouped together on a single level. When that level is a basement or upper story, their rescue becomes much simpler. Then, no amount of horizontal fire through the first floor will affect them. And the other upper stories and roof can normally be secured by the members of single team with almost no chance of shooting each other.

The floor that contains the noncombatants/hostages presents more of a problem. That's because interior walls are normally too thin to stop a bullet. However, there is less chance of an accident when the civilians lie flat on the floor, all upright rescuers shoot horizontally, and all prone rescuers shoot slightly upwards. GIs can be trained to do this. Additionally, the liberal use of flash/bangs and concussion grenades will normally put any adversary into a compromising stance. To further prevent accidents, the attackers can be armed with pellet-throwing shotguns. If the civilians' location can be pre-ascertained, then two assault teams should be able to approach that location from different directions without entering each other's zone of fire. Only required is a little route planning. In barricade situations, U.S. policemen face that kind of risk all the time.

Once the two assault teams have rescued the civilians, they can then attack outwards without masking each other's fire. At some point, all miscreants will be forced downward in the building. Once they reach the bottom floor, their only option will be to surrender. That's because the outside teams can now safely shoot them from all windows and doors.

Clearing a building in such a manner seems reasonable. But still at issue is whether the noncombatants can be reached in time. No number of well-placed snipers can adequately neutralize their guards. Only someone who had secretly entered the building and was hiding nearby could do that. Such things happen all the time in the Orient. That's largely because of *ninjutsu,* and its regional equivalents. Virtually every Asian army has people who could accomplish such a mission. Under certain circumstances, so could a daring pair of U.S. military scout/snipers. They would try right before dawn. Should they encounter resistance, an all-out assault would immediately ensue to reinforce them.

Final Reconnaissance and Noncombatant Protection

Over the years, many Asian armies have reconnoitered rural objectives from within.[76] That they can also secretly enter a building should come as no surprise, because *ninjutsu* includes many fortress entry techniques. Among them are the following: (1) crawling through sewers and airshafts; (2) ascending a drainpipe; (3) stone or brick wall climbing; (4) pole or tree climbing; (5) moving along horizontal pole, rope, or "leaping ladder"; (6) moving unobstrusively through a window; and (7) bypassing sentries.[77] Most buildings are readily accessible at night through upstairs windows or ventilation ducts. Once inside, the infiltrator has only to locate the civilians and hide nearby (like in a closet). While a single *ninja* could more easily do this, two U.S. infiltrators are recommended so they can cover each other's movement by fire. Any unsuppressed shot would then summon the cavalry.

Doing the Unexpected with Minimal Assets

What's "unexpected" will wholly depend on the objective's defenders. With America's massive air assets, urban hostage-takers automatically expect an assault from the air. (See Figures 9.2 and 9.3.) If they have RPGs, such an assault becomes unreasonably dangerous. Therefore, this chapter will focus on other options. Among the most intriguing is a "front-end-loader" assault.[78] While busting through the main gate, the massive earth-mover keeps its bucket low to protect the driver. Then, as the building is reached, it raises that bucket up to disgorge an assault team onto the second floor. In this way, rapid approach, frontal protection, and upper-floor entry are all accomplished at once.

Figure 9.2: Hostage-Takers Expect a Helicopter Assault
(Source: FM 90-10-1 [1982], p. F-13)

Figure 9.3: Ways to Discourage an Attack from the Air
(Source: FM 90-10 [1979], p. D-4)

165

Of course, the foes during a standard U.S. military city-clearing operation would expect much less. They would prepare for a ground-level assault from the front with no preliminary reconnaissance. To counter that expectation, one could "demonstrate" at the building's bottom front, while sneaking tiny elements around both flanks to assault its upper floors. There is now a crossbow-fired grappling hook. By looping a thin line through its eyelet, one can position a fully rigged plastic block and tackle at a building's top without ever leaving the ground. Then, one or two people on the ground could quickly pull others up. With standard-issue optics, U.S. grunts are also good enough marksmen to function as snipers. A pair with a radio could cover all but the most heavily contested of maneuvers.

How Such an Assault Might Work

Over the next few pages, a typical urban attack scenario will be depicted. The assault objective is of a size that would require about 40 men to seize. (See Figures 9.4 through 9.6.) It is known to contain women and children as well as enemy combatants. As with many such structures around the world, this one is inside a walled compound. That wall represents not only a barrier, but also an envelopment route. It's easier to scale than to breach, and scaling it would better protect the element of surprise. All assault teams will carry collapsible ladders so as not to automatically telegraph their individual roles. One team is also toting a funny-looking crossbow.

From the building's recent infiltration (Figure 9.7), it is known that all noncombatants are in a second-floor interior room and that all infiltrators are beneath that floor's staircase. (If the civilians can only be located through electronic surveillance, they must be saved from execution by one of the assault teams.)

All seven assault teams have secretly positioned themselves around the compound. With the rising of the sun, they attack. Only two will penetrate the building, and one of those two has the sun at its back. Both climb to their respective floors as another blows open the front door. It and the remaining teams do not enter. Instead, they cover the ground floor by fire. (See Figures 9.8 through 9.12).

After entering the second story, the two penetration teams go by the most direct route to the room containing noncombatants.

Figure 9.4: Objective Compound from the Front
(Source: FM 90-10-1 [1982], p. 3-35)

Figure 9.5: Objective Compound from the Back
(Source: FM 90-10 [1979], p. G-4)

As per SAS method, buddy pairs move in leapfrog fashion. If either team encounters resistance, both crawl the rest of the way. To overcome that resistance, they toss stun grenades and shoot upwards into it. By so doing, they remove any chance of fratricide. (See Figures 9.13 and 9.14.) Peeking around corners is best done at ground level anyway.

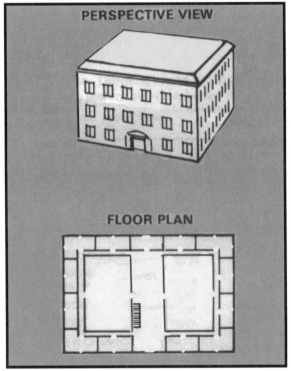

Figure 9.6: Enemy-Controlled Building
(Source: FM 90-10-1 [1982], p. C-15)

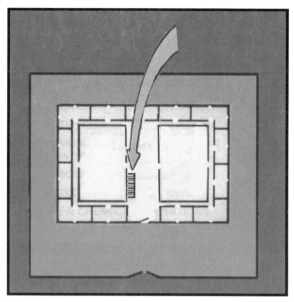

Figure 9.7: How Building Already Infiltrated

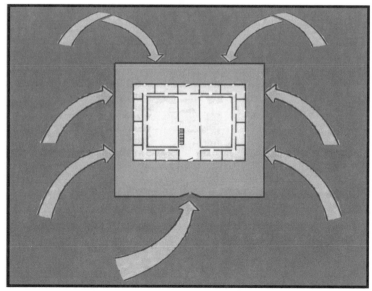

Figure 9.8: Compound Attacked from All Directions at Once

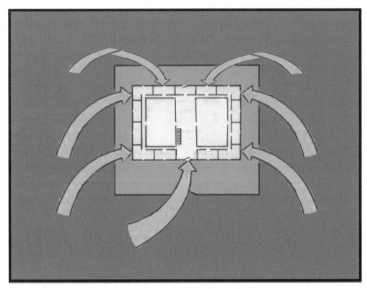

Figure 9.9: All Assault Teams Move to Bottom-Floor Aperture

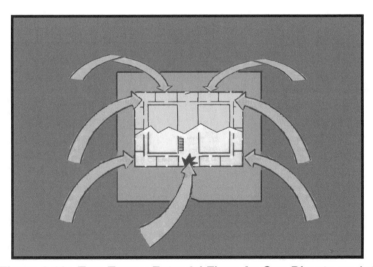

Figure 9.10: Two Teams Enter 2d Floor As One Diverts on 1st

Figure 9.11: Ladders to Make Entry Quicker
(Source: FM 90-10-1 [1982], pp. B-5, B-21)

IT IS ASSUMED THAT ANY NONCOMBATANTS WILL
LIE NEAR THE FLOOR DURING AN ACTIVE ASSAULT.

SNIPERS ARE COVERING BY FIRE 2D-FLOOR WINDOWS
TO BE PENETRATED ON OPPOSITE SIDES OF BUILDING.

PENETRATION TEAMS ARE TWO OF THE SEVEN THAT
QUIETLY VAULT COMPOUND WALL & RUSH BUILDING.

THE TWO USE LADDERS AS FRONT TEAM BLOWS DOOR.

UNLIKE STANDARD MILITARY ASSAULT, THE TWO DON'T
PRECEDE ENTRY WITH FRAGMENTATION GRENADES.

FOE STILL CONFUSED AS TO PENETRATION POINTS.

FIRST MAN UP EACH LADDER PEAKS INTO ROOM (AS IN
PIEING IT OFF) WHILE SNIPER & BUDDIES COVER HIM.

IF HE SEES FOE DURING THAT PEAK, HE SLIDES
BACK DOWN LADDER & TRIES ANOTHER WINDOW.

IF ROOM SEEMS EMPTY, HE ENTERS (KEEPING STUN
GRENADE & AUTOMATIC WEAPON AT THE READY).

IF SHOT AT, HE TOSSES STUN GRENADE WHILE DIVING
FOR COVER & THEN FIRES A BURST UPWARDS.

Figure 9.12: Window Entry Sequence

Acquiring the Roof

It takes a 55-foot-long ladder to reach the top of a three-story building. That long a ladder is not only hard to carry, but it also exposes its climbers to more enemy fire. If that structure's roof has a perimeter wall or gutter, a crossbow-fired grappling hook makes a better option. After a plastic block-and-tackle assembly has been

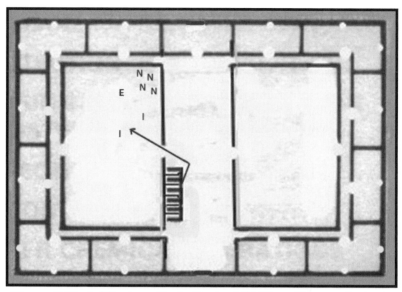

Figure 9.13: Infiltrators Go to Protect 2d-Floor Noncombatants

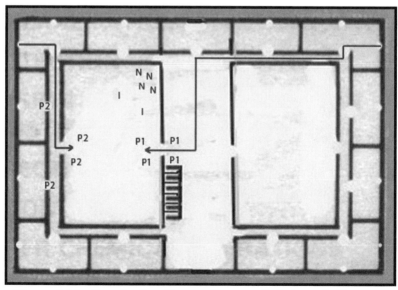

Figure 9.14: Penetration Teams Move to Reinforce Infiltrators

hauled into place, it can quickly move people to the rooftop. Should the block and tackle not be available, there is always rope-climbing equipment. (See Figures 9.15 through 9.17.)

First, the roof must be searched for mines. Then, any without a built-in stairwell will have to be breached with explosives. That detonation should stun any third-floor enemy long enough for the roof team to drop down. The third story can then be cleared in the usual way, because all civilians are on the floor below.

Completing the Mission

After locating and evacuating the civilians, the two second-floor teams go off along different hallways to finish clearing that story. As the foes are forced downward onto the first floor, they encounter fire from outside teams. Those teams are shooting horizontally from behind exterior walls. There is little chance of them hitting each other or anyone upstairs. (See Figure 9.18)

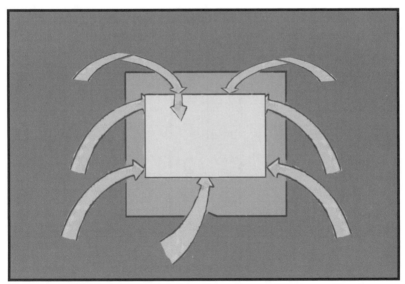

Figure 9.15: Most of One Rear Team Climbs to Roof

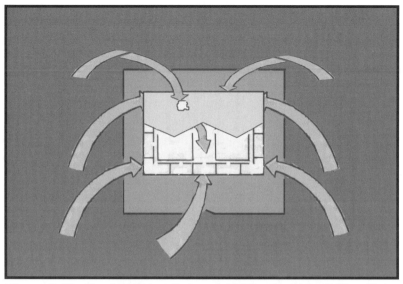

Figure 9.16: Roof Element Enters 3d Floor through Ceiling Hole

Figure 9.17: Only Non-Hostage Floors Are Cleared Standing Up
(Source: FM 90-10-1 [1982], p. B-27)

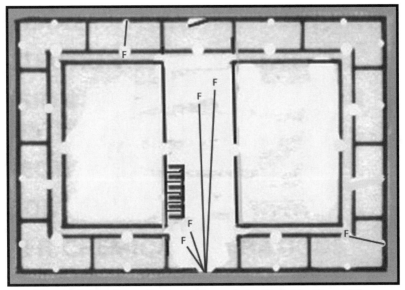

Figure 9.18: Foes Pushed Down into Outside-Team Fire

Then, only left is physically to account for everyone involved. Some may be wounded, and others hiding. (For a step-by-step summary of the entire method, see Figure 9.19.)

A More Infantry-Friendly Version

Clearly, the above method is better suited for hostage rescue specialists than for line infantrymen facing an enemy strongpoint with civilians inside. With a little practice, an infantry platoon could do something similar in the heat of urban combat. Three squads could concurrently attack the same building from different directions, as long as all three planned to enter a different floor. That way, there would be no dangerous stairs to negotiate. And the building's exterior walls would prevent those three from shooting each other on the way in. (See Figure 9.20.)

Where civilians are to be safeguarded, machineguns can't be used to suppress enemy fire. Instead, a few infantry marksmen must function as snipers to provide overhead covering fire for all maneuver elements. That fire would consist of single well-aimed

INFILTRATE OR ELECTRONICALLY SURVEIL BUILDING TO FIND LIKELY WHEREABOUTS OF FOES & HOSTAGES.

SEPARATE SNIPERS WILL COVER APPROACHES (FROM EVERY DIRECTION) OF SEVEN LADDER-TOTING TEAMS.

ALL QUIETLY SWARM INTO COMPOUND & MOVE TO HOUSE APERTURES; REAR TEAM GRAPPLES TO ROOF.

TWO JUXTAPOSED SIDE TEAMS CLIMB LADDERS WHILE OTHERS PREPARE TO MAKE 1ST-FLOOR BREACHES.

FRONT TEAM BLOWS MAIN DOOR, AS TWO SIDE TEAMS ENTER 2D-FLOOR WINDOWS & OTHERS BREAK GLASS.

MEANWHILE, A REAR TEAM HAS USED CROSSBOW TO SHOOT GRAPPLING HOOK/PULLEY ASSEMBLY TO ROOF.

ONCE BLOCK & TACKLE WITH HEAVIER LINE IN PLACE, PEOPLE ON GROUND PULLED OTHERS TO ROOFTOP.

ROOF ELEMENT BLOWS HOLE, DROPS ONTO 3D FLOOR, & THEN CLEARS /WATCHES IT.

MEANWHILE, BOTH 2D-FLOOR ELEMENTS HAVE MOVED TOWARD HOSTAGES ALONG NON-INTERSECTING PATHS.

AFTER FINDING CIVILIANS & ANY INFILTRATORS, THEY EVACUATE THEM THRU PREVIOUSLY USED WINDOW.

THEN, BOTH 2D-FLOOR ELEMENTS ATTACK OUTWARDS.

ONLY PLACE FOR FOE TO GO IS DOWN. AS THEY REACH 1ST FLOOR, OUTSIDE PEOPLE TAKE THEM UNDER FIRE.

AFTER UPPER FLOORS SECURED, SIDE TEAM PUSHES HOLDOUTS THROUGH FRONT & REAR ZONES OF FIRE.

Figure 9.19: Sequence to Save Civilians in Barricade Situation

shots. If those marksmen were positioned just above the ground-level approaches to the objective, they could fire into all but basement windows without much chance of hitting a civilian or one of their own. (See Figure 9.21.)

Of course, snipers would not be enough at the building's front. That assault element will meet far more resistance than in a police hostage situation—namely, enemy machinegun (MG) and rocket-propelled grenade (RPG) fire. That fire could be temporarily suppressed with explosions on the outer surface of the building from either shoulder-fired multi-purpose assault weapons (SMAWs) or anti-tank weapons (like the AT-4). (See Figures 9.22 and 9.23.)

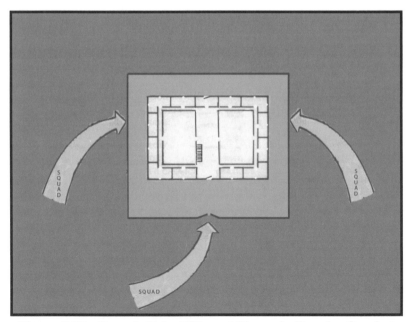

Figure 9.20: Squads Take Different Floors in Regular Combat

Figure 9.21: Initial Rushes Covered by Marksmen (Not MGs)
(Source: FM 90-10-1 [1982], p. B-29)

Figure 9.22: More Suppression for Foe RPG Launcher or MG
(Source: FM 90-10-1 [1982], p. B-35)

179

Line infantry squads may not have ladders. Then, the one wanting to enter the second floor would toss a rope-rigged grappling hook through a window. (See Figures 9.24 and 9.25.) The first man up the rope quickly peeks into the room. If he draws fire, he slides back down and tries another window. If he doesn't draw fire but still suspects trouble, he tosses in a couple of concussion grenades before scrambling through the opening (a physically demanding exercise that must be practiced ahead of time). Then, by staying close to the floor and firing slightly upwards, he eliminates any resistance without endangering civilians.

The roof squad will need a grappling-hook-firing crossbow and light-weight block and tackle or rope-climbing equipment (either is easily purchased over the internet). It must also have explosives to enter the third floor. Once all top floors have been cleared, the front squad can finally enter the building to search the first floor and basement. The latter is where civilians most often hide. (See the entire attack sequence in Figure 9.26.) Once all civilians have been removed, enemy holdouts can be enveloped from either top or bottom. (See Figure 9.27.) Now, there are fewer restrictions on how

Figure 9.23: Surface Blasts during Heavily Contested Assault
_(Source: FM 90-10 [1979], p. G-2)

Figure 9.24: The Rope Climb and Entry
(Source: FM 90-10-1 [1982], pp. B-16, B-18)

Figure 9.25: Another Way In
(Source: Courtesy of Sorman Information and Media, from Soldf: Soldaten i falt, @2001 by Forsvarsmakten and Wolfgang Bartsch, Stockholm, p. 292)

OCCUPY BUILDINGS ON EITHER SIDE OF OBJECTIVE.

SINGLE SQUADS IN EACH WILL ATTACK CLOSEST SIDE OF OBJECTIVE (HIT IT FROM OPPOSITE DIRECTIONS).

MOST OF ONE TO ENTER 2D FLOOR; MOST OF OTHER TO GO TO ROOF WITH SPECIAL CLIMBING EQUIPMENT.

FOR BOTH, SMAW & SNIPER WILL STAY BEHIND TO SUPPRESS ANY RESISTANCE DURING MANEUVER.

FRONTAL ASSAULT SQUAD MUST EXPECT MG & RPG FIRE AS IT ENTERS FORWARD PART OF COMPOUND.

AT-4, SMAW, & SNIPERS STAND READY TO BLAST ITS SOURCE AS THAT SQUAD MOVES TOWARD MAIN DOOR.

THE FRONTAL ASSAULT IS INITIALLY A DIVERSION.

NONE OF THE THREE MANEUVERS SUPPORTED BY MG FIRE TO LOWER THE RISK TO CIVILIAN OCCUPANTS.

ALL SQUADS INVADE COMPOUND AT ONCE. THOSE AT SIDES ENTER BUILDING; THAT IN FRONT BLOWS MAIN DOOR BUT DOES NOT ENTER.

ROOF SQUAD BLOWS HOLE & CLEARS 3D FLOOR.

IT & 2D-FLOOR SQUAD TOSS STUN GRENADES BUT SHOOT LITTLE WHILE CLEARING RESPECTIVE FLOORS.

FRONT SQUAD COVERS STAIRCASE & MAIN HALLWAY.

ONCE UPPER FLOORS ARE SECURED, FRONT SQUAD SEARCHES 1ST FLOOR & BASEMENT.

CIVILIANS SCREENED & MED-EVACED AS NECESSARY.

Figure 9.26: Sequence to Spare Civilans in Urban Combat

Figure 9.27: Envelopment Option after Civilians Are Safe
(Source: Courtesy of Sorman Info. & Media, illustration by Wolfgang Bartsch, from *SoldF: Soldaten i fält*, © 2001 by Wolfgang Bartsch, p. 301)

much firepower can be applied to a limited space. One must still follow the Geneva Conventions, however. Any holdout who raises his hands must be allowed to surrender.

Much more is also possible on defense than what U.S. forces can normally muster. As on offense, the key to a 4GW-consistent defense is to kill as few noncombatants are possible.

10 Collateral-Damage-_____ Free Defense

- Does sparing innocent life help to win hearts and minds?
- Can an outpost be defended without risk to its neighbors?

The key to minimal force is fewer high explosives.

(Source: Courtesy of Sorman Information and Media, from Soldf: Soldaten i falt, @2001 by Forsvarsmakten and Wolfgang Bartsch, Stockholm, p. 303)

What Normally Occurs on Defense

To protect any outpost, U.S. troops still rely almost entirely on firepower. Whatever they don't think their personal weapons will do, they entrust to on-call artillery and airstrikes. Their only other preparation is to fully bunker the place, remove its surrounding vegetation, and then encase it in barbed wire. If the outpost is in a particularly dangerous location, they will further mine its approaches. Because those "forward-position builders" have dutifully followed some military training syllabus, they fail to realize that their new "safe haven" has become more like a "bull's-eye-shaped

185

prison." They are now clearly visible to every enemy gunner for miles, and have too little tactical flexibility to counter any serious takeover attempt. Most could have usefully remembered two things: (1) there is such a thing as defensive maneuver; and (2) surprise can take the place of firepower. In a counterinsurgency or 4GW environment, all that shooting would have been counterproductive anyway. Outposted GIs make little progress by accidently killing their indigenous neighbors.

> [Defense Secretary Robert] Gates said Tuesday "we are lost" unless the United States can find a way not to kill so many civilians in . . . Afghanistan. . . .
> . . . "I don't think we can succeed in Afghanistan if civilians keep dying there," [Joint Chiefs of Staff Chairman] Mullen said.[1]
> —Associated Press, 28 January 2009

What's a Defensive Maneuver?

U.S. infantrymen have become so accustomed to positional warfare that many believe their only real protection from attack is a static formation. If they were Asian, they would have more choices—like from mobile or guerrilla warfare. Both involve defensive movement—not just relieving another unit in place but actually fending off an invader while changing location. Against a foe with more firepower, the Chinese progressively shifted their tiny bastions backwards in Korea.[2] Against one with short-range infiltrators, the pre-WWI Japanese deployed roving sentries between squad-sized positions.[3]

Also more prevalent in the Oriental way of defense is the element of surprise. On Iwo Jima and again in Vietnam, GIs could literally walk across a major defensive "belt" without ever realizing it was there. That's because the belt was not made of trenchlines. Instead, it was comprised of parallel strings of well-hidden, squad-sized strongpoints. Those strongpoints were offset so that each would be fronted by the interlocking machinegun fire from the two behind it. The overall result was a matrix in which all non-occupied ground was swept by deadly fire. It was such strongpoints that could take turns moving backwards under certain circumstances and have roving sentries between them in others. The first idea was pioneered by the WWI Germans and then later adopted by Japanese and Communist armies. (See Figures 10.1 and 10.2). When the strongpoint occupants finally made their presence known, their fire was brief,

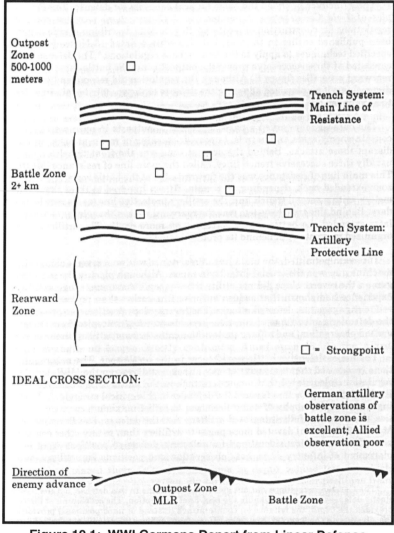

Figure 10.1: WWI Germans Depart from Linear Defense

(Source: The Changes in German Tactical Doctrine during the First World War, U.S. Army Combat Studies Inst., Leavenworth Paper No. 4 (1981), p. 14)

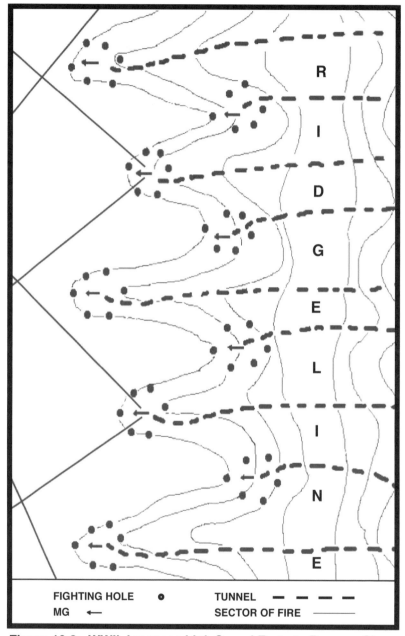

FIGHTING HOLE   ●   TUNNEL   – – – –

MG   ←   SECTOR OF FIRE ————

Figure 10.2: WWII Japanese Link Squad Forts to Reverse Slope
(Source: Poole, *The Tiger's Way*, p. 162)

accurate, and often directed backwards.[4] Within this Eastern way of doing things may lie a more "neighborhood-friendly" outposting procedure for U.S. forces. To find out, one must consider an isolated U.S. position with civilian houses nearby.

The Hypothetical Situation

Picture a platoon-sized American outpost atop the hill on Map 10.1. Here, defensive maneuver is only possible under two conditions: (1) where the entire place is abandoned during a tactical

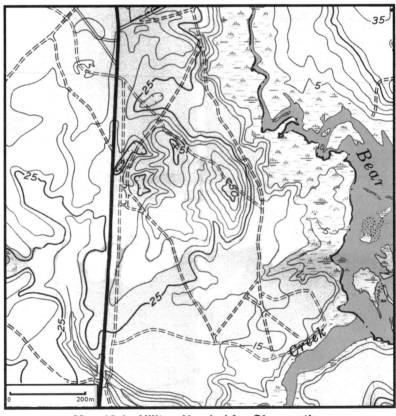

Map 10.1: Hilltop Needed for Observation
(Source: U.S. Department of the Interior Geological Survey, "Hubert Quadrangle, NC," map #34077-F2-TF-024, scale 1:24,000)

withdrawal; and (2) where a piecemeal "defense in depth" is used instead of a standard perimeter. Under enemy pressure, the former becomes nearly impossible after the approaches have been defoliated and mined. So, only the latter is viable. It would also better preserve the mission. Only missing are its particulars. This "defense in depth" would have to consist of semi-independent and fully movable entities. From history, one can see how they might cooperate.

Which Movable Entities and in What Configuration

Under extreme enemy pressure, the squad-sized strongpoints in a WWI German matrix did not fall back in any kind of predetermined sequence. (Refer back to Map 10.1.) Each was abandoned at the discretion of its NCO leader.[5] On the hypothetical hilltop, the principal American entities are therefore squads that can independently move to avoid detection. That's the only way they, as a group, will be able to continually man an observation post in enemy country.

However, the platoon as a whole may still get encircled and entrapped before its various parts can escape. It must be ready to defend itself until dark—when exfiltration becomes possible. How it plans to hold out that long is of utmost importance. It is fully committed to safeguarding all nearby inhabitants, so it must do what it has to with small arms and grenades only at short range. The enemy unit must be made to pay so dearly for every assault that it loses track of the time.

In WWII, the Japanese created inverted "V-shape" ambushes at the tops of draws. Any U.S. patrol to travel up such a draw soon found itself under fire from every direction with no place to hide. The Japanese further protected their pillbox corners with outlying, trench-fed gunpits. The resulting "X-shaped" arrangement created firesacks on all four sides of the bunker. Anyone to approach it from any side was then subjected to devastating fire from either flank. (See Figure 10.3.) The North Vietnamese had a slightly different variation on this deadly theme. To secure a rest stop or observation point, an NVA squad would form all three fire teams into a wagon wheel formation. (See Figure 10.4.) Instead of connecting trenches, it used connecting files. When atop a hill, the spokes of this wagon wheel sometimes followed fingers while its firesacks corresponded with draws. Here again, no American point men could approach the position without incurring close-range, surprise fire from either flank.

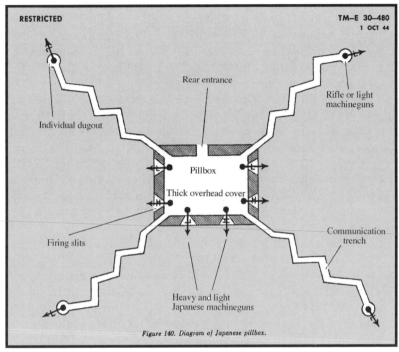

Figure 10.3: Japanese Strongpoint with Built-In Firesacks
(Source: TM-E 30-480 [1944], p. 160)

Figure 10.4: Viet Cong "Wagon Wheel" Outpost
(Source: Poole, The Tiger's Way, p. 160)

Of course, the wagon wheel formation works better against standup intruders than crawling infiltrators. To counter the latter, the formation's central observer would have to be carefully hidden and his "spoke-mates" expertly placed. The North Vietnamese probably just put their observer in a tree at the center of the formation. That way, no ground infiltrator could reach him. For barren hilltops (like those in Afghanistan), the WWII Russians had other ways of obscuring their observer. (See Figure 10.5.) As long as the hide was only manned during the day, no infiltrator could bother its occupant either.

While it's doubtful that the North Vietnamese ever rotated the spokes of their wheel to better align its firesacks with the path of an intruder, that kind of thing would be relatively easy to accomplish. Union Col. Chamberlain did something similar—with far more people—at Gettysburg's Little Round Top. There, he sent a portion of his line in a "swinging-gate" maneuver that caused follow-on Confederate attackers to think they had been outflanked by a whole new unit. Fire team or squad spokes should be able to rotate just as easily.

But the most logical direction for those spokes to move would be outboard from the wheel's hub. The personnel manning each spoke have only to turn sideways to be in column formation. Such columns could easily disperse along their respective axes (as in the Asian Cloud Battle Array [6]) and then reassemble later. Between the ends of the spokes, roving "scout-like" sentries could provide a reasonable semblance of coordination and early warning. (See Figure 10.6.)

Which Embedded Formation to Use

With two separate crests on the same hill mass (refer back to Map 10.1), an American might be tempted to form a triangular array of circular perimeters instead of linear spokes. When perfectly meshed with the microterrain, perimeters do better defend against infiltration. (See Figures 10.7 and 10.8.) But they also create a false sense of security and take too long to evacuate.

When threatened on defense (like in a perimeter setting), GIs have been traditionally trained to engage enemy forces as soon as they come into view. From atop an isolated observation post, that

Figure 10.5: Russian Observation Posts
(Source: Podgotovka Razvegchika: Sistema Spetsnaza GRU, © 1998 by A.E.Taras and F.D. Zaruz, pp. 374, 375)

can easily translate into blowing up everything and everyone for miles around. In many parts of Afghanistan, that much bombardment will only forestall the inevitable. Then, the surrounded GIs have little choice but to fight and die—for they currently lack enough skill to exfiltrate an encirclement.

To those manning each spoke of a wagon wheel outpost, the "linear ambush" better imparts what they must do to survive. When given such a mission, individual squads secretly enter enemy country. *En route* to their ambush site, they dodge enemy contact. Then after making sure their quarries are combatants, they fight by surprise and with extreme lethality from close range. Once the enemy has been sufficiently chastised, they again break contact.

Figure 10.6: The Roving Sentry
(Source: FM 7-8 [1984], p. B-4)

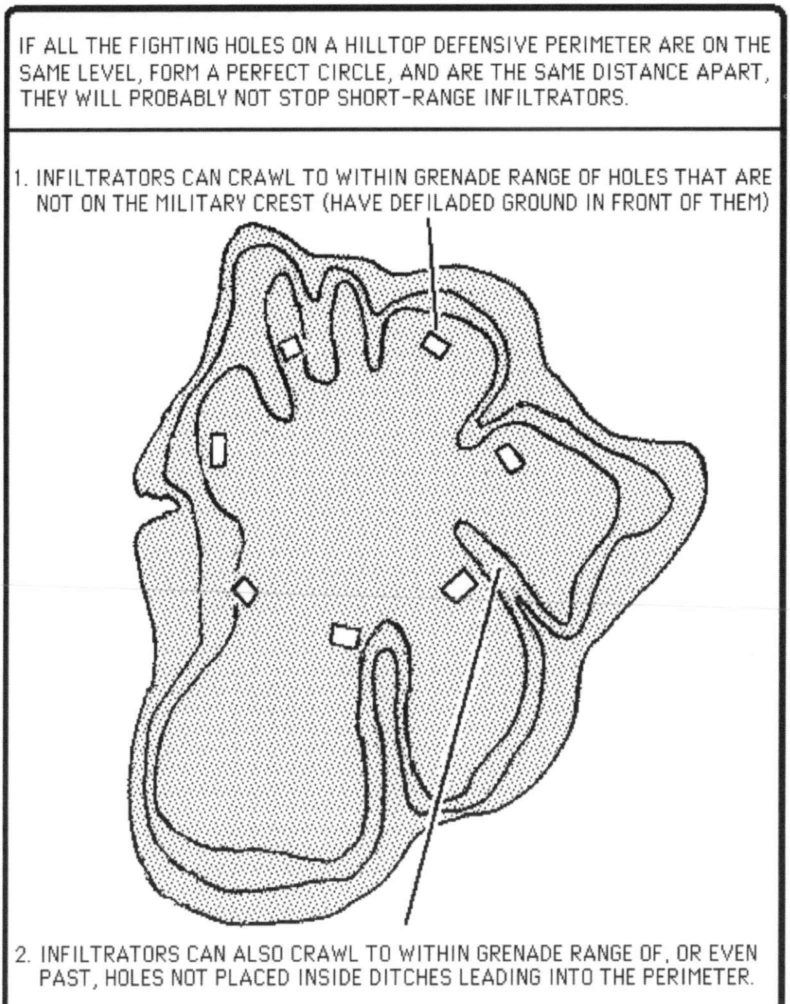

IF ALL THE FIGHTING HOLES ON A HILLTOP DEFENSIVE PERIMETER ARE ON THE SAME LEVEL, FORM A PERFECT CIRCLE, AND ARE THE SAME DISTANCE APART, THEY WILL PROBABLY NOT STOP SHORT-RANGE INFILTRATORS.

1. INFILTRATORS CAN CRAWL TO WITHIN GRENADE RANGE OF HOLES THAT ARE NOT ON THE MILITARY CREST (HAVE DEFILADED GROUND IN FRONT OF THEM)

2. INFILTRATORS CAN ALSO CRAWL TO WITHIN GRENADE RANGE OF, OR EVEN PAST, HOLES NOT PLACED INSIDE DITCHES LEADING INTO THE PERIMETER.

Figure 10.7: Wrong Way to Establish a Perimeter Defense
(Source: Poole, *The Last Hundred Yards*, p. 265)

The Way to Apply Less Force on Defense

In the 20th Century, it was supporting arms (artillery and air strikes) that killed most civilians. When an isolated U.S. outpost

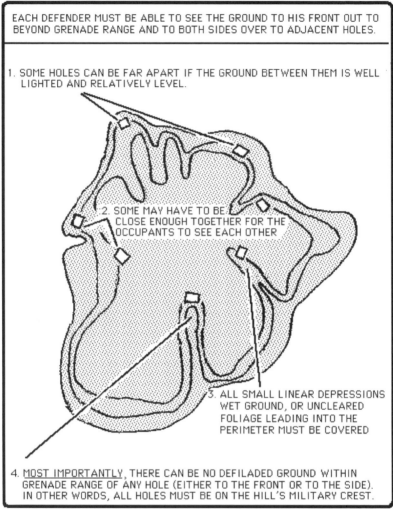

EACH DEFENDER MUST BE ABLE TO SEE THE GROUND TO HIS FRONT OUT TO
BEYOND GRENADE RANGE AND TO BOTH SIDES OVER TO ADJACENT HOLES.

1. SOME HOLES CAN BE FAR APART IF THE GROUND BETWEEN THEM IS WELL
LIGHTED AND RELATIVELY LEVEL.

2. SOME MAY HAVE TO BE
CLOSE ENOUGH TOGETHER FOR THE
OCCUPANTS TO SEE EACH OTHER

3. ALL SMALL LINEAR DEPRESSIONS
WET GROUND, OR UNCLEARED
FOLIAGE LEADING INTO THE
PERIMETER MUST BE COVERED

4. MOST IMPORTANTLY, THERE CAN BE NO DEFILADED GROUND WITHIN
GRENADE RANGE OF ANY HOLE (EITHER TO THE FRONT OR TO THE SIDE).
IN OTHER WORDS, ALL HOLES MUST BE ON THE HILL'S MILITARY CREST.

Figure 10.8: A Perimeter Defense That Will Stop Infiltrators
(Source: Poole, *The Last Hundred Yards*, p. 266)

was in danger in Vietnam, everything from B-52 carpet bombing to round-the-clock napalm was applied to all surrounding countryside. That's what has to stop. In 4GW, another way must be found to save outposts. It's true that electronic intelligence and smart munitions now somewhat decrease the danger to civilians. But, the underlying problem remains—too many high explosives in an increasingly populous world. Even if satellite imagery could tell who's only 13 years old and wearing a dress, its interpreters must still distinguish fighter from bystander. That is the nature of standoff warfare—America's favorite variant. Its alternative is short-range combat (where only small arms, grenades, and command-detonated mines are used). Because the alternative's practitioners are at the scene (as opposed to thousands of miles away behind some video monitor), they can more easily arrange for their defensive fires to harm only attackers. Their "missiles" are much smaller and can be made to harmlessly impact the ground or some other obstruction before reaching nearby residents. Those missiles can also be made to wound instead of kill.

It is short-range combat for which most Asian formations are designed. Their intent is threefold: (1) to avoid enemy notice as long as possible; (2) to surprise and overwhelm any intruders with multi-directional, close-range fire; and then (3) to change location before those intruders regroup. If a terrain feature only held strategic value as an observation point, then its occupants could move a short distance away and still continue with their mission. As soon as the foe moved on, they would reoccupy the feature.

Once the supporting-arms crutch has been discarded, there is no magical way to keep from shooting civilians. It takes constant attention to one's fields of fire. Where a civilian residence may lie along the most advantageous machinegun lane, a less advantageous lane is chosen or the whole position is moved. There are enough folds in the ground and other obstructions to adequately absorb most wayward rounds. What's really required to protect civilians is enough respect for human life to work a little harder.

Why Use a Perimeter at All?

Circular formations are not very conducive to movement. Movement is best accomplished in a column. When those in a column face sideways, they become a line. That line can direct all of its firepower forwards or backwards without endangering any member. When automatic weapons are further positioned at its ends, they can defend those ends or place interlocking fire across either front or back. In other words, the line is one of the strongest defensive formations in existence. The NVA would often defend from two parallel lines.[7] Under extreme pressure, the members of one would fall back to the other.

On the other hand, maneuver warfare enthusiasts have long talked about defending a place with an ambush matrix instead of a perimeter. Why couldn't both ideas be combined with the wagon wheel concept? What if the spokes of the wheel were not to meet at the hub, but rather begin at various distances from an invisible center. Wouldn't all still be outside of the others' principal fields of fire? Where enemy mortars are probable, one doesn't want many

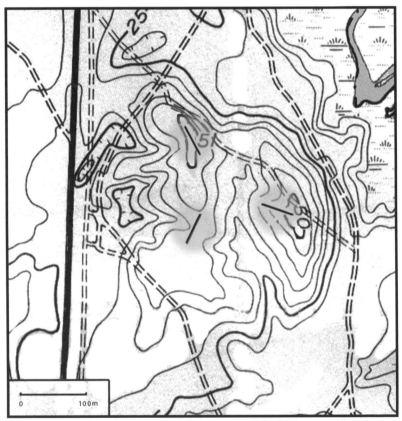

Map 10.2: Three Squads in an Extended Wagon Wheel
(Source: U.S. Department of the Interior Geological Survey, "Hubert Quadrangle, NC," map #34077-F2-TF-024, scale 1:24,000)

people at a formation's center anyway. Each spoke would then be a semi-independent linear ambush with all of its inherent combat power. (See Map 10.2 and Figure 10.9.) Then, whether or not it had to fight, it could still move away.

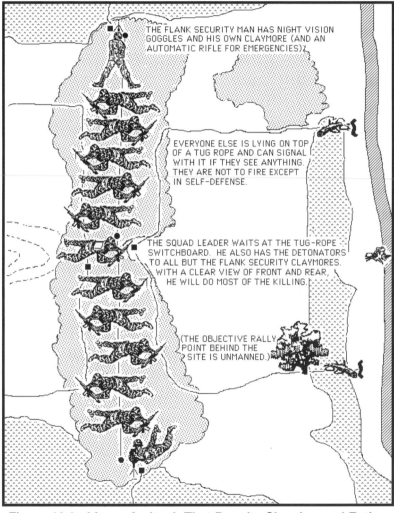

THE FLANK SECURITY MAN HAS NIGHT VISION GOGGLES AND HIS OWN CLAYMORE (AND AN AUTOMATIC RIFLE FOR EMERGENCIES).

EVERYONE ELSE IS LYING ON TOP OF A TUG ROPE AND CAN SIGNAL WITH IT IF THEY SEE ANYTHING. THEY ARE NOT TO FIRE EXCEPT IN SELF-DEFENSE.

THE SQUAD LEADER WAITS AT THE TUG-ROPE SWITCHBOARD. HE ALSO HAS THE DETONATORS TO ALL BUT THE FLANK SECURITY CLAYMORES. WITH A CLEAR VIEW OF FRONT AND REAR, HE WILL DO MOST OF THE KILLING.

(THE OBJECTIVE RALLY POINT BEHIND THE SITE IS UNMANNED.)

Figure 10.9: Linear Ambush That Permits Sleeping and Eating
(Source: Poole, *The Last Hundred Yards*, p. 169)

The Roving Sentries

No configuration of ambushes—without roving sentries between them—would provide as much overall security as a perimeter. As long as those sentries were unconventional warfare (UW) trained, they would be at little risk. Skilled at tracking, they could tell if the enemy had penetrated the inner core of the formation. Should they come into contact with that enemy, they could fall back on their

Figure 10.10: These Roving Sentries Are Trained in E&E
(Source: FM 7-8 [1984], pp. B-7, B-8)

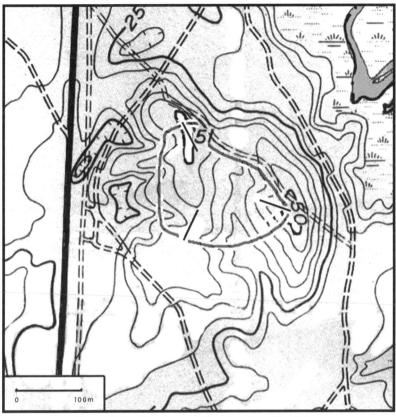

Map 10.3: Routes of the Roving Sentries
(Source: U.S. Department of the Interior Geological Survey, "Hubert Quadrangle, NC," map #34077-F2-TF-024, scale 1:24,000)

Escape and Evasion (E&E) training and link up with the rest of the platoon later. (See Figure 10.10.) A simple circular pattern would suffice for their tiny two-man patrols. (See Map 10.3.)

An Expanding Wagon Wheel

As soon as those sentries detected an enemy presence, they

201

would signal to all three squads to disperse along their respective axes. What if only two could do so successfully? Then, the third would be encircled by the enemy. (See Map 10.4.) It would fight like a linear ambush until dark and then either exfiltrate or bust through the cordon. (See Figures 10.11 and 10.12.)

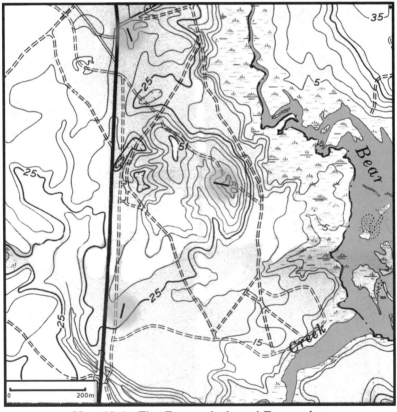

Map 10.4: The Enemy-Induced Expansion
(Source: U.S. Department of the Interior Geological Survey, "Hubert Quadrangle, NC," map #34077-F2-TF-024, scale 1:24,000)

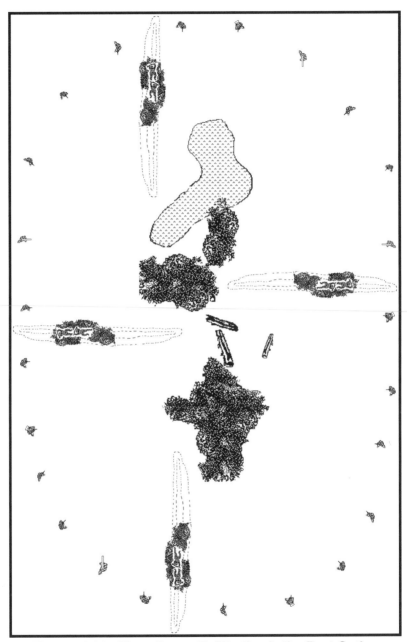

Figure 10.11: Short-Range Exfiltration Is the Best Option
(Source: FM 5-103 [1985], p. 5-10;TC 90-1 [1986], cover)

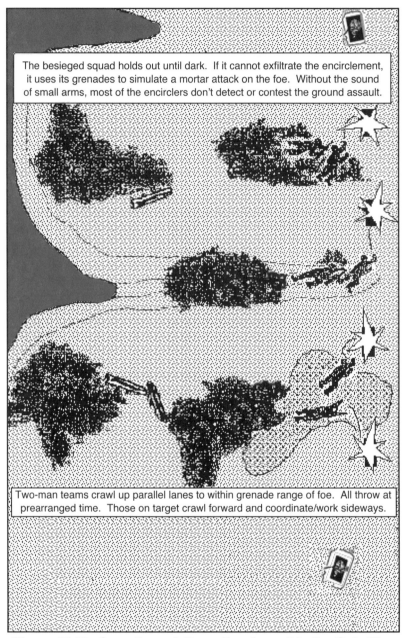

The besieged squad holds out until dark. If it cannot exfiltrate the encirclement, it uses its grenades to simulate a mortar attack on the foe. Without the sound of small arms, most of the encirclers don't detect or contest the ground assault.

Two-man teams crawl up parallel lanes to within grenade range of foe. All throw at prearranged time. Those on target crawl forward and coordinate/work sideways.

Figure 10.12: Sometimes A Deceptive Assault Is the Only Way
(Source: FM 7-70 [1986], p. 420; FM 5-103 [1985], p. 4-6; MCI 03.66a [1986], p. 2-8; FM 23-30 [1988], p. 2-8; FM 7-1183 [1976], p. 2-VII-C-4.4)

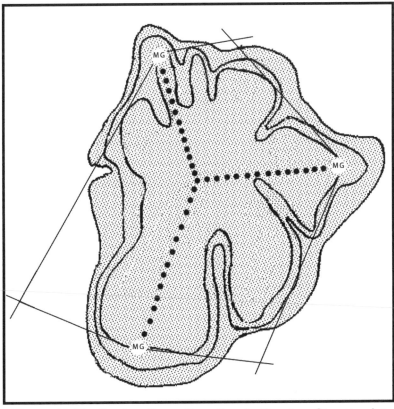

Figure 10.13: Spokes Come Together to Create a Strongpoint
(Source: Poole, *The Last Hundred Yards*, p. 265)

When the Threat Has Passed

After all three U.S. squads have escaped, the enemy will eventually lose interest in the area. Just as U.S. forces ran week-long hunts for guerrillas in many of the outlying areas of Vietnam, so too with this enemy tire of the chase. Then, the three American squads return to their hill mass like guerrillas. To initially mount the strongest defense, they first combine into a condensed wagon wheel on one crest. (See Figure 10.13.)

Such a platoon can survive deep in enemy-controlled country without doing any collateral damage or requiring rescue. (See Figure 10.14.) It does so by staying hidden and not using supporting arms when discovered. Even then, its various parts are able to restrict their own limited firepower to nearby space. None of its small-arms fire is ever directed at, or allowed to carry over into, civilian-occupied areas. Still, it is lethal enough to allow the remainder of friendly troops to escape. To resupply such a platoon, one has only to harness the latest technologies to provide a "smart" nighttime air drop from high altitude.

Figure 10.14: This Outpost Will Never Need Rescue
(Source: U.S. military website within the http://www.usafns.com/art.shtml listing, image #7-06i.gif)

206

This way of thinking from the bottom up to combine individual through squad techniques to create an obscure platoon maneuver is the essence of UW, and how the NVA was able to win in Vietnam. There is no shame in copying a former adversary. The shame is in being too prideful to learn from one. While undeniably brutal, the NVA did make full use of the South Vietnamese population.

11 Using Basic-Service _____ Volunteers

- What is the guerrilla's principal source of support?
- How can that support be most effectively offset?

Only a nation's own population can defeat an insurgency.

What's Now Required to Win at War

American enlistees are not briefed on the latest subtleties of war. They've never heard of 4GW or how their personal actions may adversely affect its outcome. At the start of the counterinsurgency operations in Iraq, U.S. leaders still thought "minimal force" too complicated a concept for young infantrymen.[1] But, just as novice policemen are taught to preserve human life, so must infantry privates. "That any foe spared today must be faced tomorrow" is the argument of fools. Until the war's underlying cause is resolved, there will always be more enemy fighters.

The job of the military professional is to win wars—not to kill people *per se*. Of late, victory has become more about mobilizing civilians than targeting antagonists. The concluding chapter has therefore been dedicated to this paradox.

Civilians cannot be mobilized without military or police assistance. North Korea has just increased its force of infiltrating commandos to 180,000. And by some estimates, the PRC now has 1,000,000 special operators trained in political and economic sabotage.[2] When widely dispersed around the world as neighborhood "commissars," that many "grass-root" 4GW experts could do a lot of damage. Within the continental U.S., drug traffickers have a similar agenda. On 12 February 2009, Phoenix was reported to be second only to Mexico City in its number of kidnappings.[3] To confront either threat, tiny contingents of American military and police will have to lead thousands of oppressed communities in their own defense. While U.S. expeditionary force commanders now know this, they have been unable to fully implement it. They can't dispatch tiny contingents to dangerous areas overseas because—unlike all North Korean riflemen [4]—their soldiers and Marines have yet receive any instruction in unconventional warfare (UW). In other words, none would have the tactical skill to dodge annihilation by a more numerous foe. To mobilize civilians, all U.S. infantrymen and law enforcement personnel will need UW training. (See Figure 11.1.)

To Win at 4GW

All insurrections have political, economic, and psychological overtones. The traditional form of Maoist revolution was no exception. To embrace "all means of resistance," it included "politicization" and "labor collectives." Its 4GW equivalents only vary in the degree of coordination between arenas. Now, any activity can have—as its sole purpose—the masking of efforts in another arena. For many years in Iraq, acts of violence successfully diverted the Coalition's attention from more important matters of governance and infrastructure.

What America's Military Can Now Share with Its Police

Part Three has been so far applying the law enforcement per-

Figure 11.1: UW-Trained GI or Paramilitary Policeman
(Source: *Courtesy of Edward Molina, copyright © 2003*)

spective to military problems. But, with the U.S. homeland now under attack, recent military lessons may help the police. Drug cartels operate in much the same way as Islamist or Communist militants—from the bottom up. They remain loose confederations of gangs so that the activities of no one gang can implicate the others, and no one boss will be irreplaceable. Those gangs feed off their respective civilian communities. Whatever they cannot earn, steal, or buy there, they simply coerce. And it is only through the collective efforts of those communities' residents that the gangs can be defeated.

211

Collocating U.S. troops with Iraqi soldiers and police in neighborhood CAPs was only part of the solution in Iraq. At the height of the Surge, no more than 100 CAPs existed within Baghdad's 100 square miles. Why, then, did the overall level of violence drop? Some action must have been equally effective in the other neighborhoods. Most got a community watch variant known as a Concerned Local Citizens (CLC) group. But these CLC groups did more than just man checkpoints. Many were assigned to public-works projects.[5] Thus, one can say they helped to provide all kinds of basic services. Such a marriage between community watch and utility functioning is particularly effective when fighting Islamists or Communists. That's because both will try to establish their own state within a state. After secretly sabotaging legitimate infrastructure, they magnanimously offer to provide their own. *Hezbollah* is known to run community service projects throughout Southern Lebanon. Al-Sadr's alternative governance of Iraq extends all the way to having his own courts.[6] And in the Colombian back country, Maoist FARC improves health care, schools, and infrastructure.[7] *Even its attack objectives are more political and economic than military. It targets the local government 27% of the time, utilities 22%, transportation 9%, police 8%, and army detachments 1%.*[8] Clearly, both the Islamists and Communists have been waging 4GW. To confront them, one needs civilian workers to accomplish non-martial endeavors.

Civilian Participation in Local Security

A community's residents have as much influence over illegal activity as its police force, but that influence must be carefully controlled. Otherwise, its law enforcement apparatus gets swamped with everything from crank phone calls to bogus arrest warrants. And then the vigilantes appear.

Normally, the inhabitants of a place elect a town council and mayor. They, in turn, provide general guidelines to a paid police force. But, that model has been occasionally modified. CLC equivalents have also occurred Stateside.

In the early nineties, the San Arias, California police department experimented with . . . the community-oriented policing (COP) concept. The city first established a committee of citizens and police to address the subject and provide guidelines for implementing the philosophy. . . . Committee members weighed in on areas such as task-organization, measures of effectiveness, training and readiness, and tactics.[9]

Not since the days of the Wild West posse, have armed U.S. citizens helped to enforce America's laws. Many of this country's personal freedoms are based on "due process." One cannot be the instrument of due process without considerable training in legal statutes, arrest procedures, and force parameters. Thus, the arming of civilians is an extremely risky proposition when it comes to counterinsurgency or 4GW.

Militias Too Easily Lose Their Way

Within the village CAP platoons of Vietnam, local militiamen did well because of their constant contact with U.S. Marine counterparts. But, without that degree of supervision, militias develop problems. The rightist AUC was formed to combat Communist FARC in Colombia. Many of its members were former policemen and soldiers who had been discharged with human-rights abuses.[10] Their business sense was no better. To augment legitimate funding, some taxed peripheral aspects of the local drug trade. Before long, the AUC was so deeply involved with the cartels that it had to be disbanded.

The AUC's undoing was greed, but what of the Nicaraguan Contras? The U.S. was finally forced to stop supporting them by both the International Court of Justice and U.N. General Assembly.[11]

Today's Trend Is Toward More Passive Security

Communities are most easily policed through constant vigilance and cumulative intelligence. In recent years, the camera has largely replaced the corner cop or watchman. But cameras cannot stop crimes from happening, only record their details. Still, no U.S. citizen would put up with the personal identification checks of an occupied Europe or Israeli West Bank. So, some other way must be found to passively defend against criminals. For example, civilian volunteers could keep logs of suspicious activity instead of calling every individual sighting in.

Photographic Intelligence

Camera technology has now reached the point where it can, at times, take the place of human intelligence gatherers.

Police Variant

Within London, not much happens these days without its particulars being recorded. In the Rampart area of L.A., cameras have made virtual patrols possible for years.

> Since the 1990's, L.A.'s MacArthur Park and the surrounding Alvarado Corridor was a known area of violent crime, narcotics sales and gang activity. The park belonged to MS-13, despite the best efforts of the police. A new approach was introduced with the "Alvarado Corridor Project". The L.A. County Rampart district's area-denial solution was threefold: flood the community with officers, monitor 24/7, and snare the drug dealers. . . . [A]reas an officer on foot could not see were covered by pan, tilt, and zoom-capable closed circuit television cameras that link to Rampart Station through the Internet. Through these links, desk personnel inside the station could conduct "virtual patrols." . . . Finally, narcotics [officers] planned and executed numerous "reverse [sting] operations": drug buys to catch dealers in the act. . . . Shootings were down by 50%, homicides by 38%, and robberies by 14%.[12]

Military Variant

In Iraq, U.S. expeditionary forces soon realized what long-range cameras could do. One particular camera may have been instrumental in the pacification of Ramadi.

> In 2006 . . . Regimental Combat Team (RCT) 5 faced a recurring problem with IEDs on a main service road (MSR) between Habaniya and Ramadi, Anbar Province. . . . [T]he insurgents had denied the RCT freedom of movement. . . . Scout Sniper Teams and patrols were immediately reported on by children, warning away any would-be IED planting teams. RCT 5 looked to the JLENS, a digital, color camera,

optimal at distances up to 4km [3.5 miles]. Planted on the roof of a headquarters bunker, the JLENS went unnoticed by insurgents. Within 90 days of installing the JLENS, Marines killed or captured over 150 insurgents along the MSR, recorded TTPs [techniques] of IED teams in the field, and amassed a veritable library of license plates, faces, and evidence for subsequent trials. In 90 days, the MSR from Habaniya to Ramadi went from a Tier 1 IED threat to no coalition or civilian casualties.[13]

Paid Informants

Since ancient times, civilian authorities have been willing to pay ordinary citizens for information about lawbreakers.

Police Variant

Informants play a big role in the solving of street crime. Every criminal investigator has a string of "snitches." While normally rewarded in dollars, such informants can receive everything from immunity from prosecution to a reduced charge on some other offense. Those already in prison are not used for this purpose. (See Figure 11.2.) They will too easily lie to obtain their release.

Figure 11.2: Jailbirds Provide No Reliable Information
(Source: *Corel Gallery* Clipart, "Totem Graphics," Justice #25C015)

SHARED EXPERIENCE IN TACTICS ────────────────────────────────

Military Variant

Deployed U.S. units could just as easily compensate local civilians for what their opponents plan, are currently doing, or have recently done. To preclude retribution, they must only have a way for tips to be passed anonymously and paid for indirectly. Who would suspect that information had been sold if some out-of-town indigenous trader were to purchase—at full price—50 of whatever the provider makes for a living?

Traffic Checkpoints

Most criminals ride to their intended target. By monitoring all vehicles in and out of that particular area, one could partially impede the process.

Police Variant

Inside the U.S., there are only occasional vehicular inspection stations. Police will sometimes throw up a roadblock to check for drivers' licenses, registrations, drinking, and fleeing felons. Where I-5 splits the narrow strip of land between the Pacific Ocean and Camp Pendleton (north of San Diego), government agents cursorily check all vehicles for illegal aliens.

Military Variant

During the Surge, Baghdad was intentionally segmented with tall walls. Then, GI contingents were assigned to these segments, just as law enforcement personnel would be to their respective beats. At some point, those walls will have to be replaced by traffic checkpoints. While ostensibly looking for bombs, their civilian operators could also reduce the amount of enemy infiltration. Through electronic license plate checks, they could quickly learn the owner's identity and address. Then, in a more controlled environment down the street, military police could more fully check the intentions of any suspicious visitor(s). As the computerized data base for neighborhood visitation grew, so would the checkpoint operators' ability to spot impending trouble.

Civilian Patrols

Police Variant

Though started in New York City in 1979, the Guardian Angels is a volunteer organization that is now active in Boston, Chicago, Philadelphia, Dallas, Houston and many other cities around the world. Because of initial attempts to train unarmed members to make citizen arrests for violent crimes, they were not initially welcomed by New York's mayor. Guardian Angels wear red berets while walking the streets or riding public transportation.[14] Where there is trouble, they now only summon police assistance by cell phone.

Military Variant

The U.S. military could hire roving civilian watchmen. In an active war zone, they might more easily survive if pretending to do something else.

Neighborhood Watches

Police Variant

Many neighborhoods in America have volunteer community watch organizations that report suspicious activity to local authorities.

Military Variant

Once inhabitants of a place become convinced that Americans are there to help, they will warn their new friends of enemy activity. But those Americans must be in permanent residence, and there must be some way to secretly alert them.

Intelligence Gathering over the Internet

Police Variant

Many American homes now have access to the internet. This

Figure 11.3: Police "Intellipedia" Editor
(Source: *Corel Gallery* Clipart, "One Mile Up," Computer #11C002)

makes possible the automatic collection of civilian input on criminal activity. For a while, the Guardian Angels tried to watch neighborhoods through their internet contacts. But, whether any police department has established a civilian-fed database on criminal activity is not known. (See Figure 11.3.) The American intelligence community has such a system, but it is only for inter-departmental sharing.

A "wiki" is a set of web pages to which anyone can contribute. The CIA's "Intellipedia" is based on wiki technology. It is a central repository through which 16 agencies collaborate on various issues. Within Intellipedia, there are three versions: (1) one accessible to most agents; (2) another secret; and (3) the last top secret. Within each version, some entrants can edit and others just view. Intellipedia's wikis are run over JWICS, SIPRNet, and Intelink-U.[15]

Military Variant

Almost everyone has heard of the "Base Hotline" for sensitive information. But to acquire and consolidate intelligence within Iraq, the U.S. military did much more.

In light of gang database successes in the U.S. and Central America, tactical intelligence collaborative (TIC) tools can pave the way for streamlined intelligence. . . . The consumer and collector is the Marine on the ground. He must have access to a real-time database that allows the company-level

intel. section to . . . submit . . . information for analysis. . . .
This . . . tactical intelligence encyclopedia would be a "who's
who" in theatre. Included could be surveillance footage,
aliases, known affiliates, as well as a collaborative tool to
query/chat. Maintenance and oversight of this tool would
rest at the brigade or higher level. To be sure, intelligence
. . . databases already exist in theatre.[16]

The Foe's Interest in Other Basic Services

Many of the Iraqi attacks have been against public infrastructure and governmental credibility. By interrupting the flow of vital
commodities (e.g., fuel) and basic services (e.g., garbage collection),
the enemy increased its popular support.

According to a *New York Times* article in late February 2005,
the Iraqi insurgents had reached a new level of coordination and
sophistication in their attempts to disrupt their capital city's basic
resources. Those resources were its supplies of crude oil, gasoline,
heating oil, water, and electricity. Iraqi and American officials said
the attack pattern demonstrated a deep understanding of the com-
plex network of pipelines, power cables, and reservoirs that carry
those resources into Baghdad.[17]

The Iraqi insurgents' way of fighting may appear amateurish,
but it has already worked in Southern Lebanon. Until the Surge,
Western occupiers were based at the edge of cities, patrolled by vehicle, and relied heavily on supporting arms. That left the individual
neighborhoods relatively devoid of security. When local residents
experienced shortages of public services and basic commodities,
they were reminded of their government's ineptitude and looked
elsewhere for help.

Throughout eastern Baghdad and most of the southern Iraqi
cities, al-Sadr and his Iranian affiliates run their own police, courts,
clinics, and food/clothing distribution points.[18] It is through their
"charities" that they do much of their military recruiting. Like
Hezbollah in Lebanon and *Hamas* in Israel, the Mahdi Army has
set up a parallel government that aspires to Shiite statehood. That
government has its own social programs, religious courts, police
patrols, and town councils.[19] This gives it quite an edge at election
time.

Like the Mahdi Army in Iraq, FARC has created a "state-within-a-state" in Colombia. It funds that state through taxes.

Now they [the FARC] tax every stage of the drug business, from the chemicals needed to process the hardy coca bush into cocaine and the opium poppy into heroin, right up to charging for the processed drugs to be flown from illegal airstrips they control.[20]
— BBC News, September 2003

Before taking an interest in drugs, FARC collected "war taxes" from the inhabitants, merchants, and landowners of the areas it controlled. During the 1970's and 1980's, it established its own schools, judicial system, health care, and agrarian economy. In essence, it too had created its own *de facto* state in southern Colombia. It now has units throughout the country, but they are strongest in remote areas. There, FARC improves health care, schools, and infrastructure.[21]

Not Every Enemy Soldier Is a Communist or *Jihadist*

Many of the opposition fighters in Iraq and Afghanistan have no other way to support their families. They are not doing their Islamic duty but simply taking the only jobs available. Instead of trying to kill them, why not just create other employment? Normally, that kind of talk leads to more billets in a friendly militia. But, it could just as easily lead to public-works jobs like those with which Franklin D. Roosevelt saved America in 1933. With his Civilian Conservation Corps, he did two things at once: (1) rebuilt infrastructure; and (2) forestalled the mischief of idle minds.[22] If the enemy had no more fighters, he would be as good as defeated. There is no dishonor in fighting him with bucks instead of bullets. Wars are not fought as an assertion of personal machismo. They are fought to restore peace. By Christian doctrine, one cannot morally wage war without sparing as many antagonists as possible.[23]

Defeating the Foe in the Non-Martial Arenas of 4GW

When one's Afghan adversary intends "death by a thousand

[tiny] cuts,"[24] one must expect to be attacked in ways that U.S. generals would not associate with combat. As already demonstrated, security is not the enemy's only basic-service interest. One must also upstage his other initiatives. That means enlisting civilian help to provide local utilities or aid within Iraq, Afghanistan, or wherever U.S. forces are deployed. The only two that really require governmental supervision are electricity and phone lines. Sewage, water, garbage collection, road maintenance, schooling, and the various emergency services are all within the purview of local citizens. If too few host-country residents wanted to volunteer, then others could be paid a subsistence wage from the U.S. defense budget. That budget should also be big enough to cover a few inoculations against disease.

Most Important to Public Health Is Water

In Africa, food, water, sewage, inoculations, and security are the most vital of the basic services. Lt.Gen. Ghormley, head of the U.S. Marine "Horn of Africa" contingent, has focused on the first four. He says his Marines are "waging peace instead of war."[25] They spend much of their time digging wells and giving inoculations.

In the city, only existing water lines should be repaired so as not to deprive other neighborhoods. (See Figure 11.4.) But, rainwater

Figure 11.4: Water and Sewage Worker
(Source: *Corel Gallery* Clipart, "Totem Graphics," 28W046)

run-off systems are not hard to build. And a well can often be activated through a little pump or generator repair. Military medics know how to make water safe to drink. Of all the public services, water is the most vital.

According to a U.N. Report in March 2006, as many as 1.1 billion people [about 1/5 the world's population] still do not have access to safe water. Sub-Saharan Africa is among the areas hardest hit by poverty, disease, and drought. The report goes on to say that diarrheal diseases and malaria kill around 3.1 million people a year in all parts of the world. The U.N. further indicated that 1.6 million of those people could be saved if they only had safe drinking water, sanitation, and hygiene.[26]

Many other public-health needs can be locally satisfied, while the central government expands its ability to support them. Besides sewage, garbage collection, and inoculations, there are others: (1) washing; (2) fuel collection for heating and cooking; (3) roof maintenance; and (4) wall caulking for protection against the cold.

Sewage

Undeveloped countries have sewer ditches instead of sewer pipes. Those ditches may be partially covered in urban areas, but they can still be cleaned out by hand. Then, it is the rain water runoff that keeps them relatively free of obstruction. (Refer back to Figure 11.4.)

Garbage Collection and General Hygiene

With increased cleanliness comes better morale. If soap or brooms are lacking, provide them. By keeping a neighborhood clear of trash, one can more easily create the impression of a viable central government. (See Figure 11.5.) In 1974, the U.S. Bureau of Land Management sponsored a program called the "Johnny Horizon Community Cleanup Campaign" to commemorate America's 200th birthday. On a cold Saturday morning in November throughout the Illinois township of Romeoville, Marine Junior Reserve Officer Training Corps (JROTC) cadets got involved. They collected all the refuse that lined that town's roadways or vacant lots and piled it into five-ton trucks belonging to Joliet's reserve artillery battery. The cadets enjoyed the visibility, and the reservists got a chance to exercise their equipment. The public response to this limited contribution to community upkeep was nothing short of phenomenal.[27] From that time forward, that JROTC unit could do nothing wrong in the eyes of Romeoville's residents.[27]

America's deployed units have no shortage of rolling stock. They could just as easily cooperate with indigenous groups to make their place of habitation more acceptable.

Medical Assistance

Unit medics have enough wherewithal to set up temporary clinics for minor injuries. Whatever they couldn't get from their supply system, American nonprofits would happily provide. Such things do wonders to cement relations with an indigenous community. With a little assistance from the chain of command and civilian volunteers, those medics could offer both first aid and inoculations (like the Marines in Djibouti did). (See Figure 11.6.)

Figure 11.5: Refuse Collector
(Source: *Corel Gallery* Clipart, "Totem Graphics," Man #28U012)

Other Emergency Services

Emergency services are important to any neighborhood or village. A fire department, ambulance service, and soup kitchen can often be assembled from salvaged equipment, donated supplies, and volunteer labor. Then, injured residents of that tiny municipality would at least be assured of a way to the hospital. Of course, how fast they get there will depend on the quality of the roads. (See Figures 11.7 and 11.8.)

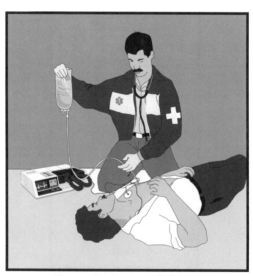

Figure 11.6: Local Clinic
(Source: *Corel Gallery* Clipart, "Tech Pool Studios," Medical #30E053)

Figure 11.7: Volunteer Fireman
(Source: *Corel Gallery* Clipart, "Tech Pool Studios," Fire #17B013)

Road Maintenance

When "up country" in either India or Burma, one still sees roads being repaired by hand with shovels and locally produced gravel.[28] That gravel is made from river stone by scores of people with tiny rock hammers.

Figure 11.8: Makeshift Ambulance
(Source: *Corel Gallery* Clipart, "Tech Pool Studios," Miscellaneous #31E002)

Charities

Having violently opposed Western decadence since the late 1920's, the Muslim Brotherhood has been linked to *al-Qaeda's* birth. Among its objectives is "building extensive social networks of schools, hospitals, and charitable organizations with Islamist ideals."[29] Those charitable organizations must be offset by others from the West. That's why protecting the workers of all Western Non-Government Organizations (NGOs) is such an important 4GW strategy.

Education

The fundamentalist *madrasas* of Pakistan have severely hindered the U.S. war effort in Afghanistan. On 14 April 2009, PBS reported that "Pakistan's state education system had collapsed." Many of the Taliban's fighters come from *madrasas* in their safe havens of Quetta and Karachi.[30] *Hezbollah* and the Mahdi Army depend upon education as well.[31] In the Gaza Strip and West Bank, *Hezbollah's* Sunni proxies distribute thousands of *Intifada* scrapbooks to underage children in an attempt to grow suicide bombers.[32] Communists prefer to "re-educate" misguided adults.[33]

GIs first encountered Muslim insurgency in the Philippine-American War around 1900. That war was in part won by giving the Filipino people instruction on English and its associated values.[34] Thus, education is essential to succeeding at either counterinsurgency or 4GW. (See Figure 11.9.)

Figure 11.9: Schooling Critical to 4GW Victory
(Source: *Corel Gallery* Clipart, "One Mile Up," Miscellaneous #31D003)

Figure 11.10: Recropping the Fields
(Source: *Corel Gallery* Clipart, "Totem Graphics," Man #28V028)

Farm and Business Loans

Where drugs have largely driven a local economy, something must take their place. Once that area had been occupied by U.S. forces, entrepreneurial loans would help to establish new crops and businesses. Otherwise, the local populace might continue to grow coca or poppies in secret or fall for enemy promises of land redistribution. Each American contingent should bankroll a few small-business or farming initiatives, like the Marines did in Iraq's Anbar Province with their "micro-loans."[35] (See Figure 11.10.)

Neighborhood Governance

In 2003, U.S. forces set up dozens of local councils to democratically govern Iraqi neighborhoods. Then, those councilmen began to die. In August 2004, four from Baghdad's Hay Somer neighborhood were killed. That neighborhood's basic services (like garbage collection) and cooperative attitude soon fell into a state of decline.[36] Before falling under Communist or Islamist control, most places of habitation would have a council or founding-father group. Reestablishing it must be a top priority. It is local leaders who must provide guidance after U.S. forces leave.

Youth Services

Wherever young men have too much spare time, there will be trouble. This is as true on the streets of America as in any overseas war zone. In Iraq and Central America, soccer leagues have helped to defuse the situation. (See Figure 11.11.)

Civilian Variant

Law enforcement on Long Island has developing gang awareness suppression and prevention programs (GASP) to reduce gang recruitment. In fact, GASP participants have contributed information leading to the conviction of 65 MS-13 members in Freeport, New York alone.[37] The Freeport Community Response Unit (CRU) deploys two detectives and community leaders to homes of gang members, confronting parents with evidence of their child's misguided activities.[38]

Figure 11.11: Soccer League
(Source: *Corel Gallery* Clipart, "Totem Graphics," Man #28W046)

Military Variant

Parallel programs to the CRU have been in operation in Honduras and are equally applicable in a counterinsurgency environment.[39]

The Shortest Route to Those "Hearts and Minds"

Insurgents get the majority of their support from the civilian population of the nation they wish to rule. After aggravating that population's hardships, Communists and Islamists pretend to provide relief. That's how they subjugate so many communities. It is incumbent upon Allied forces to provide more assistance to those communities than their opposition can. Communist and Islamist factions also require impressionable young fighters. Any act of kindness toward a child effectively lessens their recruiting base. Irrespective of political leaning, all parents worldwide want what is best for their offspring. That's why—more than anything else—child-oriented assistance helps to win over the hearts and minds of a civilian population. (See Figure 11.12.)

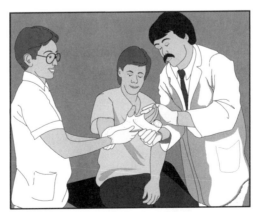

Figure 11.12: Build Public Support by Helping Youngsters
(Source: *Corel Gallery* Clipart, "Tech Pool Studios," People #34I01)

229

Throughout Africa, South America, and the Middle East, all enemy fighters are not loathsome murderers. Within Uganda's Lord's Resistance Army and Colombia's FARC, many have been kidnapped in their pre-teens.[40] Among Lebanese *Hezbollah's* suicide bombers are children who have been initially tricked with promises of money, paradise, or glory and subsequently shamed into destroying themselves.[41] Thus, a fair share of America's frontline opposition may be psychological or economic captives. As such, they must be rescued along with their beleaguered societies.

Afterword

In Quick Retrospect

Within the Introduction and Chapter One is hard evidence of many parts of the world—including Latin America—being under low-intensity 4GW attack from the PRC. While such an attack has never been officially acknowledged by the U.S. government, its existence is more that adequately detailed in *Terrorist Trail, Dragon Days,* and *Tequila Junction.* The attack's ultimate objective is obviously political, but its initial strategies are economic. America has just undergone a severe economic crisis of its own. That it occurred before the most crucial election in U.S. history should give U.S. voters adequate reason for pause. They know that the crisis was caused by a sub-prime mortgage meltdown. What they don't know is that the meltdown was exacerbated by U.S. banks granting huge loans to recent immigrants—many of them Hispanic—who had little chance of paying them back.[1] Nor do they know that most Chinese banks did not participate in the program nor badly suffer from the crisis.[2] All of this may be pure coincidence. But in a highly complicated and quickly changing world, some degree of introspection is always necessary. U.S. leaders need to wake up to the fact that an emerging superpower has the following attributes: (1) unlimited funding; (2) little if any regard for human rights; (3) a completely different vision of world progress; (4) a cultural history of military deception; (5) an atheistic outlook on life; and (6) a paranoid fear of both organized religion and Western democracy. That superpower's so-far successful formula for expansion has included the following: (1) so flooding each nation's economy with low-price trade goods as to run its local manufacturers out of business; (2) indirectly providing political advice to its leftist candidates; (3) indirectly funding those candidates through non-traceable sources; and then (4) acquiring diplomatic concessions through conditional loans.

Incontrovertible Evidence of a New Kind of War

Since the horrific events of 9/11, most U.S. first-responder, police, and security personnel have solely focused on domestic terrorism. Unfortunately, America now has a foe who needs no explosives, toxins, or bullets to do her harm. The most widely accepted guidebook on such options is *Unrestricted Warfare*.[3] Published in 1999 by the Chinese PLA, it discusses everything from "plane hijackings,"[4] "tall buildings,"[5] and "a major explosion at the World Trade Center,"[6] to "electricity network . . . paralyzed,"[7] "hacking into websites,"[8] and "paralyzed . . . computer systems throughout the United States."[9] Many of these things have already come to pass. It was hackers from China who caused the massive power outages in the Northeastern United States in 2003 and Florida in 2007. A U.S. Strategic Command consultant has further asserted there were 37,000 breaches of government and private computer systems in fiscal 2007 and almost 80,000 computer attacks against the Department of Defense.[10] While there is no hard evidence of Chinese government instigation, that is the overall consensus of opinion.

For "street-savy" policemen, such things often fall under the category of "someone else's business." But electric grids depend upon the power station in every community. And computer networks are easier to invade during a break-in. So, these and other dangers to America's operational infrastructure are every bit the counterterrorists' concern. The next major threat to America may be different from the last. It may masquerade as a crime wave but actually be the main offensive in a 4GW attack. The best recent example of 4GW is what Iran was caught doing in Iraq. Just as traditional military procedures were not enough to win there, neither can traditional law enforcement procedures single-handedly thwart the criminal aspect of a 4GW attack on America. To achieve the latter, all security establishment players (whether police or military) must work together more closely. Among other things, this will involve the continuous sharing of small-unit techniques.

While U.S. leaders were busy chasing Osama bin Laden, the following events have occurred: (1) Nepal has elected a Maoist prime minister;[11] (2) the Democratic Republic of the Congo has traded its mineral output to China for a 1,000-mile road;[12] and (3) a million Chinese workers have been spotted in the coastal lowlands of Venezuela.¹³ Individually, these things may seem relatively unimportant. But, in the context of current world history, they are very disturbing. There are only six rightist regimes now left in all of Latin America, and Mexico and Peru came very close to going Socialist in the last election.¹⁴ Thus, in this Hemisphere, the political arena appears to be of most interest to the 4GW aggressor. Who or what is ultimately behind this assault on freedom is difficult to determine because most of the political advice has come from Cuba, and the funding from Venezuelan-oil or local-drug proceeds. The rapid spread of MS-13 may be the first outward indicator of something similar happening in America. Everyone knows that drugs are involved, but why are those young thugs trying so hard to influence local politics? And from where does their managerial advice spring? The answers to these questions may affect the future lifestyle of many Americans.

In Nepal, this new way of interfering in other people's business went so far as to stray into the "psychological arena." No outright terror was involved, but the region will be so destabilized by Nepal's new Maoist regime as to give China several alternative wartime oil routes.

> The Maoists' success came not just from Maoist sympathizers, but also from Nepali [sic] youths who wanted a new political force in power after seeing former political parties not deliver for decades, says . . . a political scientist at Nepal's biggest university.
> "The voters generally did not vote for their ideology, but for change," he says. "It became a fashion, a reaction to the nonperformance of other political parties."¹⁵
> — *Christian Science Monitor,* 21 August 2008

And so, after one of the most important elections in American history, all U.S. law enforcement personnel should be especially wary of any lessening of public safety. By fully embracing globalization, their nation has become increasingly prone to foreign meddling.

The Two Most Obvious Foes

Besides an inane tendency to equate less reverence for God

233

with more personal freedom, Americans only have two enemies—Islamic militants and Communist expansionists. Many U.S. citizens are so disdainful of organized religion as not to realize its alternative. Crime is nothing more than extraordinary levels of sin. Its perpetrators so hate mainstream society that they lay around nights scheming how to harm it. Islamist and Communist subversives share that same goal—by both having to destabilize the targeted population.

The standard Islamist formula goes as follows: (1) rabble rousing; (2) infrastructure destruction; and (3) constantly demonstrating that the incumbent government can neither maintain order nor provide other basic services.

The Western Hemisphere variant of the Communist method looks very similar: (1) making false promises to the working class; (2) accusing the incumbent regime of corruption; (3) supporting an opposition candidate through drug proceeds or foreign funding; and (4) infrastructure obstruction through strikes and riots.

In both methods, the targeted-nation's police establishment must bear the brunt of the onslaught. To further overload those police, both Islamists and Communists use organized crime as a strategic tool.

What It Will Take for the U.S. Military to Help

America's whole public safety effort has been based on what pairs of policemen can collectively accomplish on their respective neighborhood "beats." The U.S. military establishment is too large-unit oriented to be much good at such a widely dispersed mission. Until, it starts paying more attention to the independent actions and strategic contributions of riflemen, buddy teams, fire teams, and squads, it will be largely unable to help with the internal defense of America. Every rifle company commander must be ordered to develop—through "tactical experimentation"—more surprise-oriented and opportunistic squads. He will never achieve that by continuing to push the memorization of standardized methods. It is most easily done through the "bottom-up" training method in the Appendix to *Tequila Junction*. (See Figure A.1.)

This method gives every company's NCOs enough practice at initiative and tactical-decision making, while concurrently modernizing their tactical techniques. It takes no extra time to

Figure A.1: The Under-Appreciated View from the Bottom
(Source: U.S. military website within the *http://www.usafns.com/art.shtml listing, image #1-38-49.jpg*)

implement and can be wholly conducted during physical training (PT) and routine delays in the unit's regular operating schedule. In that publication's Foreword, M.Gen. Ray Smith USMC (Ret.) specifically identifies this method as being superior to what the Marines currently do. That's because no amount of "force-fed" field skills can sufficiently cultivate initiative and tactical-decision making. There are no longer any Vietnam veterans left on active duty, so no one even knows what world-class tactical technique looks like any more. To become fully capable at 3GW or 4GW, they may have to assimilate some of the same short-range maneuvers with which East Asian armies have traditionally compensated for too little firepower. Even the maneuvers of impromptu guerrillas have a better chance of surprising someone than their own.

The above-mentioned training process has already been fully tested in the active-duty establishment. It provides a painless and enjoyable way to mend a chronic problem. Its only alternative is to massively overhaul the whole bureaucratic mess. Top-down organizations tend to be the least proficient at what their lowest echelons do. Such things are difficult to admit while struggling to complete a military career. Only the exceptional few will readily admit to their beautiful mistress's flaws.

The problem is simply one of perception—"bottom-up" versus "top-down." If one's foe and lowest subordinates think "bottom-up," then failing to consider that perspective can be very costly in short-range battle. But for those who have dedicated their lives to attaining rank (whether commissioned or enlisted), there is only one acceptable way of looking at things. If they have never been personally on the receiving end of world-class technique, they have a hard time appreciating it. In the current rash of unpleasantries, *Hezbollah* special operators have nearly figured some of it out. But luckily, no Muslim militant faction has yet to discover how to assault like the German Stormtroopers of WWI. That is not true of the Asians, however. The Japanese, Red Chinese, North Koreans, and North Vietnamese have all employed a similar attack sequence since WWII. It entails concussion grenades in the midst of a mortar barrage. Until the U.S. military shifts its emphasis from "high-tech" fire superiority to minimal force, it can only marginally help with the policing of America (or any foreign country for that matter).

As for Afghanistan

Afghanistan's problems may seem more straightforward than those in Iraq, but they have yet to be solved by any occupier. Here, much of the trouble springs from Pakistani soil. Everyone knows the opium growing must stop, but there is no way to get winter wheat to market. While the North Atlantic Treaty Organization (NATO) alliance will have a better chance of succeeding with Musharraf gone, it still must contend with numerous radical elements within Pakistani society and a historically autonomous ISI. It is here that 120,000 Soviets could not get the job done after amassing the following record.[16]

• Occupying Afghanistan for 10 years.

- Losing 15,000 dead or missing and tens of thousands wounded.[17]
- Leaving a million Afghans dead and at least that many injured.[18]
- Displacing half of the Afghan population.[19]
- Facing foes who were, for the most part, not funded by drugs.

NATO forces will better succeed in Afghanistan, if they can somehow end the heroin production and associated corruption throughout the Karzai regime. With the proceeds from that heroin, the Taliban can buy everything from advanced anti-aircraft missiles to short-range-infiltration instructors. Then, keeping the supply lines open will be as hard for NATO forces as it was for the Soviets. There is a common-sense solution, but it flies squarely in the face of standard U.S. military procedure. To counteract the loss of supplies from convoy ambushes, U.S. troops must learn to live off the land—i.e., buy what they need through the local economy. There is no shortage of light-infantry wherewithal in this part of the world. Of course, that would take more attention to small-unit tactical excellence than in the past and require more delegation of authority to NCOs. And it won't make the U.S. arms and equipment manufacturers very happy either.

Because of the lack of vegetation in Afghanistan, U.S. military leaders may be tempted to stick with their "death from the sky" routine. It didn't work after Vietnam was defoliated, but neither was the same amount of aerial and satellite surveillance available at the time. It won't work now in Afghanistan because the mission is again one of counterinsurgency. A strong hand has always been needed in this part of the world, but Muslims have little respect for stand-off warfare and take considerable exception to its inevitable mistakes. Thus, "death from the sky" accomplishes little against a bottom-up organization and invariably alienates its main source of support—the overall population. All the Taliban has to do is to move around in two's and three's among the civilian populace and then mass right before an attack. Unless U.S. planners try something different soon, this wild and precipitous region could turn into as big an abyss for American forces as it was for the Russians. After all, both armies do operate in much the same way.[20]

The Taliban and Hekmatyar get manpower indirectly from two of Pakistan's largest religious parties—*JUI [Jamiat Ulema*

237

i-Islam] and *JI [Jamaat i-Islami],* respectively.[21] Yet, since early 2008, there have been more than thirty U.S. drone missile attacks against terrorist sites on Pakistani soil despite that government's complaints that they incense the overall population.[22]

America's best chance in the region necessarily involves three steps: (1) ceasing all NATO air strikes on Pakistani soil; (2) only rarely resorting to the supporting-arms crutch inside Afghanistan; and (3) establishing CAP platoons throughout the southeastern (or opium-growing) part of the latter nation. These platoons would be manned by U.S. infantrymen with special training in unconventional warfare and police procedure. Instead of "infidel" occupiers, they would be foreign-aid workers in the economic and law enforcement sectors. Whenever things got too dicey, they would disappear into the ground or temporarily revert to guerrilla tactics. The Taliban are no more tactically sophisticated than were the *mujahideen.* They would be unable to root out such well-intended and elusive aid workers. And that part of the country would stop growing the opium that funds their insurgency.

More importantly, those American CAP platoons would be shortstopping 90% of the heroin that could potentially undermine their homeland. Now that most of the Golden Triangle product has been interdicted, the Hong Kong triads will need a massive new source and unwatched new conduits to fully prey on U.S. society. That source will be Afghanistan. Its heroin will most likely flow down through Taliban-controlled Quetta to Karachi,[23] and then on to Hutchison Whampoa port facilities at Manzanillo, Ensenada, and Lazaro Cardenas, Mexico.[24] Islamabad has traditionally had such loose control over southern Pakistan that the drugs will have no trouble reaching Karachi.[25] As a backup, they can always wend their way down the new road and rail network to the Chinese naval base at Gwadar.[26] Either way, there shouldn't be any shortage of COSCO shipping. To win at 4GW, one must minimally realize the extent of the enemy alliance.

> Islam forbids the use of opium . . . but the [Afghan] militants now justify the drug production by saying it's not for domestic consumption but rather to sell abroad as part of a holy war against the West.[27]
> — McClatchy Newspapers, 10 May 2009

Appendix:
China's Takeover of Nepal

The whole thing got started about 1990 when leftist-inspired "pro-de-mocracy" demonstrations erupted on the streets of Kathmandu. To restore order, King Birendra agreed to a new democratic Constitution. While the Nepal Congress Party (NCP) then won the first democratic election, its government was soon defeated by a no-confidence motion. New elections led to the formation of a Communist regime. When it too was dissolved (presumably by the king) in 1995, the Nepal Communist Party (Maoist) began an armed insurrection in the rural areas of this mountainous nation. It was aimed at abolishing the monarchy and establishing a "people's republic."[1]

In June 2001, all but the crown prince of the ruling family were murdered, and the crown prince declared king. For over two years, the Nepalese government attempted peace talks with the rebels after declaring cease-fires. Each time, the Maoists would break the truce and resume fighting. After trying several different prime ministers, Nepal's king finally disbanded the parliament in February 2005, claiming that it wasn't doing enough to quell the Maoist revolt.[2] In November of that year, the Maoists reentered the political arena within a seven-party alliance.

> The Maoists entered into a 12-point understanding last November, committing to multiparty democracy, with the seven-party alliance that called for the current strike.[3]
> — *Christian Science Monitor,* 18 April 2006

After massive "pro-democracy" demonstrations in Kathmandu in April 2006, Nepal's king agreed to reactivate the parliament and "return executive powers to the people." On the 21st of that month, the seven-party alliance rejected the king's offer to return to the parliamentary system. Their most influential member desired nothing short of a complete end to the monarchy and all of its trappings.[4] In addition to "unconditional constituent-assembly elections,"[5] the Maoists wanted immunity from attack! To "promote unity," they curtailed all street violence and implicitly acknowledged that they had arranged the protests.[6] To capitalize on the king's initial concession, the Maoists then agreed to lift the blockades of all major highways into Kathmandu—providing the political parties were further allowed to rewrite the constitution to limit the monarchy's power.[7] At this point, the king still controlled the army. On 4 May, the Nepalese cabinet dropped all terrorism-related charges against the Communist insurgents.[8] Still, Maoist chairman Pranchanda's principal demand had not yet been met—"unconditional constituent assembly elections."[9] On 12 May, under the advice of a seven-party-alliance commission and threat of renewed violence, the Nepalese parliament finally bowed to the pressure.

> [Parliament] arrested five senior ministers of the king, restricted the rest from leaving Kathmandu, and suspended chiefs of three security agencies: the regular police, the armed police, and the central intelligence department. The parties have also indicated their intent to end the king's control over the Army.[10]
> — *Christian Science Monitor,* 15 May 2006

On 16 June 2006, the two sides signed a deal "dissolving both the parliament and rebel-run local governments" so that a new Constitution could be written and coalition government formed. The Maoists still insisted that the [10,000 man] [Nepalese People's Liberation Army] [NPLA] was the legitimate state army while the Nepalese army was the "residue of a rejected regime."[11] With the urging of probable handlers, Pranchanda next objected to the Nepalese prime minister's request for U.N. involvement in the proceedings.[12] It is as if a slow-motion coup were in progress under the guise of democratic reform. While the West was engrossed in Iran's nuclear grandstanding, China was quietly stealing the crown jewel of Southeast Asia.

Then Nepal's Maoist guerrilla war shifted into its "political phase." In November 2006, Nepalese Maoist rebels signed the "most hopeful" of three peace accords since 2001. They would be allowed to help govern the country after "locking up" their weapons.[13] Unfortunately, a mutual restriction to barracks was also part of the deal.

> The deal calls for the rebels and government forces to be confined to their bases with their weapons locked up under U.N. supervision.[14]
> — *Christian Science Monitor,* 10 November 2006

This agreement and an interim parliament containing 73 Maoists were to lay the ground work for the election of a Constituent Assembly in June of the following year. Still, confining the legitimate Nepalese forces to their barracks would do little to provide the local security that a fair election demands.[15] Pranchanda again dropped his call for a "Communist republic" and seemed ready to accept a multi-party democracy.[16] But like his counterparts in southern Africa, he was only interested in a "single-party democracy." When the interim parliament tried to appoint a few ambassadors to foreign countries without the Maoists' approval in late December 2006, Pranchanda warned of a nationwide strike.[17] This was no idle threat. His last "strike" in April—when the security forces could leave their barracks—had led to 19 days of mayhem and death.[18] Now, the "Fierce One's" bragging and excesses clearly suggested the unseen presence of a powerful and greedy mentor.

> Pranchanda . . . proclaimed that even countries arrogant with power [i.e., Western] would be forced to study Nepal's 21st-Century revolution, a mix of armed uprising and nonviolent protests. . . .
> . . . Despite the accord, their [the Maoists'] excesses, in the form of abductions, [combatant] recruiting, and forced labor, continue.[19]
> — *Christian Science Monitor*, 5 December 2006

Here "recruiting and forced labor" refer to the induction of underage soldiers into the Maoist army. Already in control of 75% of the country, the Maoists had firmly established their own courts and other governance and taxation systems in most outlying areas.[20] The parallels of this "alternative governance system" to those of Nasrallah in Lebanon and al-Sadr in Iraq are striking and quite possibly no coincidence.

In January 2007, a few Maoist leaders entered parliament under the terms of a temporary Constitution. In April, more former rebels came into the political mainstream by joining the interim government.[21]

On 3 May 2007, all Communists in Nepal's government brashly demanded the immediate dissolution of its monarchy. Unhappy with delays in the parliamentary elections that were to have decided the monarchy's fate, Pranchanda threatened more mass protests.[22] To meet the rebels' demands for taking part in the upcoming elections, the reinstalled parliament took the army away from the king and nullified provisions of the existing Constitution on 18 May. Even this was not enough for Pranchanda. He had long contended that even a ceremonial role for the monarchy "goes against the people's desire for a republic."[23] With catch phrases carefully designed to appease the West, he doggedly pursued the monarchy's total removal. In September, he repeated his demand that the monarchy be scrapped. This gave the hard-pressed incumbent leaders of Nepal an excuse to further postpone the constituent assembly elections.[24] Still, the individual freedoms of Nepal's wonderful people were very much in jeopardy.

In October 2007, the U.N.'s Secretary-General seemed totally oblivious to the unfolding tragedy. He urged Nepal's competing parties "to sink their differences to save the peace process." In December, the Nepalese parliament finally approved abolition of the monarchy as part of another peace deal with Maoists, who subsequently agreed to rejoin the government apparatus. In April 2008, Maoist rebels won the largest block of seats in elections to the new constituent assembly, but failed to achieve an outright majority.[25]

241

That constituent assembly was tasked with writing a new Constitution.[26] Two months later, the Maoist ministers resigned from the cabinet in a spat over who should become the next head of state. In July (shortly after King Gyanendra's departure), a non-Maoist became Nepal's first president. His appointment triggered a fresh political crisis, and Pranchanda announced that his party would oppose the new government.[27]

The rest is history. On 18 August 2008, "a former Maoist guerrilla was sworn in . . . as Nepal's first prime minister . . . [after being] picked . . . by a special assembly meant to write a new Constitution and double as an interim parliament."[28] One can only imagine how Pranchanda managed to fill just enough seats at the proper time to achieve what he had been seeking all those years.

Notes

SOURCE NOTES

Illustrations:

Maps on pages 10, 21, 28, 64, 79, 87, and 107 reprinted after written assurance from GENERAL LIBRARIES OF THE UNIVERSITY OF TEXAS AT AUSTIN that they are in the public domain.

Tables on pages 53 and 54 reproduced with permission of "STREET GANGS MAGAZINE." Copyright © 2009 by Streetgangs.com. All rights reserved.

Map on page 62 reproduced with permission of the POLICE FOUNDATION, Washington, D.C., and DAPHNE SAWYER. This illustration is by Daphne Sawyer while with the Fairfax County Police Department and appears in "Crime Mapping News," volume 6, issue 3, summer 2004. Copyright © 2004 by Daphne Sawyer. All rights reserved.

Pictures on pages 123, 139, 181, 183, 185, and 209 reproduced with permission of the SWEDISH ARMED FORCES and written assurance from Sorman Information/Media that the illustrator can no longer be contacted, from *Soldf: Soldaten I Falt,* by Forsvarsmakten, with illustrations by Wolfgang Bartsch. These pictures appear on pages 144, 200, 292, 301, 303, and 307 of the Swedish publication. Copyrights © 2001 by Wolfgang Bartsch. All rights reserved.

Map on page 130 reproduced after being unable to contact THE GIOI PUBLISHERS, Hanoi, from *The Ho Chi Minh Trail,* by Hoang Khoi and The Gioi. This illustration appears on page 26 of the Vietnamese publication. Copyright © 2001 by Gioi Publishers. All rights reserved.

Picture on page 152 reproduced after asking permission of
BRITISH BROADCASTING CORPORATION NEWS ONLINE,
London, from the following article(s): "SAS Storm
the Embassy." Copyright © 2000 by BBC. All rights
reserved.

Text:

244

ENDNOTES

Disclaimer

1. H. John Poole, *Tactics of the Crescent Moon: Militant Muslim Combat Methods* (Emerald Isle, NC: Posterity Press, 2004), chapt. 8; Bush Administration admission, on ABC's Nightly News, 12 April 2008.
2. H. John Poole, *Terrorist Trail: Backtracking the Foreign Fighter* (Emerald Isle, NC: Posterity Press, 2006), Introduction; ABC's Nightly News, 30 November 2008; Senior member of Gen. Petraeus' staff, on CBS's "Sixty Minutes," 22 February 2009.

Preface

1. *Encyclopedia Britannica Online* and *Wikipedia Encyclopedia,* s.v. "Vladimir Lenin" and "Red Terror."
2. "The War of the World: The Clash of Empires," PBS, 30 June 2008.
3. *Encyclopedia Britannica Online* and *Wikipedia Encyclopedia,* s.v. "Vladimir Lenin."
4. "How Many Did the Communist Regimes Murder," Univ. of Hawaii study, by R.J. Rummel.
5. "Stalin's Mass Murders Were 'Entirely Rational' Says New Russian Textbook Praising Tyrant," by Will Stewart, *Daily Mail* (London), 3 September 2008.
6. AFP-published estimate in *Twentieth Century Atlas—Death Tolls;* Jean-Louis Margolin estimate and Richard L. Walker, "The Human Cost of Communism in China," 1971 study for U.S. Congress, in *The China Threat,* by Bill Gertz (Washington, D.C.: Regnery Publishing, 2000), p. xxi; *Wikipedia Encyclopedia,* s.v. "Cultural Revolution"; R.J. Rummel, *Death by Government* (n.p., n.d.), pp. 100-101, in *China: The Gathering Threat,* by Constantine Menges (Nashville, TN: Nelson Current, 2005), p. 54.

Introduction

1. Nicholas Blandford, "Lebanon Defuses Crisis," *Christian Science Monitor,* 22 May 2008, pp. 1, 11; Andrew Lee Butters, "Welcome to Hizballahstan," *Newsweek,* 26 May 2008, pp. 30, 31.
2. ABC's Nightly News, 26 January 2006; Ramit Plushnick-Masti, AP, "Militant Groups Join Forces, Get Hezbollah Help," *Jacksonville Daily News* (NC), 28 October 2003, p. 1A.

248

3. Kim Gamel, AP, "Iraqi Cleric Orders His Forces off the Streets," *Jacksonville Daily News* (NC), 31 March 2008, pp. 1A, 6A; NPR's "Morning Edition" News, 31 March 2008.

4. "China Winning Resources and Loyalties of Africa," *The Financial Times* (UK), 28 February 2006.

5. Daniel Pepper, "Congolese Hopeful Ahead of July 30 Vote," *Christian Science Monitor,* 29 June 2006, p. 7.

6. "China's 'Comprehensive Warfare' Strategy Wears Down Enemy Using Non-Military Means," *Geostrategy-Direct,* 2 August 2006.

7. "A Former Maoist Guerrilla Was Sworn in Monday As Nepal's First Prime Minister," World News in Brief, *Christian Science Monitor,* 19 August 2008.

8. GlobalSecurity.org and *Wikipedia Encyclopedia,* s.v. "Naxalite."

9. Ibid., s.v. "West Bengal" and "Kolkata."

10. Bikash Sangraula, "Nepal's Ex-Guerrillas Take On Civilian Rule," *Christian Science Monitor,* 21 August 2008, p. 7.

11. Ibid.

12. NPR's "Morning Edition" News, 22 April 2009; "Zuma's Missing Years Come to Light," *The Times* (UK), 22 February 2009; *Wikipedia Encyclopedia,* s.v. "Jacob Zuma"; Poole, *Terrorist Trail,* pp. 17-38, 197-208, 223-246.

13. "The Congo's Killing Fields," by Kevin Clarke, *U.S. Catholic,* July 2008; "45,000 Die Each Month in Congo," World Briefs Wire Reports (AP), *Jacksonville Daily News* (NC), 23 January 2008, p. 4A.

14. "China in Angola: An Emerging Energy Partnership," by Paul Hare, Jamestown Foundation, *China Brief,* vol. 6, issue 22, 8 November 2006; "China and Angola Strengthen Bilateral Relationship," by Loro Horta, *Power and Interest News Report,* 23 June 2006.

15. *China's Rising Power in Africa,* Part 3, "China, Congo Trade for What the Other Wants," by Gwen Thompkins, NPR, 30 July 2008.

16. Ibid.

17. Scott Baldauf, "In Congo, a Doctor Keeps Helping As Victims Keep Coming," *Christian Science Monitor,* 24 October 2008, pp. 1, 11.

18. Scott Baldauf, "Congo's Riches Fuel Its War," *Christian Science Monitor,* 4 November 2008, pp. 1, 10.

19. "Two Weeks after Being Asked for Help, Angola's Government Said," World News in Brief, *Christian Science Monitor,* 13 November 2008; "Angolan, Congolese Troops Join Forces," World Briefs Wire Reports (AP), *Jacksonville Daily News* (NC), 7 November 2008.

20. "While Congo's Government Is 'Open for Dialogue' with All," World News in Brief, *Christian Science Monitor,* 5 November 2008, p. 7.

21. Scott Baldauf, "What Does Congo's Nkunda Want," *Christian Science Monitor,* 14 November 2008, p. 6; Scott Baldauf and Jina Moore, "Congo's Risky Push to Crush Rebels," *Christian Science Monitor,* 26 January 2009, p. 6.

22. "Islam in Africa Newsletter," vol. 1, no. 1, May 2006, by Moshe Terdman and Reuven Paz, Project for the Research of Islamist Movements (Israel); "Tribal Militants Claimed Responsibility for Another Attack on an Energy Installation," World News in Brief, *Christian Science Monitor,* 8 June 2006, p. 7.

23. Longtime owner of Khartoum hotel, in conversation with author on 31 May 2006; "China in Angola," by Hare; "China and Angola Strengthen Bilateral Relationship," by Loro Horta, *Power and Interest News Report,* 23 June 2006.

24. *China's Rising Power in Africa,* "Series Overview," by Didrik Schanche, NPR, 28 July 2008.

25. Ibid., Part 4, "Chinese-Built Zambian Smelter Stirs Controversy," by Ofeibea Quist-Arcton, NPR, 1 August 2008.

26. Ibid., Part 5, "Army of Shopowners Paved China's Way in Africa," by Ofeibea Quist-Arcton, NPR, 1 August 2008.

27. *Tehran's War of Terror and Its Nuclear Delivery Capability,* by Stephen E. Hughes (Victoria, Canada: Trafford Publishing, 2007), p. 151; *Wikipedia Encyclopedia,* s.v. "Panama."

28. Bill Gertz, "Chinese Military Trains in West," *Washington Times,* 15 March 2006.

29. Ibid.

30. H. John Poole, *Tequila Junction: 4th-Generation Counterinsurgency* (Emerald Isle, NC: Posterity Press, 2008), pp. 72-75; *Wikipedia Encyclopedia,* s.v. "Jacobo Arenas."

31. "Transnational Activities of Chinese Crime Organizations," by Glenn E. Curtis, Seth L. Elan, Rexford A. Hudson, and Nina A. Koll, Fed. Research Div., Library of Congress, April 2003.

32. *CIA — The World Factbook,* s.v. "China."

33. "Chavez Eyes China, Russia, More on 'Strategic'-Interest Tour," from Agence-France Presse, 20 September 2008.

34. Simon Romero, "Cocaine Trade Helps Rebels Re-ignite War in Peru," *New York Times,* 17 March 2009.

35. Sara Miller Llana, "El Salvador Joins Latin Leftward Tilt," *Christian Science Monitor,* 17 March 2009, pp. 1, 11.

36. China's State Commission of Science, Technology and Industry for National Defense, as quoted in "Chinese Military to Make Billions through Capitalism," *Geostrategy Direct,* 16 January 2008.

37. "Who Needs the Panama Canal," by Robert Morton, *Washington Times,* Nat. Weekly Ed., 1-8 March 1999, as reprinted in *World Tribune,* 4 March 1999; Adm. Alejandro Kenny, "China's Presence in Latin America: A View on Security from the Southern Cone," *Military Review,* September/October 2006; Gertz, *The China Threat,* pp. 76, 78, 80, 91, 92.

38. "Ecuador Offers Concession of Manta Air Base to China, Declines to Renew Contract with U.S.," by Vittorio Hernandez, AHN News (Ecuador), 26 November 2007.
39. Poole, *Tequila Junction,* Part One.
40. "Organized Crime Slayings More Than Double in Mexico," World Briefs Wire Reports (AP), *Jacksonville Daily News* (NC), 9 December 2008.
41. FMFM 1-3A, *A Tactical Handbook for Counterinsurgency and Police Operations,* draft copy, 12 August 2008.
42. ABC's Nightly News, 25 March 2009.

Chapter 1: *Far Too Much Foreign Activity on U.S. Soil*

1. Mark Gregory, "U.S. Under Chinese Hack Attack," *BBC News Online,* 30 April 2001; Kevin Anderson, "U.S. Fears Chinese Hack Attack," *BBC News Online,* 28 April 2001.
2. Lisa Hoffman, Scripps Howard, "Chinese Hackers," *Jacksonville Daily News* (NC), 15 June 2008, p. 6A; Gregory, "U.S. Under Chinese Hack Attack."
3. Shane Harris, "China's Cyber-Militia," *National Journal Magazine,* 31 May 2008.
4. Ibid.
5. Ibid.; "Computers Get Hacked," National Briefs Wire Reports (AP), *Jacksonville Daily News* (NC), 12 June 2008.
6. *Unrestricted Warfare, b*y Qiao Liang and Wang Xiangsu (Beijing: PLA Literature and Arts Publishing House, February 1999), FBIS translation over the internet; Jon Swartz, "Chinese Hackers Seek U.S. Access," *USA Today,* 11 March 2007; John Wagley, "Foreign Hackers are Overwhelming U.S. Government Computers, Says Analyst," *Security Management,* 19 December 2008.
7. Abdel Bari Atwan, *The Secret History of Al-Qa'ida* (London: Abacus, 2006), p. 122.
8. Harris, "China's Cyber-Militia."
9. Ibid.
10. Ibid.
11. John Wagley, "Foreign Hackers are Overwhelming U.S. Government Computers, Says Analyst," *Security Management,* 19 December 2008.
12. Richard Clarke (former U.S. antiterrorism czar), on ABC's Nightly News, 25 April 2009.
13. Bill Gertz, *The China Threat: How the People's Republic Targets America* (Washington, D.C.: Regnery Publishing, 2000), p. 12; "Power and the People," PBS's *China from the Inside,* Part I, NC Public TV, 10 January 2007; *CIA—The World Factbook,* s.v. "China."

14. "The Lobotomist," PBS's *American Experience,* NC Public TV, 16 February 2009.

15. *National Drug Threat Assessment (for) 2009,* "Heroin," NDIC, December 2008.

16. "Do I Look Dangerous to You," Part I, Partners in Crime Series, by Frederic Dannen, *The New Republic,* 14 & 21 July 1997.

17. Ibid.

18. Ibid.

19. "A Means of Maintaining Social Order," Part II, Partners in Crime Series, by Frederic Dannen, *The New Republic,* 14 & 21 July 1997; *Unrestricted Warfare, by* Liang and Xiangsu.

20. "A Means of Maintaining Social Order," by Dannen.

21. "Do I Look Dangerous to You," by Dannen.

22. Rohan Gunaratna, *Inside al-Qaeda: Global Network of Terror* (Lahore: Vanguard, 2002, pp. 164, 165; "Transnational Activities of Chinese Crime Organizations," by Curtis, et al, p. 25.

23. Al Santoli, "The Panama Canal in Transition: Threats to U.S. Security and China's Growing Role in Latin America," American Foreign Policy Council Investigative Report, 23 June 1999; Roger Faligot, *The Chinese Mafia in Europe* (Paris: Calmann-Levy, 2001), pp. 142-143, as quoted in "Transnational Activities of Chinese Crime Organizations," by Curtis, et al, p. 23.

24. Royal Canadian Mounted Police, "Beneath the Dragon's Shadow" in "Transnational Activities of Chinese Crime Organizations," by Curtis, et al, p. 24.

25. "Transnational Activities of Chinese Crime Organizations," by Curtis et al, p. 28.

26. "Asian Transnational Organize Crime and Its Impact on the United States," by James O. Finckenauer and Ko-lin Chin, U.S. Dept. of Justice Special Report, January 2007, as retrieved from its National Inst. of Justice website in September 2008.

27. "Hong Kong Triads after 1997," *Trends in Organized Crime,* vol. 8, no. 3, March 2005; *Wikipedia Encyclopedia,* s.v. "Wo Shing Wo."

28. "Transnational Activities of Chinese Crime Organizations," by Curtis et al, p. 11.

29. "Operation Hardtac," FBI Case Study, 1998, as retrieved from its website in October 2008.

30. "Transnational Activities of Chinese Crime Organizations," by Curtis et al, p. 28.

31. "Asian Organized Crime and Terrorist Activity in Canada, 1999-2002," by Neil S. Helfand, Fed. Research Div., Library of Congress, July 2003, pp. 25, 26.

32. Joshua Quittner, "The Hottest Software in Town," *Time,* 5 June 1995; *Wikipedia Encyclopedia,* s.v. "Wah Ching."

33. "Transnational Activities of Chinese Crime Organizations," by Curtis, et al, p. 27.

34. Ibid., p. 63.

35. Ibid., p. 24, 25.

36. Ibid., pp. 23.

37. Ibid., p. 26.

38. NPR's "Morning Edition" News, 5 November 2008 and 6 January 2009; NPR's "Marketplace Morning Report," 13 January 2009.

39. H. John Poole, *Dragon Days: Time for "Unconventional" Tactics* (Emerald Isle, NC: Posterity Press, October 2007), *Terrorist Trail,* and *Tequila Junction.*

Chapter 2: *More Than Just a Crime Wave*

1. Abraham Lincoln, in *American Quotations,* by Gordon Carruth and Eugene Ehrlich (New York: Wings Books, 1992), pars. 12:67, 12:68.

2. "Department of Justice Launches New Law Enforcement Strategy to Combat Increasing Threat of International Organized Crime," Dept. of Justice and FBI Press Releases, 23 April 2008, as retrieved from their websites in October 2008.

3. Peter Ford, "China's Buying Spree in Global Fire Sale," *Christian Science Monitor,* 23 February 2009, pp. 1, 11; NPR's "Marketplace Morning Report," 24 March 2009.

4. Peter Ford, "China's Economy Cools," *Christian Science Monitor,* 21 October 2008, p. 11.

5. "Russia's Economy Is Protected against a Sharp Change," World News in Brief, *Christian Science Monitor,* 21 November 2008, p. 7.

6. *Unrestricted Warfare,* by Liang and Xiangsu, pp. 191, 223 (footnote 2).

7. Ibid.

8. Poole, *Tequila Junction,* pp. xxx, 11, 117, 144.

9. Pineda Cruz, "Al-Qaeda's Unlikely Allies in Central America," in *Unmasking Terror,* vol. II, ed. Christopher Heffelfinger (Washington, D.C: Jamestown Foundation, 2006), p. 459; Robert Clifford, Head of MS-13 National Gang Task Force, as quoted in "U.S. Steps Up Battle against Salvadoran Gang MS-13," by Danna Hartman, *USA Today,* 23 February 2005; "Asian Transnational Organized Crime and Its Impact on the United States," by Finckenauer and Chin; "Gang-Related Gun Battle Kills Three in Southern Mexico," from AP, 23 September 2004.

10. *National Drug Threat Assessment (for) 2008,* "Drug Transportation," NDIC, October 2007; *National Drug Threat Assessment (for) 2009,* "National Drug Threat Summary" and "Heroin"; "Transnational Activities of Chinese Crime Organizations," by Curtis, et al, p. 23.

11. "Central America: An Emerging Role in the Drug Trade," STRATFOR Global Intelligence, 26 March 2009; NPR's "Morning Edition" News, 23 March 2009.
12. "Mexico's Drug Cartels," by Colleen W. Cook, CRS Report for Congress, Order Code RL34215 (Washington, D.C: Library of Congress, 25 February 2008, pp. CRS-8, CRS-9, CRS-13; "Mexico's Internal Drug War," Power and Interest News Report (PINR), 14 August 2006, as retrieved from its website in July 2007; *Wikipedia Encyclopedia,* s.v. "Guzman-Loera" and "Los Negros."
13. *Mexico—Country Profile for 2003,* U.S. Department of Justice, Drug Enforcement Administration, Nov. 2003; *National Drug Threat Assessment (for) 2008,* "Drug Transportation," endnote; *Wikipedia Encyclopedia,* s.v. "Joaquin Guzman-Loera," "Ismael Zambada-Garcia," "Juan Jose Esparragosa-Moreno," and "Los Negros"; "Mexico's Counter-Narcotics Efforts under Fox—December 2000 to October 2004," by Larry Stores, CRS Report for Congress, Order Code RL32669 (Washington, D.C: Library of Congress, 10 November 2004); U.S. Dept. of State website, s.v. "Ismael Zambada-Garcia"; FBI website, s.v. "Ignacio Coronel Villareal"; Alfredo Corchado and Laurence Iliff, "Ex-Rivals' Merge to 'Megacartel' Intensifies Brutality in Mexico, *Dallas Morning News,* 17 June 2008.
14. "Portrait of a Mexican Drug Lord," *CBS Online News,* 24 October 2003.
15. *National Drug Threat Assessment (for) 2008,* "Cocaine—Strategic Findings"; Ginger Thompson, "U.S. Indicts Suspected Drug Kingpin," World Briefing, *New York Times,* 28 October 2004.
16. *National Drug Threat Assessment (for) 2008,* "Drug Trafficking Organizations—Overview."
17. *Mexico—Country Profile for 2003,* "Armando Valencia Organization"; *Attorney General's Report to Congress on the Growth of Violent Street Gangs in Suburban Areas,* April 2008, "Suspected Connections between Gangs and Drug Trafficking Organizations," Appendix C, as retrieved from the NDIC website in October 2008.
18. *National Drug Threat Assessment (for) 2008,* "Heroin—Strategic Findings."
19. Ibid., "Drug Trafficking—Overview" and "Drug Trafficking Organizations—Overview."
20. Ibid.
21. "Do I Look Dangerous to You," by Dannen.
22. Santoli, "The Panama Canal in Transition."
23. "Transnational Activities of Chinese Crime Organizations," by Glenn E. Curtis, et al; "FBI Priorities," as retrieved from minneapolis.fbi.gov in August 2008.

24. *Attorney General's Report to Congress on the Growth of Violent Street Gangs in Suburban Areas,* "National-Level Street, Prison, and Outlaw Motorcycle Gang Profiles," Appendix B, as retrieved from the NDIC website in October 2008. (The original document will henceforth be cited as *Attorney General's Report.)*

25. *National Drug Threat Assessment (for) 2009,* "Drug Trafficking Organizations."

26. *Attorney General's Report,* "Gang-Drug Trafficking Organization Connections Affecting Suburban Areas."

27. Ibid., Appendix C; *Weak Bilateral Law Enforcement Presence at the U.S. / Mexico Border,* Committee on the Judiciary, U.S. House of Representatives (isbn #1422334414), 17 November 2005, pp. 11, in *Wikipedia Encyclopedia,* s.v. "Los Negros."

28. Amy O'Neill Richard, "International Trafficking in Women to the United States," Center for the Study of Intelligence, November 1999, p. 13, in "Asian Organized Crime and Terrorist Activity in Canada, 1999-2002," by Helfand, p. 16.

29. Danna Harman, "U.S. Steps Up Battle against Salvadoran Gang MS-13," *USA Today,* 23 February 2005; "National Drug Intelligence Center, ESRL Times research, n.d., map "MS-13map2.gif."

30. "The MS-13 Threat: A National Assessment," FBI Headline Archive, 14 January 2008, as retrieved from its website in October 2008.

31. "Al Qaeda Seeks Tie to Local Gangs," *Washington Times,* 28 September 2004; N.C. Aizenman, "Latino Gang Study Finds Few Links to Overseas Groups," *Washington Post,* 8 February 2007.

32. "FBI Announces Coordinated Law Enforcement Action against Gangs," FBI Press Release, 8 September 2005, as retrieved from its website in October 2008.

33. *National Gang Threat Assessment (for) 2009,* Nat. Gang Intel. Center in collaboration with NDIC, January 2009, Appendix C; Arian Campo-Flores, "MS-13," *Newsweek,* 28 March 2008.

34. "How We're Ganging Up on MS-13: And What You Can Do to Help," FBI Press Release, 13 July 2005, as retrieved from its website in October 2008.

35. "A Close-Up of MS-13: FBI Executive Visits El Salvador," FBI Headline Archive, 19 April 2006, as retrieved from its website in October 2008.

36. "Going Global on Gangs: New Partnership Targets MS-13," FBI Headline Archive, 10 October 2007, as retrieved from its website in October 2008.

37. "The MS-13 Threat: A National Assessment"; *National Gang Threat Assessment (for) 2009,* Appendix B.

38. Ibid.; "MS-13 Gang," Detention and Prevention of Violence," as retrieved from KeysToSaferSchools.com in August 2008.

39. "The Maras: A Menace to the Americas," by Frederico Breve (former Minister of Defense of Honduras), *Military Review,* July/August 2007; eMachine during January 2007, in "2008 Street Gangs Discussion on Bloods, Crips, 18th Street, MS 13 . . . ," as retrieved from streetgangs.com in August 2008.

40. *National Gang Threat Assessment (for) 2009,* "Street Gangs"; "MS-13 National Gang Task Force," powerpoint presentation, n.d., as retrieved from scm.oas.org on 11 March 2009; *Wikipedia Encyclopedia,* s.v. "18th St. Gang."

41. *Attorney General's Report,* Appendix B.

42. Ibid.; "Gangs and Drugs in the United States," NDIC, July 2003, in *National Gang Threat Assessment (for) 2005,* National Alliance of Gang Investigators Assoc., in partnership with FBI Nat. Drug. Intell. Center, n.d., p. 1.

43. "Country Profiles," *BBC News Online,* s.v. "Timeline: El Salvador"; "At Least 31 Killed in Guatemala Prison Gang War," MSNBC, 15 August 2005.

44. Pineda Cruz, "Al-Qaeda's Unlikely Allies in Central America," *Unmasking Terror,* vol. II, p. 459.

45. Harman, "U.S. Steps Up Battle against Salvadoran Gang MS-13."

46. Ibid.

47. "Nicaragua Corredor de Armas," by Elizabeth Romero, *La Prensa,* 17 April 2005; *Wikipedia Encyclopedia,* s.v. "Revolutionary Armed Forces of Colombia."

48. "America's Most Dangerous Gang—MS13—Violent, Vicious, and Spreading Fast," by Shelly Feuer Domash, *Police Magazine,* 20 February 2005.

49. Harman, "U.S. Steps Up Battle against Salvadoran Gang MS-13"; "The Maras: A Menace to America," by Breve, p. 90; "Topics: MS-13, Gangs, Illegal Immigration, Americans, Security," from AP, in *The Lexington Dispatch,* 4 April 2005.

50. "Asian Transnational Organized Crime and Its Impact on the United States," by Finckenauer and Chin, p. 137.

51. *National Gang Threat Assessment (for) 2005,* National Alliance of Gang Investigators Assoc., in partnership with FBI Nat. Drug. Intell. Center, n.d., p. 33.

52. "Drugs and Crime Gang Profile: Mara Salvatrucha," NDIC, November 2002, in "National Gang Threat Assessment (for) 2005," p. 29.

53. Ibid.

54. "Asian Organized Crime and Terrorist Activity in Canada, 1999-2002," by Helfand, in *National Gang Threat Assessment (for) 2005,* p. 3.

55. *National Gang Threat Assessment (for) 2005,* p. 2.

56. Streetgangs.com and *Wikipedia Encyclopedia,* s.v. "Wah Ching."

57. Ibid.
58. Ibid.
59. Ibid.; "Asian Gangs in Los Angeles County" and "Hispanic Gangs in Los Angeles County," as retrieved from streetgangs.com in May 2009.
60. Thomas Davidson, "Terrorism and Human Smuggling Rings . . . ," in *Unmasking Terror*, vol. III, ed. Jonathan Hutzley (Washington, D.C: Jamestown Foundation, 2007), p. 501.
61. *National Drug Threat Assessment (for) 2008*, "Illicit Finance."
62. Ibid., "Heroin—Strategic Findings."
63. "Asian Transnational Organized Crime and Its Impact on the United States," by Finckenauer and Chin, p. 13.
64. "Chinese Transnational Organized Crime: The Fuk Ching," by James O. Finckenauer, Nat. Inst. of Justice, United Nations Activities, n.d.
65. "MS-13 Gang," Detention and Prevention of Violence"; "Report: MS-13 Gang Hired to Murder Border Patrol," as retrieved from DailyBulletin.com in October 2008.
66. *National Drug Threat Assessment (for) 2008*, "Drug Transportation."
67. "Al Qaeda Seeks Tie to Local Gangs."
68. *National Drug Threat Assessment (for) 2008*, "Drug Transportation."
69. *Attorney General's Report*, "National-Level Gang-Drug Trafficking Organization Connections"; "Gangs and Drugs in the United States," NDIC, July 2003, in *National Gang Threat Assessment (for) 2005*, p. 1.
70. *Attorney General's Report*, Appendix B.
71. "History of the Mexican Mafia Prison Gang," *Police Magazine*, July 2007; "American Me," 126 min., Universal Studios, 2002, DVD, isbn #0-7832-3360-4.
72. Ibid.
73. *National Gang Threat Assessment (for) 2005*, pp. 7, 8; "Mexican Mafia: Prison Gang Profile," as retrieved from insideprison.com in May 2006; *Wikipedia Encyclopedia*, s.v. "Mexican Mafia."
74. *Attorney General's Report*, "Gang-Drug Trafficking Organization Connections Affecting Suburban Areas."
75. *National Gang Threat Assessment (for) 2005*, p. 31.
76. "The Maras: A Menace to the Americas," by Breve, p. 89; *Attorney General's Report*, "National-Level Gang-Drug Trafficking Organization Connections Affecting Suburban Areas" and Appendix C.
77. *National Gang Threat Assessment (for) 2005*, p. 9.
78. Robert Hart and Paul McNulty, as quoted in "A Reputation," by Cara Buckley, *New York Times*, 19 August 2007.
79. "History of the Mexican Mafia Prison Gang."
80. *Attorney General's Report*, Appendix B.

81. Ibid., Appendix C.

82. Ibid.

83. Ibid., Appendix B.

84. "FBI Announces Coordinated Law Enforcement Action against Gangs."

85. *National Gang Threat Assessment (for) 2005,* pp. 16, 20; "A Reputation," by Cara Buckley, *New York Times,* 19 August 2007.

86. "Mexican Mafia: Prison Gang Profile."

87. "Asian Transnational Organized Crime and Its Impact on the United States," by Finckenauer and Chin, p. 135.

88. "Asian Criminal Enterprises," FBI's Organized Crime Section, as retrieved from its website in September 2008.

89. Fas.org and *Wikipedia Encyclopedia,* s.v. "triads."

90. "Transnational Activities of Chinese Crime Organizations," by Curtis, et al, pp. 27, 28; *National Drug Threat Assessment (for) 2008,* "Southwest Border Region Drug Transportation and Homeland Security Issues."

91. Amy O'Neill Richard, "International Trafficking in Women to the United States," Center for the Study of Intelligence, November 1999, p. 14. in "Asian Organized Crime and Terrorist Activity in Canada, 1999-2002," by Helfand, p. 26.

92. "Asian Organized Crime and Terrorist Activity in Canada, 1999-2002," by Helfand, p. 1.

93. *Attorney General's Report,* "Gang-Drug Trafficking Organization Connections Affecting Suburban Areas."

94. Ibid., Appendix B.

95. Ibid., Appendix C.

96. Ibid., "National-Level Gang-Drug Trafficking Organization Connections Affecting Suburban Areas," Appendix C; *Wikipedia Encyclopedia,* s.v. "triads" and "Wo Hop To."

97. "Asian Organized Crime," Internat. Crime Threat Assessment, 2000," in "Asian Organized Crime and Terrorist Activity in Canada, 1999-2002," by Helfand, p. 25.

98. Fas.org and *Wikipedia Encyclopedia,* s.v. "List of Chinese Criminal Organizations."

99. Ibid., "Tung Group."

100. "Asian Transnational Organize Crime and Its Impact on the United States," by Finckenauer and Chin, p. 136.

101. "Chinese Transnational Organized Crime: The Fuk Ching," by Finckenauer, p. 1.

102. Ibid.

103. *National Drug Threat Assessment (for) 2009,* "Gangs."

104. "Chinese Transnational Organized Crime: The Fuk Ching," by Finckenauer, p. 3.

105. "Asian Organized Crime and Terrorist Activity in Canada, 1999-2002," by Helfand, p. 22.

106. "Transnational Activities of Chinese Crime Organizations," by Curtis, et al; Mario Daniel Montoya, "War on Terrorism Reaches Paraguay's Triple Border," p. 14, from *Inside al-Qaeda,* by Gunaratna, p. 166.

107. Rory Stewart, "How to Save Afghanistan," *Time,* 28 July 2008, p. 31.

108. *National Drug Threat Assessment (for) 2008,* "Heroin—Strategic Findings."

109. "International Operations," as retrieved from the Hutchison Whampoa website in October 2008.

110. "Fence Impacts Border Town Culture, Relationships," by Jason Beaubien, Part Five of series *The U.S.-Mexican Border: A Changing Frontier,* NPR's "Morning Edition" News, 5 December 2008.

111. *National Drug Threat Assessment (for) 2008,* "National Drug Threat Summary."

Chapter 3: *Too Much for U.S. Police to Handle?*

1. "Successes in the Fight Against Drugs," DEA New Release, March 2008.

2. Lisa Hoffman, Scripps Howard, "Cocaine Use Is on the Rise in the U.S.," *Jacksonville Daily News* (NC), 1 November 2007, p. 4A; ABC's Nightly News, 5 July 2008.

3. Stewart, "How to Save Afghanistan," p. 31.

4. *Crime Mapping News,* Police Foundation, vol. 6, issue 3, Summer 2004, p. 1.

5. "Highlights of the 2006 National Youth Gang Survey," as retrieved from the Institute for Intergovernmental Research website in October 2008.

6. *National Gang Threat Assessment (for) 2009,* "National Gang Threat Summary."

7. "Fact Sheet: Department of Justice Comprehensive Efforts to Fight Gang Violence," U.S. Dept. of Justice, 24 June 2008, as retrieved from its website in October 2008.

8. Santoli, "The Panama Canal in Transition"; Gertz, *The China Threat,* p. 94.

9. "Mexico's Internal Drug War"; "International Operations."

10. "Department of Justice Launches New Law Enforcement Strategy to Combat Increasing Threat of International Organized Crime."

11. Leslie Miller, "Cross-Border Trucking Plan Draws Criticism," from AP, 24 February 2007; Mark Stevenson, "Mexico Protests U.S. Decision to End Mexican Truck Program by Raising Tariffs on U.S. Goods," from AP, 16 March 2009.

12. *National Drug Threat Assessment (for) 2008,* "Cocaine—Strategic Findings."

13. "Probation and Parole in the United States, 2006," Revised Bureau of Justice Statistics Bulletin #NCJ220218, by Lauren E. Glaze and Thomas P. Bonczar, U.S. Dept. of Justice, 2 July 2008, p. 2, from *Wikipedia Encyclopedia,* s.v. "Incarceration in the United States"; "Correctional Populations," U.S. Dept of Justice, Bureau of Justice Statistics, as retrieved from its website in October 2008.

14. "World Prison Population List," seventh ed. (October 2006), by Roy Walmsley, King's College London, International Centre for Prison Studies, as retrieved from the Australian Government's Institute of Criminology website in October 2008; "One in 100: Behind Bars in America 2008," The Pew Center on the States, and "New Incarceration Figures," The Sentencing Project: Research and Advocacy for Reform, 2006, both from *Wikipedia Encyclopedia,* s.v. "Incarceration in the United States."

15. "California's Growing Prison Crisis," by Sonja Steptoe, *Time,* 21 June 2007; "California's Crisis in Prison Systems a Threat to Public Longer Sentences and Less Emphasis on Rehabilitation Create Problems," by John Pomfret, *Washington Post,* 11 June 2006, p. A03.

16. Mark Sappenfield and Anand Gopal, "Rise in Crime, Kidnapping, Tops Afghan's Worries," *Christian Science Monitor,* 25 November 2008, p. 5; Poole, *Tequila Junction,* chaps. 2, 6, and 8.

17. *National Drug Threat Assessment (for) 2008,* "Drug Trafficking Organizations—Overview."

18. *Attorney General's Report,* "Appendix C"; *National Gang Threat Assessment (for) 2009,* "Street Gangs."

19. Ibid., "National-Level Gang-Drug Trafficking Organization Connections."

20. *National Drug Threat Assessment (for) 2008,* "Cocaine—Strategic Findings"; *Attorney General's Report,* "National-Level Gang-Drug Trafficking Organization Connections."

21. "Los Angeles International Chiefs of Police Summit on Transnational Gangs," DEA Press Release, 3 March 2008, as retrieved from its website in October 2008.

22. "Hispanic Gangs in Los Angeles County," as retrieved from streetgangs.com in May 2009.

23. "Asian Gangs in Los Angeles County," as retrieved from streetgangs.com in May 2009.

24. *National Gang Threat Assessment (for) 2005,* p. 33.

25. *Crime Mapping News,* p. 2.

26. *National Drug Threat Assessment (for) 2008,* "Southwest Border Region Drug Transportation and Homeland Security Issues"; *Wikipedia Encyclopedia,* s.v. "Mexican Mafia."

27. *National Drug Threat Assessment (for) 2008,* "Drug Trafficking Organizations."

28. "Suspected Gang Members Arrested in North Carolina," CNN, 24 July 2008.

29. "Topics: MS-13, Gangs, Illegal Immigration, Americans, Security, NC," from AP, in *Lexington Dispatch,* 4 April 2005.

30. "National Youth Gang Center Related Articles," Inst. for Intergovernmental Research, from its website's "state-by-state" listing.

31. *National Drug Threat Assessment (for) 2008,* "Drug Trafficking Organizations."

32. Ibid., "Southwest Border Region Drug Transportation and Homeland Security Issues."

33. *Truth Be Tolled,* Turf Special Edition, by William H. Molina, Storm Pictures LLC, 2008, 99 minutes, DVD # 7-44773-0133-2.

34. *National Drug Threat Assessment (for) 2008,* "Drug Trafficking Organizations."

35. Lt. Fred Leland, Walpole Police Dept., in telephone conversation with author on 20 November 2008.

36. "Cities in Which Mexican DTOs Operate within the United States," NDIC, Situation Report #2008-S0787-005, 11 April 2008.

37. *Attorney General's Report,* "Appendix C" and "National-Level Gang-Drug Trafficking Organization Connections"; *National Gang Threat Assessment (for) 2005,* p. 1; *Wikipedia Encyclopedia,* s.v. "Los Negros."

38. "The Maras: A Menace to the Americas," by Breve, p. 89; *Attorney General's Report,* "National-Level Gang-Drug Trafficking Organization Connections Affecting Suburban Areas" and "Appendix C."

39. Max G. Manwaring, "Street Gangs: The New Urban Insurgency" (Carlisle, PA: U.S. Army Strategic Studies Inst., March 2005), pp. 13, 14.

40. "Ex-Crime Chief Arrested in Mexico," *BBC News on Line,* 21 November 2008.

41. "Top Mexico Police Officer Resigns," *BBC News on Line,* 2 November 2008.

42. "Attorney General Mukasey Announces Charges against Los Angeles Gang Members and the Formation of an Additional Safe Streets Task Force to Combat Gang Violence," DEA Press Release, 26 March 2008.

43. Lomi Kriel, "SAPD to Get $557,000 to Fight Gangs," *San Antonio Metro,* 30 October 2008, pp. 1B, 5B.

44. *Attorney General's Report,* "Executive Summary."

45. Manwaring, "Street Gangs: The New Urban Insurgency," pp. 13, 14.

Chapter 4: *Border Crisis Too Big for Govt. Agencies*

1. "Transnational Activities of Chinese Crime Organizations," by Curtis, et al, p. 23.
2. "New York Drug Threat Assessment (for) 2002," NDIC, n.d., as retrieved from the NDIC website in October 2008.
3. "Mexico's Internal Drug War," by Sam Logan, *Power and Interest News Report (PINR)*, 14 August 2006; *National Drug Threat Assessment (for) 2008*, "Drug Transportation."
4. Arian Campo-Flores and Monica Campbell, "Bloodshed on the Border," *Newsweek*, 8 December 2008, pp. 50-54.
5. Danelo, *The Border*, p. 186.
6. "Economy, Drug Wars Hurt Cross-Border Business," by Jason Beaubien, Part Four of series *The U.S.-Mexican Border: A Changing Frontier*, NPR's "Morning Edition" News, 4 December 2008; Campo-Flores and Campbell, "Bloodshed on the Border," pp. 50-54.
7. David J. Danelo, *The Border: Exploring the U.S.-Mexican Divide* (Mechanicsburg, PA: Stackpole Books, 2008), pp. 47, 63; *National Drug Threat Assessment (for) 2008*, "Drug Transportation."
8. Gerardi Ruiz Mateos (Mexico's Economy Secretary), as quoted in "Mexico Protests U.S. Decision to End Mexican Truck Program by Raising Tariffs on U.S. Goods," by Mark Stevenson, from AP, 16 March 2009.
9. Jerome R. Corsi, "Premeditated Merger: Mexican Trucks to Enter U.S. in 15 Seconds," *World Net Daily*, 17 April 2007.
10. Danelo, *The Border*, pp. 58, 63
11. Press Release, U.S. Immigration and Customs Enforcement, n.d., in *The Border*, by Danelo, p. 102.
12. Danelo, *The Border*, pp. 63, 64.
13. "Fence Impacts Border Town Culture, Relationships," by Beaubien; Davidson, "Terrorism and Human Smuggling Rings . . . ," *Unmasking Terror*, vol. III, p. 501; "Vias Ferreas de la Republica Mexicana," Instituto Nationale de Estadistica, from Univ. of Texas at Austin library, map designator "railroads.gif."
14. Fly2houston.com and *Wikipedia Encyclopedia*, s.v. "George Bush Intercontinental Airport."
15. Memorandum for the record by H.J. Poole.
16. Danelo, *The Border*, pp. 50-55.
17. Ibid., pp. 49, 50.

18. Ibid., p. 207.

19. Ibid., pp. 74, 75.

20. Ibid., p. 94.

21. Ibid. pp. 104, 105.

22. Poole, *Tequila Junction,* pp. 129, 130; *Wikipedia Encyclopedia,* s.v. "Pablo Acosta" and "Amado Carrillo Fuentez."

23. Danelo, *The Border,* pp. 108, 109.

24. Ibid., pp. 112-113, 124-129.

25. Ibid., pp. 131-153.

26. "Deported Immigrants Struggle to Re-Enter U.S." and "Agents Use High- and Low-Tech Tracking at Border," by Jason Beaubien, Parts Two and Three, *The U.S.-Mexican Border: A Changing Frontier,* NPR's "Morning Edition" News, 2-3 December 2008; "Economy, Drug Wars Hurt Cross-Border Business," by Beaubien; "Mexico's Drug Cartels," by Cook, p. CRS-8; *National Drug Threat Assessment (for) 2008,* "Drug Transportation," endnote.

27. Danelo, *The Border,* pp. 163-170.

28. Memorandum for the record by H.J. Poole.

29. *Attorney General's Report,* "Number of Street Gang Members along the U.S.-Mexico Border," Appendix E.

30. Danelo, *The Border,* p. 208.

31. Sara Miller Lhana, "As Mexico's Drug War Rages, Military Takes Over for Police," *Christian Science Monitor,* 5 December 2008, pp. 1, 12.

32. Ibid.

33. "Drug Deaths, Violence Plague Border in Tijuana," by Jason Beaubien, Part One, *The U.S.-Mexican Border: A Changing Frontier,* NPR's "Morning Edition" News, 1 December 2008.

34. *Attorney General's Report,* "Executive Summary."

35. "Drug Deaths, Violence Plague Border in Tijuana," by Beaubien.

36. "Mexicali Called Hub for Smuggling Chinese into the United States," *Geostrategy-Direct,* 22 February 2005; "Smuggled Chinese Travel Circuitously," by Irene Jay Liu, NPR's "Morning Edition" News, 20 November 2007; "Terror Hoax Uncovers Border Threat," by David Hancock, CBS's Online News, 7 February 2005.

37. "Mexicali Called Hub for Smuggling Chinese into the United States."

38. "Smuggled Chinese Travel Circuitously," by Irene Jay Liu, NPR's "Morning Edition" News, 20 November 2007; Santoli, "The Panama Canal in Transition."

39. Joe Cummings, "Mexicali's Chinatown," as retrieved from url, http://www.cpamedia.com/history/sharks_fin_tacos/on 25 October 2008, in Wikipedia Encyclopedia, s.v. "Mexicali."

40. Poole, *Dragon Days,* p. 310.
41. T.J. Bonner, Border Patrol Union President, as quoted in *The Border,* by Danelo, p. 191.
42. David von Drehe, "A New Line in the Sand," *Time,* 30 June 2008, p. 34; Danelo, *The Border,* chapt. 9.
43. "Tunnels beneath U.S. Borders Proliferation," Federation of American Scientists (Washington, D.C.), as posted and retrieved from their website, fas.org, on 23 February 2009.
44. "7 Large Tunnels Beneath U.S.-Mexican Border Raising Security Concerns," *Fox Online News,* 30 January 2007; Randal C. Archibold, "Officials Find Drug Tunnel With Surprising Amenities," *New York Times,* 27 January 2006.
45. "Agencies Work Together to Find More Tunnels in Arizona," U.S Border Patrol News Release, 16 December 2008.
46. Ibid.
47. Danelo, *The Border,* p. 157.
48. "Statistics on Mexican Army Incursions," El Paso Intelligence Center, 2005, in *The Border,* by Danelo, p. 193.
49. Danelo, *The Border,* p. 193.
50. "Country Profile: Mexico," Library of Congress, Fed. Research Div., July 2006.
51. Photograph caption, in "A Model Counterinsurgency: Uribe's Colombia (2002-2006)," by Thomas A. Marks," *Military Review,* March-April 2007, p. 42; *Tequila Junction,* by Poole, p. 192.
52. Danelo, *The Border,* p. 206.
53. CBS's "Sixty Minutes," 22 February 2009.
54. Campo-Flores and Campbell, "Bloodshed on the Border," p. 53.

Chapter 5: *The 4GW Policing Requirement*

1. William S. Lind, in a letter to the author on 9 May 2009.
2. Stewart, "How to Save Afghanistan," p. 31.
3. ABC's Nightly News, 16 April 2009.
4. "Grisly Slayings Are Bringing Mexican Drug War to the U.S.," from AP, *Jacksonville Daily News* (NC), 19 April 2009, pp. A1, A7.
5. Lisa Hoffman, Scripps Howard, "Cocaine Use Is on the Rise in the U.S.," *Jacksonville Daily News* (NC), 1 November 2007, p. 4A; ABC's Nightly News, 5 July 2008.
6. Max Hastings, *The Korean War* (New York: Touchstone, 1987), p. 196; *Wikipedia Encyclopedia,* s.v. "Operation Ripper" and "Matthew Bunker Ridgway."
7. Memorandum for the record by H.J. Poole.
8. Danelo, *The Border,* chapt. 3.

Chapter 6: *Law Enforcement Not Military's Job in Past*

1. Sam Dagher, "Baghdad Safer, But It's a Life behind Walls," *Christian Science Monitor,* 10 December 2007, pp. 1, 11.
2. Sam Dagher, "Baghdad Strategy: 'Preserve Gains'," *Christian Science Monitor,* 30 January 2008, p. 6.
3. Poole, *Tequila Junction,* p. 163.
4. *Korea—the Unknown War* (London: Thames TV in assoc. with WGBH Boston, 1990), "An Entirely New War" segment, PBS, NC Public TV, n.d. [The source documentary will henceforth be cited as *Korea—the Unknown War.]*
5. Hastings, *The Korean War,* p. 196.
6. "An Entirely New War," *Korea—the Unknown War.*
7. Brig.Gen. Edwin Simmons USMC (Ret.), in "An Entirely New War," *Korea—the Unknown War.*
8. PFC Win Scott, as quoted in *The Korean War: Pusan to Chosin, An Oral History,* by Donald Knox (San Diego: Harcourt Brace Jovanovich, 1985), p. 291.
9. "North Korea Handbook," *PC-2600-6421-94* (Washington, D.C.: U.S. Dept. of Defense, 1994), p. 3-91.
10. Smith, "Triumph in the Philippines," pp. 259-260; Connaughton, et al, "The Battle for Manila," p. 109; "37th Div. Report after Action," p. 45; and Frankel, "The 37th Infantry Division in World War II," p. 27; in "The Battle of Manila," by Thomas M. Huber (Ft. Leavenworth, KS: Combat Studies Inst., U.S. Army Cmd. & Gen. Staff College, n.d.).
11. Rt.Hon. George Younger M.P., future British Defense Minister (then member of Argyll & Southern Highlanders), in "An Entirely New War," *Korea—the Unknown War.*
12. R.W. Thompson, *Daily Telegraph,* as quoted in *The Korean War,* by Hastings, p. 112.
13. H. John Poole, *The Tiger's Way: A U.S. Private's Best Chance for Survival* (Emerald Isle, NC: Posterity Press, 2003), p. 292.
14. "Many Roads to War," *Korea—the Unknown War.*
15. Gregory Henderson, U.S. Vice Counsel to Korea 1948-1950, in "Many Roads to War," *Korea—the Unknown War.*
16. "An Arrogant Display of Strength," *Korea—the Unknown War.*
17. Chung Il-Wan, S. Korean Constabulary, in "An Arrogant Display of Strength," *Korea—the Unknown War.*
18. Www.korean-war.com, s.v. "South Korean Army."
19. Ibid. and *Wikipedia Encyclopedia,* s.v. "The Jeju Uprising."
20. Bert Hardy, photographer for the *Picture Post,* in "There is No Substitute for Victory," *Korea—the Unknown War.*

21. Memorandum for the record by H.J. Poole.
22. *Guatemala* (N.p.: Lonely Planet Publications, 2007), history section.
23. Simon Watts, "Guatemala Secret Files Uncovered," *BBC News Online,* 5 December 2005.
24. Lt.Col. Robert W. Lamont, "'Urban Warrior'—A View from North Vietnam," *Marine Corps Gazette,* April 1999, p. 33.
25. Rod Nordland, "Al-Sadr Strikes," *Newsweek,* 10 April 2006, pp. 45-47; ABC's Nightly News, 26 March 2006.
26. Max Boot, Frederick Kagan, and Kimberly Kagan, "How to Surge the Taliban," Op-Ed piece, *New York Times,* 13 March 2009.

Chapter 7: *Modern Infantrymen Need Police Training*

1. "East Turkestan Islamic Movement (ETIM)," by Seva Gunitskiy, Center for Defense Info., 9 December 2002; *Wikipedia Encyclopedia,* s.v. "East Turkestan Islamic Movement (ETIM)"; *Washington Post,* 27 August 2002, in *Tide of Terror: America, Islamic Extremism, and the War on Terror,* by Carl Hammer (Boulder, CO: Paladin Press, 2003), p. 485.
2. *MSN Encarta Encyclopedia,* s.v. "Geneva Conventions"; *Wikipedia Encyclopedia,* s.v. "Geneva Conventions" and "Protocol I."
3. Ibid.
4. Ibid.
5. *MSN Encarta Encyclopedia,* s.v. "Geneva Conventions"; *Wikipedia Encyclopedia,* s.v. "Geneva Conventions" and "Protocol II"; "Protocol Additional to the Geneva Conventions of 12 August 1949, and Relating to the Protection of Victims of Non-International Armed Conflicts (Protocol II), 8 June 1977," Internat. Humanitarian Law—Treaties and Documents, Internat. Red Cross, n.d.
6. Ibid., list of Protocol II signatories, as retrieved from the following url: http://www.icrc.org/ihl.nsf/WebSign?ReadForm&id=475&ps=P.

Chapter 8: *Foiling Foe's Resupply and Reinforcement*

1. David Kilcullen, *The Accidental Guerrilla* (Oxford: Oxford Univ. Press, 2009), in "How is Afghanistan Different from Al Anbar," by Carter Malkasian and Gerald Meyerle (N.p.: CNA Analysis and Solutions, 14 February 2009), p. 3.

2. Wright and Baker, "Iraq, Jordan See Threat to Election from Iran," *Washington Post,* 8 December 2004, p. A01; Annia Ciezadlo, "Intrigue, Power Plays as Iraq Campaign Season Starts," *Christian Science Monitor,* 16 December 2004; "Iraq's Most Feared Terror Chief Declared a Fierce War on Democracy," World News in Brief, *Christian Science Monitor,* 24 January 2005, p. 20.

3. ABC's Morning News, 14 December 2005.

4. CBS's "Sixty Minutes," 1 March 2009.

5. Eric Hammel, *Fire in the Streets: The Battle for Hue, Tet 1968* (Pacifica, CA: Pacifica Press, 1991), p. 29.

6. "Probable Cause," Congressional Research Service Memorandum, 30 January 2006, as retrieved from www.fas.org on 12 March 2009.

7. Memorandum for the record by H.J. Poole.

8. Ibid.

9. Hoang Khoi and The Gioi, *The Ho Chi Minh Trail* (Vietnam: The Gioi Publishers, 2001), "Truong Son Network of Strategic Routes: 1973-75" map, p. 70.

10. Memorandum for the record by H.J. Poole.

11. Ibid.

12. Texas resident, in telephone conversation with author in late 2008.

13. "Nicaragua Corredor de Armas," by Elizabeth Romero, *La Prensa,* 17 April 2005; *Wikipedia Encyclopedia,* s.v. "Revolutionary Armed Forces of Colombia"; "DEA Boosts Its Role in Paraguay," by Jack Sweeney, *Washington Times,* 21 August 2001.

Chapter 9: *Civilian-Saving Attack on a Building*

1. *Patterns of Global Terrorism, 2003* (Washington, D.C.: U.S. Dept. of State, April 2004); Amir Mir, *The True Face of Jihadis* (Lahore: Mashal Books, 2004), pp. 95,96, 103; Mariane Pearl, *A Mighty Heart: The Inside Story of the Al Qaeda Kidnapping of Danny Pearl* (New York, Scribner, 2003), pp. 72-74.

2. "Smoking Al Qaeda Out of Karachi," by B. Raman, South Asia Analysis Group, Paper No. 519, 14 September 2002; "Dawood Gang Provided Logistics to Lashkar Militants," Press Trust of India, NDTV website (Mumbai), 29 November 2008; *Wikipedia Encyclopedia,* s.v. "Dawood Ibrahim"; "Dawood's Drug Net Financed 26/11: Russian Intelligence," NDTV website (Mumbai), 18 December 2008; Craig Whitlock and Karen DeYoung, "Attributes Suggest Outside Help," *Washington Post,* 28 November 2008, p. 1.

3. James S. Milford (former Deputy Administrator of the DEA), in *Tehran's Wars of Terror,* by Hughes, p. 200.

4. Sudip Mazumdar, "Captors of the Liberated Zone," *Newsweek*, 18 May 2009, Maoist activity map on p. 43.

5. "Terrorist Attacks in Mumbai, India, and Implications for U.S. Interests," by Alan Kronstadt, CRS Report R40087 (Washington, D.C.: Library of Congress, 19 December 2008); Ramola Talwar Badam, "10 Young Men Started Mumbai's 60 Hours of Terror," from AP, 30 November 2008; "Mumbai Coordinated Shootings," *Significant Terrorist Event Report*, vol. 1.2, 26 November 2008, as retrieved from www.intelcenter.com (Alexandria, VA) in December 2008.

6. "Mumbai Terrorist Amped Up on Steroids, Amphetamines," by Richard Esposito, *ABC Online News*, 5 December 2008; "Terrorist Attacks in Mumbai, India, and Implications for U.S. Interests," by Kronstadt; "Transcript: Mumbai Gunmen Were Commanded by Phone," from AP, 7 January 2009; "Five Mumbai Terrorists May Have Escaped Capture," *Fox Online News*, 1 December 2008; ABC's Nightly News, early December 2008.

7. "Five Mumbai Terrorists May Have Escaped Capture," *Fox Online News*, 1 December 2008

8. "Mumbai Terrorist Amped Up on Steroids, Amphetamines," by Esposito.

9. Craig Whitlock and Karen DeYoung, "Attributes Suggest Outside Help," *Washington Post*, 28 November 2008, p. 1.

10. "Dawood Gang Provided Logistics to Lashkar Militants," Press Trust of India, NDTV website (Mumbai), 29 November 2008.

11. Ravi Nessman, AP, "Gunmen Tied to Pakistan," *Jacksonville Daily News* (NC), 1 December 2008, pp. 1A, 2A.

12. Ramola Talwar Badam, "10 Young Men Started Mumbai's 60 Hours of Terror," from AP, 30 November 2008.

13. Rajdeep Sardesai, "26/11: Terror Comes Precariously Close," from Reuters. 5 December 2008.

14. "Five Mumbai Terrorists May Have Escaped Capture."

15. "Blueprint on a Brilliant Raid," by Steve Macko, *ENN Daily Intel. Rpt.*, vol. 3, no. 114, 24 April 1997; *Wikipedia Encyclopedia*, s.v. "Japanese embassy hostage crisis."

16. "Blueprint on a Brilliant Raid," by Macko.

17. *Wikipedia Encyclopedia*, s.v. "Japanese embassy hostage crisis."

18. Steve Macko, "Day 3 of the Peru Hostage Crisis," Emergency Net News Service, 19 December 1996, in *Wikipedia Encyclopedia*, s.v. "Japanese embassy hostage crisis."

19. "Blueprint on a Brilliant Raid," by Macko; *Wikipedia Encyclopedia*, s.v. "Japanese embassy hostage crisis."

20. Ibid.; "Peruvian President Shows Model of Japanese Residence," *BBC News Online*, 11 December 1997.

21. "Peruvian President Shows Model of Japanese Residence."

22. *Wikipedia Encyclopedia*, s.v. "Japanese embassy hostage crisis."

23. "Blueprint on a Brilliant Raid," by Macko.
24. DIA Intel. Info. Rpt., 10 June 1997, in *Wikipedia Encyclopedia,* s.v. "Japanese embassy hostage crisis."
25. Lamont, "Urban Warrior—A View from North Vietnam," p. 33.
26. "Peru Hostage Crisis Comes to a Violent End," by Steve Macko, *ENN Daily Intel. Rpt.,* vol. 3, no. 113, 23 April 1997.
27. "Blueprint on a Brilliant Raid," by Macko.
28. "Fujimori-Cerpa, A Test of Wills," by Steve Macko, *ENN Daily Intel. Rpt.,* vol. 3, no. 112, 22 April 1997.
29. "Blueprint on a Brilliant Raid," by Macko; *Wikipedia Encyclopedia,* s.v. "Japanese embassy hostage crisis."
30. Bill D. Ross, *Iwo Jima: Legacy of Valor* (New York: Vintage, 1986), p. 333; Col. Joseph H. Alexander, *Closing In: Marines in the Seizure of Iwo Jima,* Marines in World War II Commemorative Series (Washington, D.C.: Hist. & Museum Div., HQMC, 1994), p. 46.
31. "SAS Storm the Embassy" and "Six Days of Fear," Siege at the Iranian Embassy series, *BBC News Online,* 26 April 2000; "Blueprint on a Brilliant Raid," by Macko; Jon E. Lewis, *SAS Combat Handbook* (London: Lyons Press, 2002), pp. 275-282.
32. Leroy Thompson, *Hostage Rescue Manual: Tactics of the Counter-Terrorist Professionals* (London: Greenhill Books, 2006), pp. 111, 132.
33. Ibid., p. 133.
34. Ibid.
35. Ibid., pp. 91, 99, 123.
36. Ibid., pp. 22, 23.
37. Ibid., pp. 25, 107, 108.
38. Ibid., p. 14.
39. Ibid., p. 173.
40. Ibid., p. 111.
41. Ibid., p. 41, 72.
42. Ibid., pp. 97-99.
43. Ibid., p. 62.
44. Ibid., p. 133.
45. Ibid., pp. 20, 74, 116, 130.
46. Ibid., pp. 74, 76.
47. Ibid., p. 73.
48. Ibid., pp. 73, 130-134.
49. Ibid., pp. 75, 133.
50. Ibid., p. 24.
51. Ibid., p. 15.
52. Memorandum for the record by H.J. Poole.
53. Mark V. Lonsdale, *Raids: A Tactical Guide to High Risk Warrant Service* (Los Angeles: Spec. Tactical Training Unit, 2005), p. 10.
54. Ibid., pp. 67, 97.

55. Ibid., pp. 96, 100, 104.
56. Ibid., pp. 12, 69.
57. Ibid., pp. 84, 160.
58. Ibid., pp. 118, 161.
59. Ibid., p. 161.
60. Ibid. p. 188.
61. Ibid., pp. 70-75.
62. Ibid., p. 86.
63. Ibid., p. 92.
64. Ibid., p. 48.
65. Ibid., p. 90.
66. Ibid., p. 11.
67. Ibid., p. 11.
68. Ibid, p. 84.
69. Ibid., pp. 92, 93.
70. Ibid., p. 92.
71. Ibid., pp. 86. 91.
72. Ibid., p. 92.
73. Ibid., p. 70.
74. Keith William Nolan, *Operation Buffalo: USMC Fight for the DMZ* (New York: Dell Publishing, 1991), pp. 76-79.
75. David H. Hackworth and Julie Sherman, *About Face* (New York: Simon & Schuster, 1989), p. 594.
76. Michael Lee Lanning and Dan Cragg, *Inside the VC and the NVA: The Real Story of North Vietnam's Armed Forces* (New York: Ivy Books, 1992), pp. 211, 212; H. John Poole, *One More Bridge to Cross: Lowering the Cost of War* (Emerald Isle, NC: Posterity Press, 1999), chapt. 11.
77. Poole, *The Tiger's Way,* table 2.2; Poole, *Dragon Days,* fig. 16.8.
78. Attributed to Rodney Walker.

Chapter 10: *Collateral-Damage-Free Defense*

1. Anne Gearan, AP, "Gates Sees Limit on Force in Afghanistan," *Jacksonville Daily News* (NC), 28 January 2009, pp. 1A, 2A.
2. Maj. Scott R. McMichael, "The Chinese Communist Forces in Korea," in "A Historical Perspective on Light Infantry," *Leavenworth Research Survey No. 6* (Ft. Leavenworth, KS: Combat Studies Inst., U.S. Army Cmd. & Gen. Staff College, 1987), p. 70.
3. *Night Movements,* trans. and preface by C. Burnett (Port Townsend, WA: Loompanics Unlimited, n.d.), originally published as Japanese training manual (Tokyo: Imperial Japanese Army, 1913), p. 73.

4. Lt.Col. Whitman S. Bartley, *Iwo Jima: Amphibious Epic* (Washington, D.C.: Hist. Branch, HQMC, 1954), p. 140; Memorandum for the record by H.J. Poole.
5. Bruce I. Gudmundsson, *Stormtrooper Tactics: Innovation in the German Army, 1914-1918* (Westport, CT: Praeger Pubs., 1989), p. 94.
6. H. John Poole, *Phantom Soldier: The Enemy's Answer to U.S. Firepower* (Emerald Isle, NC: Posterity Press, 2001), p. 37.
7. Lanning and Cragg, *Inside the VC and the NVA*, pp. 206-208.

Chapter 11: *Using Basic-Service Volunteers*

1. Organizational White Paper, published at the start of U.S. counterinsurgency operations in Iraq (Camp Pendleton, CA: I MEF, n.d.).
2. NPR's "Morning Edition" News, 23 February 2009; "Wushu & Sanda," *Fight Quest*, Discovery Channel, 28 December 2008.
3. ABC's Nightly News, 12 February 2009.
4. Joseph S. Bermudez, Jr., *North Korean Special Forces* (Annapolis: Naval Inst. Press, 1998), p. 147.
5. Dagher, "Baghdad Safer, But It's a Life Behind Walls," pp. 1, 11; Dagher, "Baghdad Strategy: 'Preserve Gains'," p. 6.
6. Nordland, "Al-Sadr Strikes," pp. 45-47; ABC's Nightly News, 26 March 2006.
7. "Colombia's Civil War," PBS's *Online News Hour*, 2003.
8. The Memorial Inst. for the Prevention of Terrorism (MIPT) Knowledge Base, s.v. "FARC."
9. Paul M. Walters, "Community Oriented Policing," *FBI Law Enforcement Bulletin*, vol. 62, issue 11, November 1993, in FMFM 1-3A, pp. 9, 10.
10. "Nations Hospitable to Organized Crime and Terrorism," by LaVerle Berry, Glenn E. Curtis, John N. Gibbs, Rex A. Hudson, Tara Karacan, Nina Kollars, and Ramon Miro, Fed. Research Div., Library of Congress, October 2003, p. 171.
11. "Country Profiles," *BBC News Online*, s.v. "Nicaragua" and "Timeline: Nicaragua."
12. Chief William Bratton, "Returning the Alvarado Corridor/MacArthur Park to the Community," Press Conference, 11 March 2004, in FMFM 1-3A, pp. 8, 9.
13. Brig.Gen. L. D. Nicholson, USMC, "Distributed Operations in the Current Operating Environment," Expeditionary Warfare School Lecture, Quantico, VA, February 2008, in FMFM 1-3A, p. 20.
14. Guardianangels.org and *Wikipedia Encyclopedia*, s.v. "Guardian Angel."

15. C.G. Lynch, "Three Things the CIA Learned about Implementing an Enterprise Wiki," *CIO Magazine,* 10 June 2008; *Wikipedia Encyclopedia,* s.v. "wiki" and "Intellipedia."

16. Major Greg Thiele, Expeditionary Warfare School Lecture, Quantico, VA, 29 February 2008, in FMFM 1-3A, p. 19.

17. James Glanz, "The Conflict in Iraq," *New York Times,* 21 February 2005.

18. "Iran Role in the Recent Uprising in Iraq," Special Dispatch No. 692, 9 April 2004, from Middle East Media Research Inst.

19. Scott Baldauf, "Sadr Loyalty Grows, Even as Sistani Returns," *Christian Science Monitor,* 26 August 2004, p. 6.

20. "Colombia's Most Powerful Rebels," *BBC News on Line,* 19 September 2003.

21. "Colombia's Civil War," PBS's *Online News Hour,* 2003.

22. Www.archives.gov and *Wikipedia Encyclopedia,* s.v. "Civilian Conservation Corps."

23. Pope John Paul II, *Crossing the Threshold of Hope* (New York: Alfred A. Knopf, 1995), pp. 205, 206.

24. Gen. Akhtar Rehman, Pakistani ISI Head, as quoted in *The Silent Soldier: The Man Behind the Afghan Jehad,* by Brigadier Mohammad Yousaf, (South Yorkshire, UK: Pen & Sword Books, n.d.).

25. ABC's Morning News, early 2006.

26. "U.N.: Fifth of the World Lacks Clean Water," World Brief Wire Reports (AP), *Jacksonville Daily News* (NC), 7 March 2006, p. 7A.

27. Memorandum for the record by H.J. Poole; *Wikipedia Encyclopedia,* s.v. "Johnny Horizon."

28. Memorandum for the record by H.J. Poole.

29. Patrick Poole, "The Muslim Brotherhood 'Project'," *Front Page Magazine,* 11 May 2006.

30. PBS's "Frontline World," 14 April 2009.

31. Lt.Cmdr. Youssef H. Aboul-Enein, "The Hezbollah Model: Using Terror and Creating a Quasi-State in Lebanon," *Marine Corps Gazette,* June 2003, pp. 34, 35; ABC's Nightly News, 26 March 2006; Nordland, "Al-Sadr Strikes," pp. 45-47.

32. Julie Stahl, "'Paradise Camps' Teach Palestinian Children to Be Suicide Bombers," Cybercast News Service, 23 July 2001.

33. *CIA — The World Factbook,* s.v. "Cambodia"; Suzy Kim, "Saying I Do Willingly This Time," *Christian Science Monitor,* 16 January 2007, p. 20.

34. Col. Pat Rotchford USMC (Ret.) — three-year resident of the Philippines — in conversation with the author in February 2009.

35. Tony Perry, "U.S. 'Micro-Loan' Effort Yields Big Results in Iraqi Province," *Los Angeles Times,* 22 February 2008.
36. Dan Murphy, "Iraq's Neighborhood Councils Are Vanishing," *Christian Science Monitor,* 25 February 2005, pp. 1, 5.
37. Michael E. Woodward, Freeport Police Dept., *Labor,* 4 June 2007, p. 2, in FMFM 1-3A, p. 15.
38. Ibid., pp. 5-8, in FMFM 1-3A, p. 15.
39. "The Maras: A Menace to the Americas," by Breve, pp. 93, 94, in FMFM 1-3A, p. 15.
40. GlobalSecurity.org, s.v. "FARC" in "Colombia's Civil War"; *Patterns of Global Terrorism, 2003 Report,* "Lord's Resistance Army."
41. Mark Clayton, "Reading into the Mind of a Terrorist," *Christian Science Monitor,* 30 October 2003, p. 11; Ilene Prusher, "As Life Looks Bleaker, Suicide Bombers Get Younger," *Christian Science Monitor,* 5 March 2004, pp. 1, 5; ABC's Nightly News, 26 March 2004.

Afterword

1. Christopher Goffard and Jennifer Delson, "When Dream Homes Become Nightmares," *L.A. Times,* B-4 edition, 8 October 2007; Wall Street auditor, in blog entry to *New York Post* website, in response to "Illegals and the Mortgage Mess," by Malkin, n.d.
2. Simon Montlake, "Why Asian Banks Are Stronger Than U.S. Banks," *Christian Science Monitor,* 7 October 2008, pp. 1, 10; Olivia Chung, "China Succor for Foreign Lenders," *Asia Times,* 10 July 2008.
3. *Unrestricted Warfare,* by Liang and Xiangsui.
4. Ibid., p. 54.
5. Ibid., p. 158.
6. Ibid., p. 144.
7. Ibid., p. 146.
8. Ibid., p. 144.
9. Ibid., p. 133.
10. Harris, "China's Cyber-Militia."
11. Sangraula, "Nepal's Ex-Guerrillas Take On Civilian Rule."
12. *China's Rising Power in Africa,* Part 3, "China, Congo Trade for What the Other Wants," by Thompkins.
13. U.S. oil company executive who lives within the Venezuelan community, in conversation with author on 20 August 2008.
14. Poole, *Tequila Junction,* p. 184.
15. Sangraula, "Nepal's Ex-Guerrillas Take On Civilian Rule," p. 7.

16. BBC News, as broadcast over NPR, 13 December 2008.
17. Patrick Jackson, "Analysis: Moscow's Doomed Invasion," *BBC News Online,* 17 December 2004.
18. Ibid.
19. "Timeline: Moscow's Afghan War," *BBC News Online,* 17 December 2004.
20. Poole, *The Tiger's Way.*
21. H. John Poole, *Militant Tricks: Battlefield Ruses of the Islamic Insurgent* (Emerald Isle, NC: Posterity Press, 2005), chapt. 6.
22. NPR's "Morning Edition" News, 13 March 2009; PBS's "Frontline World," 14 April 2009.
23. Joe Klein, "The Aimless War," *Time,* 22 December 2008, p. 26.
24. Hutchison Whampoa website, www.hutchison-whampoa.com.
25. Poole, *Dragon Days,* chapt. 7.
26. Niazi, Assoc. for Asian Research, "Gwadar: China's Naval Outpost on the Indian Ocean," in *Wikipedia Encyclopedia,* s.v. "Gwadar."
27. "Everyone Wants Cut in Afghan Drug Trade," from McClatchy Newspapers, *Jacksonville Daily News* (NC), 10 May 2009, p. A8.

Appendix: *China's Takeover of Nepal*

1. "Country Profiles," *BBC News Online,* s.v. "Nepal: Timeline."
2. ABC's Nightly News, 25 April 2006.
3. Bikash Sangraula, "Key Role of Nepal Security Forces," *Christian Science Monitor,* 18 April 2006, p. 6.
4. Bikash Sangraula, "Pressure Rises on Nepal's King," *Christian Science Monitor,* 24 April 2006, pp. 1, 10, 11; ABC's Nightly News, 20-22 April 2006.
5. Bikash Sangraula, "In Nepal's Democratic Revival, Maoist Rebels Dubious," *Christian Science Monitor,* 26 April 2006, pp. 1, 11.
6. Sangraula, "Pressure Rises on Nepal's King," pp. 1, 10.
7. "The Blockade of Major Highways in Nepal . . . ," World News in Brief, *Christian Science Monitor,* 27 April 2006, p. 7.
8. "Nepalese Cabinet Declares Cease Fire," World Briefs Wire Reports (AP), *Jacksonville Daily News* (NC), 4 May 2006, p. 5A.
9. Sangraula, "In Nepal's Democratic Revival, Maoist Rebels Dubious," pp. 1, 11.
10. Bikash Sangraula, "Nepal's Parliament Sets Fast-Paced Agenda," *Christian Science Monitor,* 15 May 2006, pp. 1, 12.
11. Bikash Sangraula, "Rebel Visit Moves Nepal Closer to Peace," *Christian Science Monitor,* 19 June 2006, pp. 1, 10.
12. Bikash Sangraula, "Nepalese Hit the Streets—Again—for a Change," *Christian Science Monitor,* 27 June 2006, pp. 6, 7.

13. Dharma Adhikari, "Joy and Caution in Nepal's Peace Deal," *Christian Science Monitor,* 5 December 2006, p. 9.

14. "A Deal That Will Bring Communist Rebels into the Government of Nepal," World News in Brief, *Christian Science Monitor,* 10 November 2006, p. 7.

15. Bikash Sangraula, "Nepal's Decade of War Draws to a Close," *Christian Science Monitor,* 9 November 2006, p. 6.

16. Adhikari, "Joy and Caution in Nepal's Peace Deal," p. 9.

17. "There Will Be No Year-End Strike in Nepal," World News in Brief, *Christian Science Monitor,* 26 December 2006, p. 7.

18. Bikash Sangraula, "Popular Protests Ignite Nepal," *Christian Science Monitor,* 11 April 2006, p. 6; Sangraula, "Nepal's Decade of War Draws to a Close," p. 6.

19. Adhikari, "Joy and Caution in Nepal's Peace Deal," p. 9.

20. Bikash Sangraula, "Nepal's Children Forced to Fight," *Christian Science Monitor,* 28 July 2006, p. 7.

21. "Country Profiles," *BBC News Online,* s.v. "Nepal: Timeline."

22. "A Two-Week Ultimatum Was Issued by Communists," World News in Brief, *Christian Science Monitor,* 3 May 2007, p. 7.

23. Bikash Sangraula, "Nepal's Parliament Asserts Power," *Christian Science Monitor,* 19 May 2006, p. 4.

24. "Country Profiles," *BBC News Online,* s.v. "Nepal: Timeline."

25. Ibid.

26. Sangraula, "Nepal's Ex-Guerrillas Take On Civilian Rule," p. 7.

27. "Country Profiles," *BBC News Online,* s.v. "Nepal: Timeline."

28. "A Former Maoist Guerrilla Was Sworn in Monday As Nepal's First Prime Minister."

Glossary

ABC	American Broadcasting Company	U.S. TV network
ACE	Automated Customs Environment	U.S. border crossing procedure
AK-47	Russian and Chinese weapon designator	Eastern-bloc assault rifle
AP	Associated Press	U.S. news service
AT-4	Anti-tank weapon designator	U.S. hand-held tank killer
ATF	Alcohol, Tobacco, and Firearms	U.S. firearms control agency
AUC	Autodefensas Unidas de Colombia	Colombia's rightist paramilitaries
BBC	British Broadcasting Company	British electronic media network
CAP	Combined-Action Platoon	One squad each of U.S. infantry, local police, & indigenous army or militia (with no overall leader)
CIA	Central Intelligence Agency	U.S. spy organization
CLC	Concerned Local Citizens	Neighborhood watch program in Iraq
COP	Community-oriented policing	Local-citizen-assisted town policing concept

COSCO	China Ocean Shipping Company	PLA's civilian fleet
CPC	Communist Party of China	China's ruling party
CRU	Community Response Unit	Gang parent liaison program
C-TPAT	Customs Trade Partnership against Terrorism	U.S. customs program to facilitate international trade
D.C.	District of Columbia	Site of U.S. capital
DEA	Drug Enforcement Administration	U.S. narcotics monitoring bureau
DoD	Department of Defense	U.S. military establishment
DPRK	Democratic People's Republic of Korea	North Korea
DRC	Democratic Republic of the Congo	Equatorial African nation, once Zaire
DTO	Drug Trafficking Organization	Crime faction that deals in narcotics
E&E	Escape and Evasion	Ability to elude a pursuer
EME	Letter "M" in Spanish	Mexican Mafia from California
EMI	Letter "M" in Spanish	Mexican Mafia from Texas
FARC	Fuerzas Armadas Revolucionarias de Colombia	Maoist rebels from Colombia
FAST	Free and Secure Trade	U.S. Customs truck monitoring procedure
FATA	Federally Administered Tribal Areas	Pakistan area next to Afghanistan

FBI	Federal Bureau of Investigation	U.S. criminal-monitoring agency
FDLR	Forces Democratiques de Liberation du Rwanda	Rwanda genocide culprits
FMCSA	Federal Motor Carrier Safety Administration	U.S. trucking safety agency
FMFM 1-3A	Fleet Marine Field Manual designator (proposed draft)	Counterinsurgency & Police Handbook
FMLN	Farabundo Marti National Liberation Front	El Salvador's new ruling leftist party
14-K	Hong Kong triad designator	PLA-affiliated triad
4GW	4th-Generation Warfare	War that is waged in religious, economic, martial, & political orbs simultaneously
GASP	Gang Awareness Suppression & Prevention	Local police program
GI	Government issue.	Colloquial term for U.S. enlisted person
I	Interstate highway designator	U.S. roadway prefix
ID	Identification	Classification/name
IED	Improvised Explosive Device	Remote-control bomb
Interlink-U	Internet routing network (possibly unclassified)	Military internet routing format
ISI	Interservice Intelligence	Pakistani spy agency that created Taliban
JI	*Jamaat i-Islami*	Pakistani religious party
JLENS	Joint Land Attack Cruise Missile Defense Elevated Netted Sensor	Digital camera system

JROTC	Junior Reserve Officers Training Corps	High school military orientation program
JTF-6	Joint Task Force Six	U.S. military command to help stop Mexican border smuggling
JUI	*Jamiat Ulema i-Islam*	Pakistani religious party
JWICS	Joint Worldwide Intelligence Communication System	Military internet routing format
L.A.	Los Angeles	U.S. West Coast's biggest city
LET	*Lashkar-e-Toiba*	Military wing of MDI
M-18	Mara 18, 18th Street Gang, or *Calle 18*	Central American gang now active throughout U.S.
M24	U.S. tank designator	Pre-Korean War vintage U.S. tank
MDI	*Markaz-ud-Dawa-wal-Irshad*	Pakistani Muslim fundamentalist sect
MDMA	3,4-methylenedioxy-methamphetamine	Drug with the street name of "ecstasy"
MG	Machinegun	Automatic small arm
MRTA	Tupac Amaru Revolutionary Movement	Peruvian Marxist guerrillas
MS-13	Mara Salvatrucha	Hispanic gang with Salvadorian roots now active in U.S.
MSR	Main service road	Principal overland resupply route

NAFTA	North American Free Trade Agreement	Economic pact between nations
NATO	North Atlantic Treaty Organization	European military alliance
NCO	Noncommissioned Officer	Enlisted military leader
NCP	Nepal Congress Party	Former ruling party of Nepal
NDIC	National Drug Intelligence Center	U.S. Justice Dept. section
NDTS	National Drug Threat Survey	Drug survey of local police departments
NGO	Non-Government Organization	Overseas relief group
9/11	11 September 2001	U.S. Terrorist Attack
NPLA	Nepalese People's Liberation Army	Nepal's former Communist rebels
NPR	National Public Radio	U.S. educational radio network
NVA	North Vietnamese Army	U.S. foe in Vietnam
NWFP	North-West Frontier Province	Pakistan area next to Afghanistan
OMG	Outlaw Motorcycle Gang	Motorcycle club involved in crime
PBS	Public Broadcasting System	U.S. educational TV network
PFC	Private First Class	Second enlisted rank in U.S. military
PLA	People's Liberation Army	PRC's military arm (covers intell., navy, air, missiles, ground)

POE	Point of Entry	U.S border crossing location
PRC	People's Republic of China	Mainland China
PT	Physical Training	Daily military exercise session
RCT	Regimental Combat Team	Regiment-sized military task force
RDX	Explosive designator	Nitroamine
RFID	Radio Frequency Identification	U.S. border-crossing procedure
RPG	Rocket Propelled Grenade (Launcher)	Eastern-bloc bazooka
S-1	Headquarters staff designator	Administrative section in U.S. military command
S-2	Headquarters staff designator	Intelligence section in U.S. military command
S-3	Headquarters staff designator	Training/Operations section in U.S. military command
S-4	Headquarters staff designator	Logistics section in U.S. military command
SAS	British Special Air Service	British special operators
2GW	2nd-Generation Warfare	Based on attacking concentrations of enemy soldiers; U.S. has high-tech variant
SIPRNet	Secret Internet Protocol Router Network	Military internet routing format

SMAW	Shoulder-fired multi-purpose assault weapon	Modern equivalent of American bazooka, normally used for busting bunkers
SP	Shore Patrol	Pairs of U.S. troops who administratively patrol a town
SWAT	Special-Weapon Assault Team	Paramilitary police
TBA	Tri-Border Area	Corner of Argentina, Paraguay, & Brazil
3GW	3rd-Generation Warfare	Based on bypassing foe's strongpoints to ruin strategic assets instead of killing
TIC	Tactical intelligence collaborative	Database contributors
TTPs	Tactics, Techniques, & Procedures	Military methods
TV	Television	Electronic media device
U.N.	United Nations	Alliance of countries
UPS	United Parcel Service	U.S. package delivery concession
U.S.	United States	America
USCC	U.S-China Economic and Security Review Commission	U.S. agency that overseas PRC trade
USMC	United States Marine Corps	America's amphibious force
UW	Unconventional Warfare	Mostly E&E in foe-controlled area & fighting like guerrilla

VC	Viet Cong	Enemy in Vietnam
WWI	World War One	First global conflict
WWII	World War Two	Second global conflict

Bibliography

U.S. Government Publications and News Releases:

"Agencies Work Together to Find More Tunnels in Arizona." U.S Border Patrol News Release, 16 December 2008. As retrieved from its website, cbp.dhs.gov, on 23 February 2009.

Alexander, Col. Joseph H. *Closing In: Marines in the Seizure of Iwo Jima.* Marines in World War II Commemorative Series. Washington, D.C.: Hist. & Museum Div., HQMC, 1994.

"Asian Criminal Enterprises." FBI's Organized Crime Section. As retrieved from its website, www.fbi.gov, in September 2008.

"Asian Transnational Organized Crime and Its Impact on the United States." By James O. Finckenauer and Ko-lin Chin. U.S. Dept. of Justice Special Report, January 2007. As retrieved from the National Institute of Justice website, www.ojp.usdoj.gov/nij, in September 2008.

"Attorney General Mukasey Announces Charges against Los Angeles Gang Members and the Formation of an Additional Safe Streets Task Force to Combat Gang Violence." DEA Press Release, 26 March 2008. As retrieved from its website, www.usdoj.gov/dea, in October 2008.

Attorney General's Report to Congress on the Growth of Violent Street Gangs in Suburban Areas, April 2008. As retrieved from the National Drug Intelligence Center website, www.usdoj.gov/ndic, in October 2008.

Bartley, Lt.Col. Whitman S. *Iwo Jima: Amphibious Epic.* Washington, D.C.: Hist. Branch, HQMC, 1954.

"Chinese Transnational Organized Crime: The Fuk Ching." By James O. Finckenauer. National Institute of Justice. United Nations Activities, n.d.

CIA—*The World Factbook.* As updated every three months. From its website, www.odci.gov.

Cities in Which Mexican DTOs Operate within the United States." National Drug Intelligence Center. Situation Report #2008-S0787-005, 11 April 2008. As retrieved from the NDIC website, www.usdoj.gov/ndic, in December 2008.

"A Close-Up of MS-13: FBI Executive Visits El Salvador." FBI Headline Archive, 19 April 2006.

"Correctional Populations." U.S. Dept of Justice. Bureau of Justice Statistics. As retrieved from its website, www.ojp.usdoj.gov, in October 2008.

"Country Profile: Mexico." Library of Congress. Federal Research Division, July 2006.

"Department of Justice Launches New Law Enforcement Strategy to Combat Increasing Threat of International Organized Crime." Dept. of Justice and Federal Bureau of Investigation Press Releases, 23 April 2008. As retrieved from their respective websites, www.usdoj.gov and www.fbi.gov, in October 2008.

"Fact Sheet: Department of Justice Comprehensive Efforts to Fight Gang Violence." U.S. Dept. of Justice, 24 June 2008. As retrieved from its website, www.usdoj.gov in October 2008.

"FBI Announces Coordinated Law Enforcement Action against Gangs." FBI Press Release, 8 September 2005. As retrieved from its website, www.fbi.gov, in October 2008.

"FBI Priorities." As retrieved from minneapolis.fbi.gov in August 2008.

FMFM 1-3A. *A Tactical Handbook for Counterinsurgency and Police Operations.* Draft copy, 12 August 2008.

"Going Global on Gangs: New Partnership Targets MS-13." FBI Headline Archive, 10 October 2007. As retrieved from its website, www.fbi.gov, in October 2008.

"How We're Ganging Up on MS-13: And What You Can Do to Help." FBI Press Release, 13 July 2005. As retrieved from its website, www.fbi.gov, in October 2008.

Manwaring, Max G. "Street Gangs: The New Urban Insurgency." Carlisle, PA: U.S. Army Strategic Studies Institute, March 2005.

McMichael, Maj. Scott R. "The Chinese Communist Forces in Korea." From "A Historical Perspective on Light Infantry." *Leavenworth Research Survey No. 6.* Ft. Leavenworth, KS: Combat Studies Institute, U.S. Army Cmd. & Gen. Staff College, 1987.

Mexico — Country Profile for 2003. U.S. Dept. of Justice, Drug Enforcement Administration, November 2003.

"Mexico's Counter-Narcotics Efforts under Fox — December 2000 to October 2004." By Larry Stores. Congressional Research Service (CRS) Report for Congress. Order Code RL32669. Washington, D.C: Library of Congress, 10 November 2004.

"Mexico's Drug Cartels." By Colleen W. Cook. Congressional Research Service (CRS) Report for Congress. Order Code RL34215. Washington, D.C: Library of Congress, 25 February 2008.

"MS-13 National Gang Task Force." Powerpoint presentation, n.d. As retrieved from scm.oas.org on 11 March 2009.

"The MS-13 Threat: A National Assessment." FBI Headline Archive, 14 January 2008. As retrieved from its website, www.fbi.gov, in October 2008.

National Drug Threat Assessment (for) 2008. National Drug Intelligence Center, October 2007. As retrieved from the DEA website, www.usdoj.gov/dea, in October 2008.

National Drug Threat Assessment (for) 2009. National Drug Intelligence Center, December 2008. As retrieved from the NDIC website, www.usdoj.gov/ndic, in March 2009.

National Gang Threat Assessment (for) 2005. National Alliance of Gang Investigators Assoc. In partnership with FBI and National Drug Intelligence Center, n.d.

National Gang Threat Assessment (for) 2009. National Gang Intelligence Center in collaboration with National Drug Intelligence Center, January 2009. As retrieved from the NDIC website, www.usdoj.gov/ndic, in March 2009.

"Nations Hospitable to Organized Crime and Terrorism." By LaVerle Berry with Glenn E. Curtis, John N. Gibbs, Rex A. Hudson, Tara Karacan, Nina Kollars, and Ramon Miro. Federal Research Division, Library of Congress, October 2003.

"New York Drug Threat Assessment (for) 2002." National Drug Intelligence Center, n.d. As retrieved from the NDIC website, www.usdoj.gov/ndic, in October 2008.

"North Korea Handbook." *PC-2600-6421-94.* Washington, D.C.: U.S. Dept. of Defense, 1994.

"Operation Hardtac." FBI Case Study. As retrieved from its website, www.fbi.gov, in October 2008.

Organizational White Paper. Published at start of counterinsurgency operations in Iraq. Camp Pendleton, CA: I MEF, n.d.

Patterns of Global Terrorism, 2003. Washington, D.C.: U.S. Dept. of State, April 2004.

"Probable Cause." Congressional Research Service Memorandum, 30 January 2006. As retrieved from www.fas.org on 12 March 2009.

"Probation and Parole in the United States, 2006." Revised Bureau of Justice Statistics Bulletin #NCJ220218. By Lauren E. Glaze and Thomas P. Bonczar, U.S. Dept. of Justice, 2 July 2008. From *Wikipedia Encyclopedia,* s.v. "Incarceration in the United States."

"Terrorist Attacks in Mumbai, India, and Implications for U.S.
Interests." By Alan Kronstadt. Congressional Research Service
(CRS) Report for Congress. Order Code R40087. Washington,
D.C.: Library of Congress, 19 December 2008.
"Transnational Activities of Chinese Crime Organizations." By Glenn
E. Curtis, Seth L. Elan, Rexford A. Hudson, and Nina A. Koll.
Federal Research Division, Library of Congress, April 2003.

Civilian Publications, DVD's, and Website Resources:

"American Me." 126 minutes. Universal Studios, 2002. DVD,
isbn #0-7832-3360-4.
American Quotations, by Gordon Carruth and Eugene Ehrlich. New
York: Wings Books, 1992.
Atwan, Abdel Bari. *The Secret History of Al-Qa'ida.* London:
Abacus, an imprint of Little, Brown Book Group, 2006.
Bermudez, Joseph S. Jr. *North Korean Special Forces.* Annapolis:
Naval Institute Press, 1998.
"Country Profiles." *BBC News Online.* As available at its website,
bbc.co.uk.
Crime Mapping News. Police Foundation. Volume 6, issue 3, summer
2004.
Danelo, David J. *The Border: Exploring the U.S.-Mexican Divide.*
Mechanicsburg, PA: Stackpole Books, 2008.
Encyclopedia Britannica Online. From its website, www.britannica.com.
Gertz, Bill. *The China Threat: How the People's Republic
Targets America.* Washington, D.C.: Regnery Publishing, 2000.
GlobalSecurity.org. Alexandria, VA.
Guatemala. N.p.: Lonely Planet Publications, 2007.
Gudmundsson, Bruce I. *Stormtrooper Tactics: Innovation in the German
Army, 1914-1918.* Westport, CT: Praeger Publications, 1989.
Gunaratna, Rohan. *Inside al-Qaeda: Global Network of Terror.* Lahore:
Vanguard, 2002.
Hackworth, David H. and Julie Sherman. *About Face.* New York:
Simon & Schuster, 1989.
Hammel, Eric. *Fire in the Streets: The Battle for Hue, Tet 1968.*
Pacifica, CA: Pacifica Press, 1991.
Hammer, Carl. *Tide of Terror: America, Islamic Extremism, and
the War on Terror.* Boulder, CO: Paladin Press, 2003.
Hastings, Max. *The Korean War.* New York: Touchstone,
1987.
Huber, Thomas M. "The Battle of Manila." Ft. Leavenworth, KS:
Combat Studies Institute, U.S. Army Cmd. & Gen. Staff College, n.d.
As retrieved from CSI website, www-cgsc.army.mil/csi, in 2003.

Hutchison Whampoa website, www.hutchison-whampoa.com.

"Islam in Africa Newsletter" volume 1, number 1, May 2006. By Moshe Terdman and Reuven Paz. Project for the Research of Islamist Movements (Israel). From its website, www.e-prism.org.

John Paul II, Pope. *Crossing the Threshold of Hope.* New York: Alfred A. Knopf, 1995.

Knox, Donald. *The Korean War: Pusan to Chosin, An Oral History.* San Diego: Harcourt Brace Jovanovich, 1985.

Korean War website, www.korean-war.com.

Lanning, Michael Lee and Dan Cragg. *Inside the VC and the NVA: The Real Story of North Vietnam's Armed Forces.* New York: Ivy Books, 1992.

Lewis, Jon E. *SAS Combat Handbook.* London: Lyons Press, 2002.

Lonsdale, Mark. V. *Raids: A Tactical Guide to High Risk Warrant Service.* Los Angeles: Special Tactical Training Unit, 2005.

Menges, Constantine. *China: The Gathering Threat.* Nashville, TN: Nelson Current, 2005.

Mir, Amir. *The True Face of Jihadis.* Lahore: Mashal Books, 2004.

MSN Encarta Encyclopedia. From its website: encarta.msn.com.

"National Youth Gang Center Related Articles." Institute for Intergovernmental Research. As available from its website's "state-by-state" listing at www.iir.com/nygc/summaries.

Night Movements. Translated and preface by C. Burnett. Port Townsend, WA: Loompanics Unlimited, n.d. First published as Japanese training manual. Tokyo: Imperial Japanese Army, 1913.

Nolan, Keith William. *Operation Buffalo: USMC Fight for the DMZ* New York: Dell Publishing, 1991.

Pearl, Marianne. *A Mighty Heart: The Inside Story of the Al Qaeda Kidnapping of Danny Pearl.* New York, Scribner, 2003.

Poole, H. John. *Dragon Days: Time for "Unconventional" Tactics.* Emerald Isle, NC: Posterity Press, 2007.

Poole, H. John. *One More Bridge to Cross: Lowering the Cost of War.* Emerald Isle, NC: Posterity Press, 1999.

Poole, H. John. *Phantom Soldier: The Enemy's Answer to U.S. Firepower.* Emerald Isle, NC: Posterity Press, 2001.

Poole, H. John. *Militant Tricks: Battlefield Ruses of the Islamic Insurgent.* Emerald Isle, NC: Posterity Press, 2005.

Poole, H. John. *Tactics of the Crescent Moon: Militant Muslim Combat Methods.* Emerald Isle, NC: Posterity Press, 2004.

Poole, H. John. *Tequila Junction: 4th-Generation Counterinsurgency.* Emerald Isle, NC: Posterity Press, 2008.

Poole, H. John. *Terrorist Trail: Backtracking the Foreign Fighter.* Emerald Isle, NC: Posterity Press, 2006.

Poole, H. John. *The Tiger's Way: A U.S. Private's Best Chance for Survival.* Emerald Isle, NC: Posterity Press, 2003.

Ross, Bill D. *Iwo Jima: Legacy of Valor.* New York: Vintage, 1986.
Tehran's War of Terror and Its Nuclear Delivery Capability. By
   Stephen E. Hughes. Victoria, Canada: Trafford Publishing,
   2007.
Thompson, Leroy. *Hostage Rescue Manual: Tactics of the
   Counter-Terrorist Professionals.* London: Greenhill Books,
   2006.
Truth Be Tolled. Turf Special Edition. By William H. Molina.
   Storm Pictures LLC, 2008. 99 minutes. DVD #7-44773-0133-2.
Unmasking Terror: A Global Review of Terrorist Activities.
   Volumes I, II, and III. The first two edited by Christopher
   Heffelfinger, and the third by Jonathan Hutzley.
   Washington, D.C: Jamestown Foundation, 2005 through 2007.
Unrestricted Warfare. By Qiao Liang and Wang Xiangsui. Beijing:
   PLA Literature and Arts Publishing House, February 1999.
   FBIS translation over the internet.
Wikipedia Encyclopedia. From its website, wikipedia.org.
Yousaf, Brigadier Mohammad. *The Silent Soldier: The Man Behind
   the Afghan Jehad.* South Yorkshire, UK: Pen & Sword Books,
   n.d.

Radio and TV Documentaries:

China's Rising Power in Africa. Series. Five part series.
   NPR, 28 July - 1 August 2008.
Korea — the Unknown War. London: Thames TV in association with
   WGBH Boston, 1990. PBS. NC Public TV, n.d.
"The Lobotomist." PBS's *American Experience.* NC Public TV,
   16 February 2009.
"Portrait of a Mexican Drug Lord." *CBS Online News,* 24 October
   2003.
"Power and the People." PBS's *China from the Inside* Series. Part I.
   NC Public TV, 10 January 2007.
The U.S.-Mexican Border: A Changing Frontier. Five part series.
   NPR's "Morning Edition" News, 1-5 December 2008.
"The War of the World: The Clash of Empires." PBS, 30 June 2008.
"Wushu & Sanda." *Fight Quest.* Discovery Channel, 28 December
   2008.

Maps, Photos, and Graphics:

National Drug Intelligence Center. ESRL Times research, n.d. Map
   MS-13map2.gif.

Photograph and caption. In "A Model Counterinsurgency: Uribe's
    Colombia (2002-2006)." By Thomas A. Marks." *Military Review,*
    March-April 2007.
"Vias Ferreas de la Republica Mexicana." Instituto Nationale de
    Estadistica. Univ. of Texas at Austin library. From map designator
    "railroads.gif."

Verbal, Written, or E-mail Communications:

Leland, Lt. Fred. Walpole Police Dept. In several telephone and e-mail
    conversations with author in 2008.
Lind, William S. In a letter to author on 9 May 2009.
Longtime owner of Khartoum hotel. In conversation with author on
    31 May 2006.
Rotchford, Col. Pat USMC (Ret.)—three-year resident of the
    Philippines. In conversation with author in February 2009.
Texas resident. In telephone conversation with author in late 2008.
U.S. oil company executive who lives within the Venezuelan community.
    In conversation with author on 20 August 2008.

Newspaper, Magazine, and Website Articles:

Aboul-Enein, Lt.Cmdr. Youssef H. "The Hezbollah Model: Using
    Terror and Creating a Quasi-State in Lebanon." *Marine Corps
    Gazette,* June 2003.
Adhikari, Dharma. "Joy and Caution in Nepal's Peace Deal."
    Christian Science Monitor, 5 December 2006.
Aizenman, N.C. "Latino Gang Study Finds Few Links to Overseas
    Groups." *Washington Post,* 8 February 2007.
"America's Most Dangerous Gang—MS13—Violent, Vicious, and
    Spreading Fast." By Shelly Feuer Domash. *Police Magazine,*
    20 February 2005. As retrieved from freerepublic.com on
    10 October 2008.
Anderson, Kevin. "U.S. Fears Chinese Hack Attack." *BBC News
    Online,* 28 April 2001.
"Angolan, Congolese Troops Join Forces." World Briefs Wire Reports
    (AP). *Jacksonville Daily News* (NC), 7 November 2008.
Archibold, Randal C. "Officials Find Drug Tunnel With Surprising
    Amenities." *New York Times,* 27 January 2006.
"Asian Gangs in Los Angeles County." As retrieved from
    streetgangs.com in May 2009.
Badam, Ramola Talwar. "10 Young Men Started Mumbai's 60 Hours of
    Terror." From Associated Press, 30 November 2008.

Baldauf, Scott. "Congo's Riches Fuel Its War." *Christian Science Monitor,* 4 November 2008.

Baldauf, Scott. "In Congo, a Doctor Keeps Helping As Victims Keep Coming." *Christian Science Monitor,* 24 October 2008.

Baldauf, Scott. "Sadr Loyalty Grows, Even as Sistani Returns." *Christian Science Monitor,* 26 August 2004.

Baldauf, Scott. "What Does Congo's Nkunda Want." *Christian Science Monitor,* 14 November 2008.

Baldauf, Scott and Jina Moore. "Congo's Risky Push to Crush Rebels." *Christian Science Monitor,* 26 January 2009.

Blandford, Nicholas. "Lebanon Defuses Crisis." *Christian Science Monitor,* 22 May 2008.

"The Blockade of Major Highways in Nepal . . . ." World News in Brief. *Christian Science Monitor,* 27 April 2006.

"Blueprint on a Brilliant Raid." By Steve Macko. *Emergency News Net Daily Intelligence Report,* volume 3, number 114, 24 April 1997. As retrieved from its website, www.emergency.com, in January 2009.

Boot, Max, and Frederick Kagan and Kimberly Kagan. "How to Surge the Taliban." Op-Ed piece. *New York Times,* 13 March 2009.

Butters, Andrew Lee. "Welcome to Hizballahstan." *Newsweek,* 26 May 2008.

"California's Crisis in Prison Systems a Threat to Public Longer Sentences and Less Emphasis on Rehabilitation Create Problems." By John Pomfret. *Washington Post,* 11 June 2006.

"California's Growing Prison Crisis." By Sonja Steptoe. *Time,* 21 June 2007.

Campo-Flores, Arian and Monica Campbell. "Bloodshed on the Border." *Newsweek,* 8 December 2008.

"Central America: An Emerging Role in the Drug Trade." STRATFOR Global Intelligence, 26 March 2009.

"Chavez Eyes China, Russia, More on 'Strategic'-Interest Tour." From Agence-France Presse, 20 September 2008.

"China and Angola Strengthen Bilateral Relationship." By Loro Horta. *Power and Interest News Report,* 23 June 2006.

"China in Angola: An Emerging Energy Partnership." By Paul Hare. Jamestown Foundation. *China Brief,* volume 6, issue 22, 8 November 2006.

"China Winning Resources and Loyalties of Africa." *The Financial Times* (UK), 28 February 2006.

"China's 'Comprehensive Warfare' Strategy Wears Down Enemy Using Non-Military Means." *Geostrategy-Direct,* 2 August 2006.

China's State Commission of Science, Technology and Industry for National Defense. As quoted in "Chinese Military to Make Billions through Capitalism." *Geostrategy Direct,* 16 January 2008.

Chung, Olivia. "China Succor for Foreign Lenders." *Asia Times,*
10 July 2008.

Clayton, Mark. "Reading into the Mind of a Terrorist." *Christian
Science Monitor,* 30 October 2003.

"Colombia's Civil War." PBS's *Online News Hour,* 2003.

"Colombia's Most Powerful Rebels." *BBC News Online,*
19 September 2003.

"Computers Get Hacked." National Briefs Wire Reports (AP).
Jacksonville Daily News (NC), 12 June 2008.

"The Congo's Killing Fields." By Kevin Clarke. *U.S. Catholic,*
July 2008.

Corchado, Alfredo and Laurence Iliff. "Ex-Rivals' Merge to 'Megacartel'
Intensifies Brutality in Mexico." *Dallas Morning News,* 17 June
2008.

Corsi, Jerome R. "Premeditated Merger: Mexican Trucks to Enter U.S.
in 15 Seconds." *World Net Daily,* 17 April 2007.

Dagher, Sam. "Baghdad Safer, But It's a Life behind Walls." *Christian
Science Monitor,* 10 December 2007.

Dagher, Sam. "Baghdad Strategy: 'Preserve Gains'." *Christian
Science Monitor,* 30 January 2008.

"Dawood Gang Provided Logistics to Lashkar Militants." Press
Trust of India. NDTV.com (Mumbai), 29 November
2008.

"Dawood's Drug Net Financed 26/11: Russian Intelligence." NDTV.com
(Mumbai), 18 December 2008.

"DEA Boosts Its Role in Paraguay." By Jack Sweeney. *Washington
Times,* 21 August 2001.

"A Deal That Will Bring Communist Rebels into the Government of
Nepal." World News in Brief. *Christian Science Monitor,*
10 November 2006.

"Do I Look Dangerous to You?" Part I. Partners in Crime Series. By
Frederic Dannen. *The New Republic,* 14 & 21 July 1997. As
retrieved from http://www.copi.com/articles/triads2.html.

"East Turkestan Islamic Movement (ETIM)." By Seva Gunitskiy.
Center for Defense Information, 9 December 2002.

"Ecuador Offers Concession of Manta Air Base to China, Declines to
Renew Contract with U.S." By Vittorio Hernandez. AHN News
(Ecuador), 26 November 2007. As retrieved through
ACCESS@g2-forward.org and MILINET.

"Everyone Wants Cut in Afghan Drug Trade." From McClatchy
Newspapers. *Jacksonville Daily News* (NC), 10 May 2009.

"Ex-Crime Chief Arrested in Mexico." *BBC News Online,*
21 November 2008.

"Five Mumbai Terrorists May Have Escaped Capture." *Fox
Online News,* 1 December 2008.

Ford, Peter. "China's Buying Spree in Global Fire Sale."
Christian Science Monitor, 23 February 2009.

Ford, Peter. "China's Economy Cools." *Christian Science Monitor,*
21 October 2008.

"A Former Maoist Guerrilla Was Sworn in Monday As Nepal's First
Prime Minister." World News in Brief. *Christian Science Monitor,*
19 August 2008.

"45,000 Die Each Month in Congo, Report Says." World Briefs Wire
Reports (AP). *Jacksonville Daily News* (NC), 23 January 2008.

"Fujimori-Cerpa, A Test of Wills." By Steve Macko. *Emergency Net
News Daily Intelligence Report,* volume 3, number 112,
22 April 1997. As retrieved from its website, www.emergency.com,
in January 2009.

Gamel, Kim. Associated Press. "Iraqi Cleric Orders His Forces
off the Streets." *Jacksonville Daily News* (NC), 31 March 2008.

Gearan, Anne. Associated Press. "Gates Sees Limit on Force in
Afghanistan." *Jacksonville Daily News* (NC), 28 January 2009.

Gertz, Bill. "Chinese Military Trains in West." *Washington Times,*
15 March 2006.

Glanz, James. "The Conflict in Iraq." *New York Times,*
21 February 2005.

Goffard, Christopher and Jennifer Delson. "When Dream Homes
Become Nightmares." *L.A. Times,* B-4 edition, 8 October 2007.

Gregory, Mark. "U.S. Under Chinese Hack Attack." *BBC News Online,*
30 April 2001.

"Grisly Slayings Are Bringing Mexican Drug War to the U.S." From
Associated Press. *Jacksonville Daily News* (NC), 19 April 2009.

Harman, Danna. "U.S. Steps Up Battle against Salvadoran Gang
MS-13." *USA Today,* 23 February 2005.

Harris, Shane. "China's Cyber-Militia." *National Journal Magazine,*
31 May 2008.

"Highlights of the 2006 National Youth Gang Survey." As retrieved
from the National Youth Gang Center at the Institute for
Intergovernmental Research website, www.iir.com, in October
2008.

"Hispanic Gangs in Los Angeles County." As retrieved from
streetgangs.com in May 2009.

"History of the Mexican Mafia Prison Gang." *Police Magazine,* July
2007.

Hoffman, Lisa. Scripps Howard. "Chinese Hackers." *Jacksonville
Daily News* (NC), 15 June 2008.

Hoffman, Lisa. Scripps Howard. "Cocaine Use Is on the Rise
in the U.S." *Jacksonville Daily News* (NC), 1 November 2007.

"Hong Kong Triads after 1997." *Trends in Organized Crime,*
volume 8, number 3, March 2005.

"How Many Did the Communist Regimes Murder." Univ. of Hawaii study. By R.J. Rummel. As retrieved from its website, www.hawaii.edu, in September 2008.

"International Operations." As retrieved from the Hutchison Whampoa website, www.hutchison-whampoa.com, in October 2008.

"Iran Role in the Recent Uprising in Iraq." Special Dispatch No. 692. Middle East Media Research Institute, 9 April 2004.

Jackson, Patrick. "Analysis: Moscow's Doomed Invasion." *BBC News Online,* 17 December 2004.

Kenny, Adm. Alejandro. "China's Presence in Latin America: A View on Security from the Southern Cone." *Military Review,* September/October 2006.

Kim, Suzy. "Saying I Do Willingly This Time." *Christian Science Monitor,* 16 January 2007.

Klein, Joe. "The Aimless War." *Time,* 22 December 2008.

Kriel, Lomi. "SAPD to Get $557,000 to Fight Gangs." *San Antonio Metro,* 30 October 2008.

Lamont, Lt.Col. Robert W. "Urban Warrior—A View from North Vietnam." *Marine Corps Gazette,* April 1999.

Lhana, Sara Miller. "As Mexico's Drug War Rages, Military Takes Over for Police." *Christian Science Monitor,* 5 December 2008.

Lhana, Sara Miller. "El Salvador Joins Latin Leftward Tilt." *Christian Science Monitor,* 17 March 2009.

Lynch, C.G. "Three Things the CIA Learned about Implementing an Enterprise Wiki." International Data Group. *CIO Magazine,* 10 June 2008. As retrieved from its website, www.cio.com, on 18 February 2009.

Malkasian, Carter and Gerald Meyerle. "How is Afghanistan Different from Al Anbar?" N.p.: CNA Analysis and Solutions, 14 February 2009. As retrieved from cna.org on 18 March 2009.

Mazumdar, Sudip. "Captors of the Liberated Zone." *Newsweek,* 18 May 2009.

"A Means of Maintaining Social Order." Part II. Partners in Crime Series. By Frederic Dannen. *The New Republic,* 14 & 21 July 1997. As retrieved from http://www.copi.com/articles/triads2.html.

"Mexican Mafia: Prison Gang Profile." As retrieved from insideprison.com in May 2006.

"Mexico's Internal Drug War." By Sam Logan. *Power and Interest News Report (PINR),* 14 August 2006.

Miller, Leslie. "Cross-Border Trucking Plan Draws Criticism." From Associated Press, 24 February 2007.

Montlake, Simon. "Why Asian Banks Are Stronger Than U.S. Banks." *Christian Science Monitor,* 7 October 2008.

"MS-13 Gang." Detention and Prevention of Violence. As retrieved from KeysToSaferSchools.com in August 2008.

"Mumbai Coordinated Shootings." *Significant Terrorist Event Report,* volume 1.2, 26 November 2008. As retrieved from www.intelcenter.com (Alexandria, VA) in December 2008.

"Mumbai Terrorist Amped Up on Steroids, Amphetamines." By Richard Esposito. *ABC Online News,* 5 December 2008.

Murphy, Dan. "Iraq's Neighborhood Councils Are Vanishing." *Christian Science Monitor,* 25 February 2005.

"Nepalese Cabinet Declares Cease Fire." World Briefs Wire Reports (AP). *Jacksonville Daily News* (NC), 4 May 2006.

Nessman, Ravi. Associated Press. "Gunmen Tied to Pakistan." *Jacksonville Daily News* (NC), 1 December 2008.

"Nicaragua Corredor de Armas." By Elizabeth Romero. *La Prensa,* 17 April 2005.

Nordland, Rod. "Al-Sadr Strikes." *Newsweek,* 10 April 2006.

"One in 100: Behind Bars in America 2008." The Pew Center on the States. From *Wikipedia Encyclopedia,* s.v. "Incarceration in the United States."

"Organized Crime Slayings More Than Double in Mexico." World Briefs Wire Reports (AP). *Jacksonville Daily News* (NC), 9 December 2008.

Pepper, Daniel. "Congolese Hopeful Ahead of July 30 Vote." *Christian Science Monitor,* 29 June 2006.

Perry, Tony. "U.S. 'Micro-Loan' Effort Yields Big Results in Iraqi Province." *Los Angeles Times,* 22 February 2008.

"Peru Hostage Crisis Comes to a Violent End." By Steve Macko. *Emergency Net News Daily Intelligence Report,* volume 3, number 113, 23 April 1997. As retrieved from its website, www.emergency.com, in January 2009.

Plushnick-Masti, Ramit. Associated Press. "Militant Groups Join Forces, Get Hezbollah Help." *Jacksonville Daily News* (NC), 28 October 2003.

Poole, Patrick. "The Muslim Brotherhood 'Project'." *Front Page Magazine,* 11 May 2006. From its website, frontpagemagazine.com.

"Protocol Additional to the Geneva Conventions of 12 August 1949, and Relating to the Protection of Victims of Non-International Armed Conflicts (Protocol II), 8 June 1977." International Humanitarian Law—Treaties and Documents, International Red Cross, n.d. As retrieved from its website, www.icrc.org, on 23 March 2009.

Prusher, Ilene. "As Life Looks Bleaker, Suicide Bombers Get Younger." *Christian Science Monitor,* 5 March 2004.

Quittner, Joshua. "The Hottest Software in Town." *Time,* 5 June 1995.

"Report: MS-13 Gang Hired to Murder Border Patrol." As retrieved from DailyBulletin.com in October 2008.

"A Reputation." By Cara Buckley. *New York Times*, 19 August 2007.

Romero, Simon. "Cocaine Trade Helps Rebels Re-ignite War in Peru." *New York Times*, 17 March 2009.

"Russia's Economy Is Protected against a Sharp Change." World News in Brief. *Christian Science Monitor*, 21 November 2008.

Sangraula, Bikash. "In Nepal's Democratic Revival, Maoist Rebels Dubious." *Christian Science Monitor*, 26 April 2006.

Sangraula, Bikash. "Key Role of Nepal Security Forces." *Christian Science Monitor*, 18 April 2006.

Sangraula, Bikash. "Nepalese Hit the Streets—Again—for a Change." *Christian Science Monitor*, 27 June 2006.

Sangraula, Bikash. "Nepal's Children Forced to Fight." *Christian Science Monitor*, 28 July 2006.

Sangraula, Bikash. "Nepal's Decade of War Draws to a Close." *Christian Science Monitor*, 9 November 2006.

Sangraula, Bikash. "Nepal's Ex-Guerrillas Take On Civilian Rule." *Christian Science Monitor*, 21 August 2008.

Sangraula, Bikash. "Nepal's Parliament Asserts Power." *Christian Science Monitor*, 19 May 2006.

Sangraula, Bikash. "Nepal's Parliament Sets Fast-Paced Agenda." *Christian Science Monitor*, 15 May 2006.

Sangraula, Bikash. "Popular Protests Ignite Nepal." *Christian Science Monitor*, 11 April 2006.

Sangraula, Bikash. "Pressure Rises on Nepal's King." *Christian Science Monitor*, 24 April 2006.

Sangraula, Bikash. "Rebel Visit Moves Nepal Closer to Peace." *Christian Science Monitor*, 19 June 2006.

Santoli, Al. "The Panama Canal in Transition: Threats to U.S. Security and China's Growing Role in Latin America." American Foreign Policy Council Investigative Report, 23 June 1999.

Sappenfield, Mark and Anand Gopal. "Rise in Crime, Kidnapping, Tops Afghan's Worries." *Christian Science Monitor*, 25 November 2008.

Sardesai, Rajdeep. "26/11: Terror Comes Precariously Close." From Reuters. 5 December 2008.

"SAS Storm the Embassy." Siege at the Iranian Embassy series. *BBC News Online*, n.d.

"7 Large Tunnels Beneath U.S.-Mexican Border Raising Security Concerns." *Fox Online News*, 30 January 2007.

"Six Days of Fear." Siege at the Iranian Embassy series. *BBC News Online*, 26 April 2000.

"Smoking Al Qaeda Out of Karachi." By B. Raman. South Asia Analysis Group. Paper Number 519, 14 September 2002.

Stahl, Julie. "'Paradise Camps' Teach Palestinian Children to Be Suicide Bombers." Cybercast News Service, 23 July 2001.

"Stalin's Mass Murders Were 'Entirely Rational' Says New Russian Textbook Praising Tyrant." By Will Stewart. *Daily Mail* (London), 3 September 2008. From its website, www.dailymail.co.uk.

Stevenson, Mark. "Mexico Protests U.S. Decision to End Mexican Truck Program by Raising Tariffs on U.S. Goods." From Associated Press, 16 March 2009. As retrieved from cnsnews.com on 18 March 2009.

Stewart, Rory. "How to Save Afghanistan." *Time*, 28 July 2008.

"Suspected Gang Members Arrested in North Carolina." Cable News Network, 24 July 2008.

Swartz, Jon. "Chinese Hackers Seek U.S. Access." *USA Today*, 11 March 2007.

"Terror Hoax Uncovers Border Threat." By David Hancock. CBS's Online News, 7 February 2005.

"There Will Be No Year-End Strike in Nepal." World News in Brief. *Christian Science Monitor,* 26 December 2006.

Thompson, Ginger. "U.S. Indicts Suspected Drug Kingpin." World Briefing. *New York Times,* 28 October 2004.

"Timeline: Moscow's Afghan War." *BBC News Online,* 17 December 2004.

"Top Mexico Police Officer Resigns." *BBC News Online,* 2 November 2008.

"Topics: MS-13, Gangs, Illegal Immigration, Americans, Security." From Associated Press. In *Lexington Dispatch,* 4 April 2005.

"Transcript: Mumbai Gunmen Were Commanded by Phone." From Associated Press, 7 January 2009. As retrieved from YNetNews.com (Israel).

"Tribal Militants Claimed Responsibility for Another Attack on an Energy Installation." World News in Brief. *Christian Science Monitor,* 8 June 2006.

"Tunnels beneath U.S. Borders Proliferation." Federation of American Scientists (Washington, D.C.). As posted and retrieved from their website, fas.org, on 23 February 2009.

"A Two-Week Ultimatum Was Issued by Communists." World News in Brief. *Christian Science Monitor,* 3 May 2007.

"Two Weeks after Being Asked for Help, Angola's Government Said." World News in Brief. *Christian Science Monitor,* 13 November 2008.

"U.N.: Fifth of the World Lacks Clean Water." World Brief Wire Reports (AP). *Jacksonville Daily News* (NC), 7 March 2006.

Von Drehe, David. "A New Line in the Sand." *Time,* 30 June 2008.

Wagley, John. "Foreign Hackers are Overwhelming U.S. Government Computers, Says Analyst." *Security Management,* 19 December 2008. As retrieved from its website, securitymanagement.com, 27 December 2008.

Wall Street auditor. From blog entry to *New York Post* website. In response to "Illegals and the Mortgage Mess." By Malkin, n.d.

Watts, Simon. "Guatemala Secret Files Uncovered." *BBC News Online,* 5 December 2005.

"While Congo's Government Is 'Open for Dialogue' with All." World News in Brief. *Christian Science Monitor,* 5 November 2008.

Whitlock, Craig and Karen DeYoung. "Attributes Suggest Outside Help." *Washington Post,* 28 November 2008.

"Who Needs the Panama Canal." By Robert Morton. *Washington Times,* National Weekly Edition, 1-8 March 1999. As reprinted in *World Tribune,* 4 March 1999.

"World Prison Population List." Seventh edition (October 2006). By Roy Walmsley. King's College London, International Centre for Prison Studies. As retrieved from the Australian Government's Institute of Criminology website, www.aic.gov.au, in October 2008.

"Zuma's Missing Years Come to Light." *The Times* (UK), 22 February 2009.

About the Author

After 28 years of commissioned and noncommissioned infantry service, John Poole retired from the United States Marine Corps in April 1993. While on active duty, he studied small-unit tactics for nine years: (1) six months at the Basic School in Quantico (1966); (2) seven months as a rifle platoon commander in Vietnam (1966-67); (3) three months as a rifle company commander at Camp Pendleton (1967); (4) five months as a regimental headquarters company (and camp) commander in Vietnam (1968); (5) eight months as a rifle company commander in Vietnam (1968-69); (6) five and a half years as an instructor with the Advanced Infantry Training Company (AITC) at Camp Lejeune (1986-92); and (7) one year as the Staff Noncommissioned Officer in Charge of the 3rd Marine Division Combat Squad Leaders Course (CSLC) on Okinawa (1992-93).

While at AITC, he developed, taught, and refined courses on maneuver warfare, land navigation, fire support coordination, call for fire, adjust fire, close air support, M203 grenade launcher, movement to contact, daylight attack, night attack, infiltration, defense, offensive Military Operations in Urban Terrain (MOUT), defensive MOUT, Nuclear/Biological/Chemical (NBC) defense, and leadership. While at CSLC, he further refined the same periods of instruction and developed others on patrolling.

He has completed all of the correspondence school requirements for the Marine Corps Command and Staff College, Naval War College (1,000-hour curriculum), and Marine Corps Warfighting Skills Program. He is a graduate of the Camp Lejeune Instructional Management Course, the 2nd Marine Division Skill Leaders in Advanced Marksmanship (SLAM) Course, and the East-Coast School of Infantry Platoon Sergeants' Course.

In the 15 years since retirement, John Poole has researched the small-unit tactics of other nations and written nine other books: (1) *The Last Hundred Yards: The NCO's Contribution to Warfare,* a squad combat study based on the consensus opinions of 1,200 NCOs and casualty statistics of AITC and CSLC field trials; (2) *One More Bridge to Cross: Lowering the Cost of War,* a treatise on enemy proficiency at short range and how to match it; (3) *Phantom Soldier: The Enemy's Answer to U.S. Firepower,* an in-depth look at the highly deceptive Asian style of war; (4) *The Tiger's Way: A U.S. Private's Best Chance of Survival,* a study of how Eastern fire teams and individual soldiers fight; (5) *Tactics of the Crescent Moon: Militant Muslim*

Combat Methods, a comprehensive analysis of the insurgents' battlefield procedures in Palestine, Chechnya, Afghanistan, and Iraq; (6) *Militant Tricks: Battlefield Ruses of the Islamic Insurgent,* an honest appraisal of the so-far-undefeated *jihadist* method; (7) *Terrorist Trail: Backtracking the Foreign Fighter,* how many of the *jihadists* in Iraq can be traced back to Africa; (8) *Dragon Days: Time for "Unconventional" Tactics,* an unconventional warfare technique manual that also reveals the extent to which China may be hiding its own strategic agenda behind Muslim insurgency; and (9) *Tequila Junction: 4th-Generation Counterinsurgency,* how to fight narco-guerrillas.

As of September 2008, John Poole had conducted multiday training sessions (on 4GW squad tactics) at 39 (mostly Marine) battalions, nine Marine schools, and seven special-operations units from all four U.S. service branches. Since 2000, he has done research in Mainland China (twice), North Korea, Vietnam, Cambodia, Thailand, Russia, India, Pakistan, Iran, Lebanon, Turkey, Egypt, Sudan, Tanzania, Venezuela, and Sri Lanka. Over the course of his lifetime, he has visited scores of other nations on all five continents.

Between early tours in the Marine Corps (from 1969 to 1971), John Poole worked as a criminal investigator for the Illinois Bureau of Investigation (IBI). After attending the State Police Academy for several months in Springfield, he was assigned to the IBI's Chicago office.

Name Index